Implementing
Backup and Recovery
The Readiness Guide
for the Enterprise
(VERITAS Series)

Implementing
Backup and Recovery
The Readiness Guide
for the Enterprise
(VERITAS Series)

David B. Little
David A. Chapa

WILEY

Wiley Publishing, Inc.

Executive Publisher: Robert Ipsen
Executive Editor: Carol Long
Developmental Editor: Adaobi Obi Tulton
Editorial Manager: Kathryn Malm
Production Editor: Angela Smith
Text Design & Composition: Wiley Composition Services

This book is printed on acid-free paper. ∞

Published by Wiley Publishing, Inc., Indianapolis, Indiana
Published simultaneously in Canada

For general information on our other products and services please contact our Customer Care Department within the United States at (800) 762-2974, outside the United States at (317) 572-3993 or fax (317) 572-4002.

Wiley also publishes its books in a variety of electronic formats. Some content that appears in print may not be available in electronic books.

Library of Congress Cataloging-in-Publication Data:

ISBN: 0-471-22714-5

Printed in the United States of America

10 9 8 7 6 5 4 3 2 1

Dedicated to Overlin L. Chapa, 1933–2001

"Chapa"

Dad, I only wish I could hand you a copy of this.

Contents

Acknowledgments

I want to first thank my wife, Nancy, for all her support during this long and sometimes arduous process. Thanks for doing all the driving so I could work on the book. We can't accomplish much without a supportive family behind us and I am no exception. My kids, Dan, Lisa, Jill, Jeff, and Amanda, have always been there as well as my parents, Ray David and Jeffie Little. Thanks to you all.

I would also like to give a special thanks to my co-workers Jim Coby and Mark Erickson who were there to help and also provided content when asked. I am sure my family and my co-workers were beginning to wonder if there really was a book. I guess this is the proof.

A special thanks also goes out to Dave High who was willing to review the chapters as I completed them and took the time from his own busy schedule to provide comments and feedback. This book would never even have happened without the support of Scott Tirrell and Brad Hargett who afforded me the time as needed. I would also like to thank the following VERITAS people who were willing to review parts of the book and offer comments: Danny Dunn, Erik Moller, Bill Drazkowski, Shawn Aquino, John Moore, Terry Noonan, Jim Olson, and Hector Herrero. Charlie Van Meter and Bob Santiago skillfully provided the figures, especially the better ones.

I would like to thank the staff at John Wiley & Sons for being patient with a beginning author and taking the time to help me through some of the rough spots. The original drivers behind this entire project were Paul Massiglia and Richard Barker. They are to be either thanked or blamed.

—David B. Little

To my parents for always believing that I could do anything I put my mind to, thanks mom and dad.

Thanks to Kevin Weiss, my friend and boss, and to everyone at DataStaff for their constant encouragement.

Thanks to Peter L. Buschman, friend and co-laborer in the field of backup storage management. Your keen insights continue to challenge me to think not only outside the box but to search for an entirely new box to explore.

Thanks to Paul Massiglia at VERITAS for his sage advice as a seasoned author and to Dave Little for asking me to jump on board with this project. It's been a great experience . . . so when's the next one Dave?

Thank you must go out to Charlie Van Meter, VERITAS, and his team for taking our diagrams, pictures, and drawings and making us look good!

All the great folks at Wiley, thank you for allowing me this opportunity, especially to Adaobi Obi Tulton and Carol Long for challenging us to push forward! And Angela Smith for her diligence.

To the Starbucks in Lake Geneva, WI—many thanks! I did most of my writing after work in that little shop on a $1.83, venti coffee—no room, thank you very much. Thanks for putting up with me!

To my brother Joe, for helping me with the equations for the backup models and his all around support and prayer.

With great thanks to the many people at my church Redeemer PCA for their continued encouragement, support, and prayer through this project.

And with eternal thanks to my lovely wife Jill (I love you) for giving up so many evenings and weekends together so I could work on this book; and to our children, Ashley and Tyler (I love you two so much), who caught the writing bug and started a few of their own books while daddy was working on his.

There are many others who have helped me throughout my career, both personally and professionally, every one of them were instrumental in getting me to this point. Thanks to Kathy DeLeo, Jeff Gentges, Wendy Petty, Yuda Doron, Betty McGee, Craig Burdett, Bob Allums, Brian and Leslie Schwartz, Steve Alburty, and everyone else who has had an impact on my life.

Lastly, but certainly not least is my thanks to God; it's only by the strength of Christ that I was able to juggle so many things during this project and my busy life. Thank you.

—David A. Chapa

About the Authors

David B. Little joined VERITAS Software in April 1997. He was a support engineer and helped develop the multi-tiered support model that is a cornerstone of the world-class support organization. In 1999, he joined the Sales department as a technical product specialist. In this capacity he has traveled around the world promoting NetBackup and frequently speaking at user conferences. He also teaches NetBackup to internal VERITAS engineers and consultants as well as partners, resellers, and customers.

Prior to joining VERITAS, Dave worked at Control Data Corporation/ Control Data Systems Incorporated for almost 30 years. He worked as a software support engineer for NetBackup and various UNIX operating systems. He was also the leading support engineer for the super computers including the Cyber 205 and the ETA10.

Dave lives in Minnesota with his wife Nancy, cat Buster, and dog Astro.

David A. Chapa wears many hats at DataStaff (www.datastaff.com). In his official role he is the Consulting Manager responsible for managing the vision and direction of the consulting practices. He is also co-founder of Gray House Solutions (www.GrayHouseSolutions.com), a software company providing integrated disaster recovery solutions whose flagship product is Duplication Suite.

Prior to joining DataStaff, he held several senior level technical positions with various software manufacturers in the Backup Storage Management market space. His experience spans 18 years in the computer industry with such companies as Cheyenne Software, Unisys, OpenVision, and NSI Software, with the last 10 years focused solely on data availability and storage.

The first version of NetBackup he worked with goes all the way back to version 1.6 while he was employed with OpenVision. While at OpenVision he formally prepared and presented NetBackup Training for many large companies across the country and Canada. David is a Certified Veritas Net-Backup Instructor for both NetBackup Fundamentals Class and the Advanced NetBackup class. David is an energetic and dynamic speaker who brings a great deal of experiential knowledge, humor, and keen insight to his presentations. He has been a speaker at VERITAS Vision, Chicago Software Association's discussion on Backup Storage Management principles, and a number of user groups in the past. His Web site, www.BackupScripts.com, has built a community where sharing of ideas, scripts, tips, and concepts has provided a great deal of value to its members and best of all, it is free. Today David remains a billable consultant. He enjoys the client contact and continues to find the work challenging and stimulating as he helps his clients discover new ways to protect their digital business assets.

Introduction

Welcome to the wonderful world of backup and recovery. Since you are here, we are assuming that you have been either given the task of putting together a backup and recovery system for your organization or you are in a position where you are thinking about how backup and recovery fits within the scope of total data availability for your organization. This is a topic that has been mostly ignored or given very low priority, and until recently, you couldn't even get the young junior administrators to pay attention to backup. People are starting to realize that just about all enterprises are dependent on their data, and protecting it is equivalent to protecting the company or agency. This hasn't made backup and recovery any more exciting, but at least it has gained some well-needed recognition from upper management. The best way to view it is just like insurance. You wouldn't try to run a company without insurance even though you hope never to have to use it. The basic backup can be viewed in the same way, but as we will see as we venture further into the world of backup and recovery, it can be a bit more.

Overview of the Book and Technology

The goal in writing this book is to provide you, the reader, with enough information to be able to architect a backup and recovery system that will work for your specific needs. While there are some of you out there that would have loved a book that explored the "soft underbelly" of Net-Backup, perhaps that will come; however, we felt that the very first book highlighting this market-leading product should be more of a "best practices" approach. Which is exactly what we have done. This book will not be able to answer all your questions, nor can it provide a spreadsheet or cookie cutter formula that you can just feed data in and expect answers to come out. Believe it or not, a well-designed backup and recovery system is complicated and dependent on your specific configuration and business needs. We will cover the different areas that must be considered and arm you with the information that you will need in order to get the data necessary to allow you to architect your system. As you start to gather the information, you will have to rely on people from many different areas within your company or agency. You will need information concerning disk layouts, network topology, data structure, and a whole lot of other things we will get to in the later chapters.

How This Book Is Organized

This book is oriented as most publications: table of contents in the beginning, index at the end, appendices before the index, and a glossary mixed in there as well. Why are we bothering to state the obvious? Well, we think that when you approach a technology book, or any book for that matter, it is important to note where all of these components are first before you even read the first chapter. We often begin reading a book from page 1, Chapter 1, but rarely find ourselves picking out the gems of wisdom left there by the author (yes, we think we have one or two for your reading pleasure).

We want to offer to you a challenge: Do not start at page 1, Chapter 1 with our book; rather, after reading the introduction, read the back cover, scan intelligibly the index for terms that are of interest to you, then read the glossary and become familiar with the terms that we use in this book. Next, intelligibly scan the table of contents looking for chapters that pique your interest before you read page 1 of Chapter 1. This gives you a much clearer picture of what is ahead as you begin to read and hopefully a much more rich experience as you read not just our book, but any book.

Now on to the organization of our book. This work is separated into three parts. Part One is an introduction to backup and recovery in the enterprise. We felt it was important to lay down some foundational facts and information in Chapters 1 and 2 regarding data protection and why we would even bother to protect this data.

Part Two builds on this foundation. Here, we begin to look at the components of backup through a backup tutorial. After providing you with the background and basics, we take a more practical view of how to apply the information gathered in Part I by going through the steps of laying out, installing, and configuring a backup application. Since collectively we bring about 10 years' experience with VERITAS Software's NetBackup product specifically, we will be using NetBackup for the purposes of illustration throughout the book. NetBackup is the most installed backup and recovery solution in the UNIX space and is gaining considerable ground in the Wintel space as well.

Every site is different and unique, with different business needs and requirements. The business will drive much of the decisions for your backup plan, as you will see in our approach and some of the real-life scenarios we describe. While we won't be able to give you a step-by-step roadmap for architecting your backup and recovery system, we will provide you a firm foundation on which to build, with additional resource help on some of the components you can add to your environment to address your specific needs, thus reinforcing your backup infrastructure.

Chapters 4 to 7 really rounds out our discovery of NetBackup as a product, including discussions on its architecture, how to determine your media requirements, installation considerations, configuration, and monitoring. Chapters 8 to 9 really begin focusing more on taking NetBackup from its "stock" configuration and enhancing it through options and advanced features. Here we also offer troubleshooting tips.

In Part Three we explore the ever-explosive growth our backup enterprises face and provide suggestions for dealing with such growth. You might want to read this section before finishing your architecture because it is always a good idea to plan for the future now rather than having to react to it later. We also take some liberties in discussing the future of backup. We take a peek into the backup and recovery crystal ball and share some of the things that are being considered for the future of backup and recovery, some that are in progress, and others yet to be explored. We have elicited input from some of the best minds in the field for this information.

Lastly, we have added some very rich content in the appendices to help you in your labor. You will find a business impact analysis (BIA) planning kit, disaster recovery (DR) planning kit, NetBackup tuning guide, performance testing technical note, Command Line Interface (CLI) guide, and a glossary of terms. The planning kits, while not exhaustive, do provide you a very nice starting place if you have not performed BIAs or created DR plans at your company. The tuning guide will give you very practical methods for making sure your NetBackup environment is performing optimally.

Throughout the book we will use our personal experiences with real-life client situations to explain particular concepts or topics more clearly.

Who Should Read This Book

This book should provide helpful information for anyone who is involved in protecting the ever-growing volume of data that everyone depends on. This could be the person in the information technology (IT) or information services (IS) department, the database administrator, or the backup administrator. This could also include the value-added reseller (VAR) who is responsible for assisting his or her clients in setting up a backup and restore system. Also, anyone who currently uses VERITAS Software's Net-Backup will find this book invaluable, especially the detailed appendices. This book is also a necessity for anyone who wants to complete the ultimate computer library. There is a chapter that discusses the other major applications that are available, where we give equal billing to the "major players."

Summary

We hope you will find this work very useful as you plan, maintain, and administer your backup environments. It is our desire that the practices found in this work provide you a level of consistency in the planning, architecting, and delivery of your solutions. One thing we have learned while writing this book is that there are a variety of ways to accomplish the same task. What we have attempted to do here is to document those practices that will minimize the complexity within your environment while maintaining a highly efficient and effective solution.

In the beginning of this introduction, we welcomed you to the wonderful world of backup and recovery. However, when it comes to planning, we should really call it the wonderful world of "recovery and backup." As you will see in the pages that follow, it is the recovery requirement that defines our backup strategy, and it is our time to recovery that defines our success—not the speed of our backup. The role of the backup administrator is integral in any company; in fact, you can consider it the second most important job in your company. When does it become the first? When they can't access their data!

Introduction to Backup and Recovery in the Enterprise Environment

Backup and Recovery System Requirements Explained

A *backup* is a copy of a defined set of data, ideally as it exists at a point in time. It is central to any data protection architecture. In a well-run information services operation, backups are stored at a physical distance from operational data, usually on tape or other removable media, so that they can survive events that destroy or corrupt operational databases. Backups may be

- Kept at the data center, so that if a storage device, system, or application failure or operational error destroys vital online data, the business can restore its operational records as of a relatively recent fixed point in time. From that point, database logs can restore (nearly) up-to-date business data.

- Moved to one or more alternate sites, to protect against environmental events that destroy an entire data center. With recent backups of operational databases, a business can resume operation quickly when alternative computing facilities are available.

- Made unalterable (for example, copied onto CD-ROM) to provide durable business records for regulatory and business policy purposes when the data is no longer required online.

Backup Seems Simple . . .

Conceptually, a backup strategy is simple. A system administrator decides what data is critical for business operation, determines a backup schedule that has a minimal effect on operations, and uses a backup utility program to make the copies. The backups are stored in a safe place so they can be used to recover from a failure.

Though a backup strategy is quite simple in concept, the difficulty comes in the details. Architecting a backup and recovery strategy is more involved than most people realize. One of the most frustrating and discouraging tasks is determining where to start. What at first seems a simple task becomes daunting as you start digging deeper and realize how many elements of the backup strategy are interconnected. For example, as a system administrator of a large enterprise, chances are you would not want the burden of deciding what data is backed up when, and for how long it is kept. In fact, you may be presented with various analysis summaries of the business units or own the task of interviewing the business unit managers yourself in order to have them determine the data, the window in which backup may run, and the retention level of the data once it is stored on the backup media. This is often called a *business impact analysis* (BIA) and should yield some results that will be useful during the policy-making process. The results of these reports should also help define the recovery window, should this particular business unit suffer a disaster where data cannot be accessed or updated. Knowledge of these requirements may, in fact, change the entire budget structure for your backup environment, so it is imperative during the design and architecture phase that you have some understanding of what the business goals are with regard to recovery.

You will find that most business unit managers are not as concerned about backup as they are with recovery. As you can see from the level of complexity of our example, too often the resulting frustration may lead to inactivity where nothing gets done—or at least not done in the most effective manner. The obvious intent of a backup and recovery system is to provide data protection. Since we are setting up a system to protect the data, the next step also seems obvious: Determine how much data is in the enterprise and where it resides. This is an important part of establishing the backup and recovery system, but it does not provide enough information to architect a strategy. In addition to knowing how much data you have and where it is, you must also have a good understanding of why the data is being backed up and what the recovery requirements are. This is necessary so you can make the appropriate decisions about the overall backup and recovery strategy. The more you understand the nature of the data and the level of protection required, the better decisions you can make in setting up the entire backup and recovery environment.

The Goals of Tape Backup

You always want to keep in mind that the overall goal of tape backup is to make copies of your data that can be used to recover from any kind of data loss. The primary goals of the tape backup portion of an overall data protection strategy are to do the following:

- Understand the goals of the business in order to deliver a properly configured backup environment.
- Enable information services to resume as quickly as is physically possible after any system component failure or application error.
- Enable data to be relocated to where it's needed, when it's needed by the business.
- Meet regulatory and business policy data retention requirements.
- Meet recovery goals; in the event of a disaster, return the business to a predetermined operating level.

Each of these goals relates to a specific area of data protection and needs to be considered as we put together our overall backup strategy. Specifically, you should ask why data is being backed up. As you consider each system or group of systems, keep in mind whether the data is being backed up to protect against failure, disaster, or regulatory requirements, and if the goals of the business will be met in the event of a failure or disaster. In reality, your success as a backup administrator will not be measured by how fast you are able to back up your data but how swiftly you are able to meet the aforementioned goals. Stated simply, your success will be defined by the restorability of the data in the environment.

The Role of Tape Backup

For a personal computer user, backup typically means making a copy of the data on the computer's hard drive onto a tape or CD-ROM. Personal backup media are often labeled by hand and are "managed" by storing them in a drawer or cabinet located in the room with the computer.

In the enterprise, data protection is a little more complex. Enterprise backup must be able to do the following:

- Make copies of your data, whether organized as files, databases, or the contents of logical volumes or disks.

- Manage the backup media that contain these copies so that any backup copy of any data can be quickly and reliably located when required, and so that the media can be tracked accurately, regardless of the number.

- Provide mechanisms to duplicate sets of backed up data so that while a copy remains on-site for quick restores, another copy can be taken off-site for archival or disaster protection purposes.

- Track the location of all copies of all data accurately.

Why Is the Data Backed Up?

Why you are backing up data seems like a trivial question, but it really needs to be answered for all the data in the enterprise. Some of the most common answers to this question are as follows:

- Business requirement
- Hardware failure protection
- Disaster recovery (DR)
- Protection from application failure
- Protection from user error
- Specific service-level agreements with the users/customers (SLA)
- Legal requirements

You need to understand what data on what systems falls into each category. By interviewing the data owners, you will be better equipped to categorize the data. In most cases, the administrators know what it takes to recover the operating system and, in some cases, the database engines and other applications. However, the onus must be placed upon the data owner (customer) for the administrators to fully understand the impact to the business in the event there is a data loss (BIA). Addressing their expectations up front will save much time, money, and potential embarrassment. Several years ago, one of us was given the task of architecting a backup solution that would allow for quick recovery. "Quick" recovery is subjective, so the question asked was this: "What is your expectation of a 'quick' recovery?" Based on the response of 30 minutes, a proposal was drafted for the type of system that would need to be designed to meet this 30-minute recovery window. Soon after management reviewed the proposal, we agreed to a more realistic time frame. So you can see how this would give you an opportunity to show customers how much money their requirements will cost without you having to lose sleep in the process.

You will usually find some of the systems have fairly static data and would probably be backed up to protect against hardware failure or for DR. Other systems are very dynamic with a very active user base. Backup of this data should be considered for protection against application failure or user error. What is generally seen on systems is a mixture of these data types. The core operating system (OS) and base applications are usually static and can be rebuilt from release materials, while data used by the application can be very volatile. We will discuss each of these in more detail. Defining data types is vital, because understanding the data allows us to determine the recovery requirements. In most cases, the recovery requirements dictate the backup strategy.

Hardware Failure

Some of the data in an enterprise is backed up specifically to protect against hardware failure. You want to be sure you can recover an entire volume or database in case a disk or server fails. (The probability of doing any restore of less than an entire volume is very small.) The backup protection will be geared to this recovery requirement.

The best pure hardware failure protection is *disk mirroring*—that is, making a complete second copy of the data on disk to another disk. However, this practice does not eliminate the need for backups. For the data that falls into this category, you might consider raw volume backups where all the data in a disk volume is backed up at disk read speed. A raw partition backup is a bit-by-bit backup of a partition of a disk drive on UNIX. On Windows NT/2000, this is called a *disk-image backup*. You do not read the data via the filesystem, so you avoid adding this process to the system overhead. A raw volume backup can give you much better backup performance; however, it has some restrictions. The primary restriction is that you back up the entire volume. For example, if a 50-GB volume is only 50 percent full, a filesystem backup would result in 25 GB being backed up. However, a raw volume backup would result in 50 GB being backed up, and, accordingly, more tape being used. Then, on the restore, the entire volume is restored regardless of how much data actually resides in it. You need to take this into account when determining whether to do raw backups.

The backup strategy for this protection could be configured around the hardware layout of each system. If you know that a system will be backed up solely for hardware protection, you can lay out the system to optimize the backup and recovery performance. A lot of the data that could fall into this category is more static; it would be backed up less frequently and would usually involve full backups. This data can be entire systems within your enterprise or some of the static data that is found on more dynamic systems, such as the OS-related data or the actual applications that are loaded on a system.

Disaster Recovery

For systems that are a part of your DR strategy, you need to ensure you have all the data required to rebuild a system in an easily identified group. You must also ensure you have all the supporting data necessary to recover these systems. This can include the supporting OS data as well as everything required for the backup application in order to do full system restores. Using a vault-type solution where backups are sent off-site to be stored until needed in conjunction with the backup application greatly helps this task.

The biggest challenge here is identifying which systems and applications are critical and determining how fast they have to be back online. A part of the DR strategy should include the priority of recovering these systems. The speed of recovery can dictate some of the backup decisions. It is very likely that systems that are a part of your DR strategy might also require protection within one of the other strategies. You would actually configure your backup and recovery system to provide the necessary DR protection in addition to any other requirements. Keep in mind that when you declare a disaster it may mean you no longer have access to your primary site. So any reports, documentation, call lists, operations guides, and so on that you may require should be in an off-site location along with your DR backup media. Many DR test plans fail because of one document or component that was overlooked.

Application Failure

The data that needs protection against application corruption usually requires more frequent backups. In these instances, the use of both incremental and full backups is very important. The highest risk of application data corruption is database applications, so you should develop a specific backup strategy for these applications. Most of the backup applications can interface with the database applications to allow both full and incremental backups that can be done either hot (with the database still active) or cold (with the database shut down). The systems that require this type of data protection might also be part of your DR strategy, so they would be part of multiple strategies.

User Error

For the data that is directly user-generated or -accessed, you might want to consider a backup strategy for user error protection. This might also include mailboxes, but in these instances, the backup and recovery strategy is dictated by the mail application. The very nature of providing user error protection implies that there are many more instances of single file or directory restores, so the backup strategy needs to support this. This strategy would generally involve more frequent incremental backups. The frequency of backups is an important consideration if it involves data that users are deleting and restoring on a regular basis. You would also want to ensure the backups are configured to facilitate faster browsing and recovery.

Service Level Agreements

You might find some of the data is being backed up to meet a specific service level agreement (SLA). The backup strategy will depend on the exact agreement. It is very possible that the SLA will actually be for a recovery requirement. If that is the case, the backup strategy will be governed by these requirements. This is often the situation where there is a dedicated backup and recovery administration staff that provides this service for a particular company or agency. The other groups or business units become the customers of the backup group and could have specific SLAs. These will usually dictate the backup strategy. This is also the case in hosting centers. It is very important to determine exactly what the exact requirements are. These can involve any of the backup types mentioned, with the additional requirement to have systems or applications back online within a specific time frame. It is common to have an agreement that any request for the recovery of any file or directory must be accomplished within a given time. All of this information is required to allow you to actually put together a backup strategy.

Legal Requirements

Your company may be required by law to keep certain data for a particular time period, without exception. Then there's always the possibility that legal will be very strict in noting that certain data types are *not* to be kept more than a particular time period. These factors will further shape the way you architect the collective backup solution; for example, one server may be a member of multiple policies in order to achieve the legal requirement of its data. It is good practice to always include the legal department when determining the data retention requirements whenever possible. This is essentially a component of a business impact analysis.

Complexity in Enterprise Backup

The functions of enterprise tape backup may seem straightforward. But implementing a truly functional backup environment that meets enterprise data protection requirements can be a complex undertaking. When you design or update a backup strategy, complexity can arise for several reasons:

Ability to back up all of the data.   For the backup strategy to be useful, it must ensure that all data that can be lost is backed up. In an enterprise with large numbers of information servers, some of which may share data with others, identifying the sets of data objects to be backed up can be a significant effort.

Frequency.   Backup frequency is essentially a trade-off between resources (network and I/O bandwidth, processor capacity, tape and library hardware, and application access) and the need for the most current data possible. Again, with many information services needing data protection, finding the right balance between backup frequency and resource consumption is a challenge.

Integration of all data managers.   Enterprises with many information services are likely to use multiple data management systems (file-systems and database management systems), each with its own mechanisms for backing up data objects that it recognizes. Your task is integrating these mechanisms into a schedule that provides a consistent backup of all required data for a service and keeping them up-to-date as the service changes.

Continuous availability.   Continuous application availability is increasingly required in the today's enterprise. A variety of mechanisms enable consistent backups with minimal application downtime. Choosing among these and implementing the choice can be a complex task.

Media management.   Business or regulatory requirements can result in multiyear data retention requirements. Enterprises can find themselves responsible for maintaining backups and archives on tens or even hundreds of thousands of media (tape cartridges, optical disk platters, etc.). The procedures for managing large numbers of media can also be complex.

Management of multiple locations.   Business considerations may require that servers and data be located in multiple locations. Maintaining a consistent set of backup procedures across multiple data centers can require extensive design or management talent.

The backup component of an enterprise data protection strategy has to accommodate all of these factors.

Where Do We Start?

As you start planning your backup and recovery system, you need to start gathering detailed information on your enterprise. You need to know the network layout for all systems. If your enterprise is made up of multiple networks, you need to know how much data resides on it and the speed of each network or subnet. Obviously, it is much faster to move data across a 100-Mb/sec (100Base-T) network than a 10-Mb/sec (10Base-T) network. You need to understand the network layout and the corresponding data to help identify potential bottlenecks and take them into consideration as you architect your backup and recovery system. (This information is also necessary in determining where to put media servers and tape devices, but we will get to that in a later chapter.)

As you look at the network that makes up your enterprise, you need to understand the network speed and topology. You also need to understand the disk layout, especially for the larger file servers and database servers, or identify who has this knowledge. You should watch for bottlenecks involving the disks, as well as the networks, SCSI connections, and any other appropriate I/O paths. When considering the decisions that need to be made when architecting backup strategy, the two things you must always keep in mind are the effect on normal production and effects on restore speed and performance. This usually involves making the necessary cost trade-offs to achieve the best of all worlds.

Here are some of the steps necessary for you to gather the information needed before establishing the backup strategy:

1. Identify all the systems, noting the order in which they would need to be recovered following a disaster.

2. Identify all networks involved, including speed of network and existing load at various times throughout the 24-hour day and night.

3. Locate all existing backup-related hardware, such as tape drives and libraries.

4. Identify recovery requirements.

5. Identify data and application availability requirements during backup.

6. Determine the best way to move the data.

We discuss each of these points in a little more detail in the sections that follow.

Identify All Systems

You need to identify all systems that need to be backed up. Generally this will be most if not all of the systems in the enterprise, with the exception of user workstations. There may be some systems that are basically replicated systems and can be easily re-created. In general, it is only necessary to back up one of these systems. The following information should be gathered for all the systems:

- Amount of data
- Speed of system
- Number and type of networks
- Type of data—database or filesystem?
- Priority of recovery in DR
- Tape drive or library installed?

Identify All Networks Involved

The network layout is an important part of the information required. Identifying the layout can be very critical to establishing the backup and recovery strategy. This step addresses the potential performance bottlenecks, because slow networks are often some of the primary bottlenecks. If there is a significant amount of data on a slow network, a media server may need to be located on the network. Any systems that have large amounts of backup data, such as a system with more than 100 GB, should be considered as media servers and have direct connections to a tape drive or drives. Following is the information needed for the networks:

- Speed of network
- Amount of data residing on the systems

- Location of any backup hardware
- Current and proposed production traffic

Locate Backup Hardware

Identifying all the systems and mapping the network topology should provide an idea of the total backup requirements. Part of this information is the location of the potential backup devices. The next step is to make sure the hardware is correctly located within the enterprise. Any enterprise backup and recovery strategy should be based on an application that supports library and drive sharing to ensure the tape drives and libraries are connected throughout the enterprise in such a way as to minimize bottlenecks, as well as to gain the most use from these very expensive tape drive resources. In a pure local area network (LAN) environment, it might be advisable to physically locate the tape library or libraries close enough to the systems that have the largest amounts of data so they can be directly connected to the tape drives and therefore perform backups and restores without data being moved across the network. These systems become media servers and control access to their drives. To handle data from other LAN-based systems, you either need to add more drives and give these systems access to their own drives or use the media servers to handle the backups for the systems that do not have their own drives. Also, the systems must be physically located close enough to the tape devices to be directly connected via SCSI cables.

LEARN FROM THE ERRORS OF THEIR WAYS

Backup is a part of any data protection strategy, but there are other technologies, such as replication, that are part of it as well. The key to a sound strategy is to incorporate all the different technologies. I have been involved in too many discussions with people who were trying to recover from an outage only to discover they were not as protected as they thought. One particular case involved a company that had lost their primary server that ran their most critical application. They spent several hours trying to recover from mirrored disks, when the actual failure was filesystem corruption. Mirrors did not help in this case. Their outage was extended, but they were able to recover, since they had backups. My worst call while working in support was from a system administrator who had done a mass delete from the wrong window and had removed enough of the operating system that he could not reboot. When he asked what he had to do to recover, I told him part of the process would be to restore from his latest backup. To this, he answered that configuring for backups was on his "list of things to do."

Locate Backup Hardware—SAN Alternative

If a storage area network (SAN) is available, it can allow for more flexibility in the backup and recovery strategy. The backup hardware can be better shared amongst the large data-resident systems while still keeping the data off the production LAN. This can also allow large systems to be backed up directly to tape without making the application servers general-purpose media servers and having these systems back up other LAN-based clients.

Identify Recovery Requirements

As you identify all the systems in the enterprise, you should note the specific recovery requirements of each system. This is very helpful in setting up the backup strategy. If an order-processing application can tolerate an eight-hour outage without severe business consequences, for example, an incremental backup strategy that minimizes backup time at the expense of restore time may be appropriate. For a Web retail application, on the other hand, where every minute of downtime means permanently lost sales, a strategy that replicates data in real time might be more appropriate, even with its greater impact on application performance. The other item to note is the order in which systems need to be recovered as part of your overall disaster recovery (DR) plan.

Identify Data and Application Availability Requirements during Backup

As you assess the backup requirements of each system, you should also make sure you know which of the database applications must be kept up—remain "hot"—during the backup and which can be shut down to be backed up "cold." There are performance trade-offs involved with backing up a database while it is online, but sometimes this is necessary. This is due to the increased I/O activity, since the database activity is continuing, as well as the additional backup I/O. There are other methods of handling database backups, either hot or cold, using frozen image technologies and possibly off-host backup methods. These are discussed later in the book.

Determine the Best Way to Move the Data

You have several options for moving the data from disk to tape. Each has its own advantages and disadvantages. The methods include the following:

Files.   This involves using the operating system to read all the appropriate files within the backup set and move that data from disk to tape. This method has more operating system overhead but allows for single files to be backed up and restored. It also enables the application to check each file to determine access or modification time so incremental backups can be performed.

Volumes.   An entire volume can be backed up without reading the filesystem structure but by doing a bit-by-bit copy of the data from disk to tape. This is called a *raw backup*. This method allows for much faster data transfers but in general does not allow for single-file backups and restores. It also does not allow incremental backups. This backup method results in an entire volume being backed up, even the portions that do not contain valid data.

Block level.   If the filesystem has enough information about the files, it is possible to determine which blocks have been changed. If the backup application can interface with the filesystem, you can back up just the changed blocks. This type of backup is called *block level incremental*.

Mapped raw backup.   Some backup applications, such as VERITAS Software's NetBackup, can map a raw volume and then perform a raw volume backup while retaining the filesystem map so single files can be restored. This also allows for incremental backups. This type of backup is discussed in more detail in the section on frozen image backups in Chapter 7, "Evaluating Other Backup-Related Features and Options."

Off-host backups.   This is a mechanism where data is moved from disk to tape without the application host being directly involved in the disk reads or tape writes. This type of backup is discussed in more detail in Chapter 7.

Summary

As you learn more about the nature of the data and the reasons for backing it up, you will probably find some data or some systems that do not need to be backed up on a regular basis at all. Many people have decided that the static OS files generally do not change except when OS patches are applied or the system is reconfigured. They do not have regularly scheduled backups of this data and only perform them when applying patches or making configuration changes. Also, some systems can be easily rebuilt online from other systems, which is usually faster than a total recovery. In this case, you might only need a single backup to protect all of these systems in your enterprise. In addition, there is a cost incentive to fully understanding the data. The cost of tape media is one of the driving forces behind *not* backing up too much data, as well as the fact that backing up data that does not require it ties up tape drives that could otherwise be used for more important data.

The real key to this entire discussion on determining why the data is being backed up is to truly understand the nature of the data. In a large enterprise, it is unlikely the backup administrator will have this knowledge. You will have to get this information from the people who control the data throughout the enterprise. The best way to do this is to develop a questionnaire that you can distribute. This will help you gather the information you need to correctly architect the backup and recovery system. It is common to use this kind of tool to determine when to back up, what to back up, how long to keep the backups, and where the backups should be kept. However, as we have seen, you also need to know why certain backups must be performed. In the following chapters, we discuss the other parts of the backup equation.

Keep in mind that just because you sit down and do all of this work now, you are not "done." Things change, and you need to develop an ongoing dynamic process that lends itself to constant growth. Gathering the information that will be needed from others in the company may be time-consuming, and it may not be readily available. Formulating a backup and recovery strategy may take a while, but the first step starts with, well, a first step.

In the next chapter, we look at how your specific business requirements affect your backup and recovery strategy.

Business Requirements of Backup Systems

After determining why the data needs to be backed up and the recovery requirements, you are ready to look at how your particular business requirements come into play. You need to determine how often each type of data or each system needs to be backed up, what the restore requirements are, what the data retention policy needs to be, any security requirements, off-site storage requirements, and unique business unit requirements. All of these items must be addressed.

Developing a Backup Strategy

To start this phase of architecting your backup and recovery strategy, you need to look at the frequency of backups and the required retention of the data. This is usually controlled by the business, legal, and recovery requirements. The business requirements that generally affect the backup strategy are those that define how long specific types of data must be kept available either locally or in a storage facility. These requirements could also specify the number of copies of the data that must be retained. In some cases, there are specific business requirements regarding how often specific data is backed up. Legal requirements must also be considered, although they are usually the basis of the specific business requirements. When you are dealing with data that might fall under control of any of the many governmental regulatory agencies, you must make sure your strategy complies with all their requirements.

Business Requirements

The specific business requirements that you need to consider include the following (see Figure 2.1):

Service-level agreements to business units.   What backup and recovery guarantees do you have?

Unique requirements for specific data.   For example, all original circuit design must be kept for seven years.

Recovery time objectives.   How fast will specific systems/applications be recovered?

Recovery point objectives.   How far back in time are you willing to go to recover?

Legal Requirements

The legal requirements you need to consider are generally those imposed by governmental regulatory agencies. These typically involve specific data retention requirements for specific kinds of data. What makes this even more challenging is that these requirements can change because of changes in administrations or new laws. These can also dictate how many copies of the data must be kept and where it must be kept.

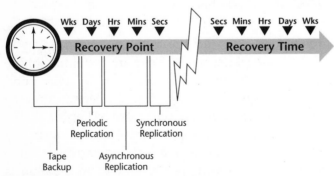

Figure 2.1   Recovery point and recovery time.

Recovery Requirements

As you build your strategy, you should make a special note of systems or applications that have special recovery requirements. These are usually covered by the business requirements but are worth mentioning again. We have found it much better to always look first at the recovery requirements when building a backup strategy, since that is probably the reason you are doing backups.

With these absolutes in mind, the next step is to take the information gathered in the first chapter and start your backup matrix. As you put this together, you should also consider the type of backup you need. Following are the different backup options:

Full backup.   This backup copies all the files and directories that are below a specified directory or filesystem to a storage unit.

Cumulative incremental backup.   Scheduled by the administrator on the master server, this option backs up files that have changed since the last successful full backup. All files are backed up if no prior backup has been done. This is very similar to a differential incremental backup, which is covered later, with one very major difference. In the event of a full system recovery, a cumulative incremental backup would require only two images: the last full backup and the most recent cumulative incremental. While this speeds the recovery process, this type of backup does require more tapes than the differential incremental and may potentially take more time, because you are backing up all the files that have changed since the last full backup.

Differential incremental backup.   Scheduled by the administrator on the master server, this option backs up files that have changed since the last successful incremental or full backup. All files are backed up if no prior backup has been done. This is what most people traditionally refer to by *incremental backup*. During a full recovery, using this type of backup could require more tapes. However, do not base your architecture decisions just on these two definitions, but rather on the information gathered during your initial discovery phase.

True image restore.   This type of backup restores the contents of a directory to what it was at the time of any scheduled full or incremental backup. Previously deleted files are ignored. You can also select Move Detection, which specifies that true image incremental backups include files that were moved, renamed, or newly installed.

EXAMPLE OF CUMULATIVE INCREMENTAL:

The example in Figure 2.2 shows the data that is included in a series of backups between January 1 and January 4. The January 1 full backup includes all files and directories in the policy file list. Each of the cumulative incremental backups include the data changed since the last full backup. If the disk fails sometime on January 4 (after the backup), the full and the last cumulative incremental are required for the recovery.

For this example: Recovery = Jan 1 (full) + Jan 4 (incr)

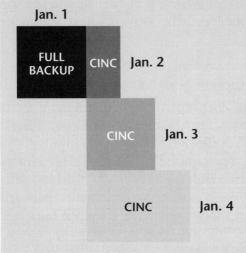

Figure 2.2 Cumulative incremental backup.

EXAMPLE OF DIFFERENTIAL INCREMENTAL

The example in Figure 2.3 shows the data that is included in a series of backups between January 1 and January 4. The January 1 backup is a full backup and includes all files and directories in the policy file list. The subsequent backups are differential incrementals and include only the data that changed since the last full or differential incremental backup. If the disk fails sometime on January 4 (after the backup), the full and all three of the incrementals are required for the recovery.

For this example:
Recovery = Jan 1 (full) + Jan 2 (incr) + Jan 3 (incr) + Jan 4 (incr)

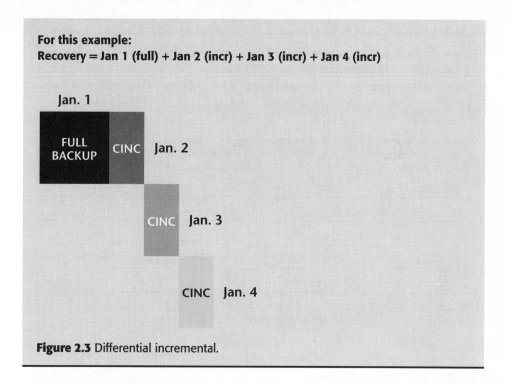

Figure 2.3 Differential incremental.

EXAMPLE OF TRUE IMAGE RESTORE WITH MOVE DETECTION

The following are examples where using move detection backs up files that otherwise would not be backed up:

♦ A file named /home/pub/doc is moved to /home/spec/doc. Here, the modification time is unchanged, but /home/spec/doc is new in the /home/spec/ directory and is backed up.

♦ A directory named /etc/security/dev is renamed as/etc/security/devices. Here, the modification time is unchanged, but/etc/security/devices is a new directory and is backed up.

♦ A file named /home/pub/doc is installed by extracting it from a UNIX TAR file. Here, the modification time is before the time of the last backup, but the doc is new in the /home/pub/ directory and is backed up.

♦ A file named docA is removed and then a file named docB is renamed as docA. Here, the new docA has the same name, but its inode number changed, so it is backed up.

NetBackup starts collecting information required for move detection beginning with the next full or incremental backup for the policy. This first backup after setting the attribute always backs up all files, even if it is an incremental.

Move detection takes space on the client and can fail if there is not enough disk space available.

EXAMPLE OF WHAT HAPPENS DURING TRUE IMAGE RESTORES

The following table shows the files backed up in the /home/abc/doc/ directory during a series of backups between 12/01/2001 and 12/04/2001. Assume that True Image Restore Information was selected for the policy that did the backups.

FILES BACKED UP IN THE HOME/ABC/DOC/ DIRECTORY*

DAY	TYPE OF BACKUP	FILES BACKED UP IN /HOME/ABC/DOC					
12/01/2001	Full	file 1	file2	dirA/fileA	dirB/fileB	file3	
12/02/2001	Incremental	file1	file2	dirA/fileA	-------	-----	
12/03/2001	Incremental	file1	file2	dirA/fileA	-------	-----	
12/04/2001	Use backup	file1	file2	dirA/fileA	-------	-----	dirC/fileC file4
12/04/2001	Incremental	file1	file2	-----	-------	-----	----- file4

Note: Dashes indicate that the file was deleted prior to this backup
*From the NetBackup 4.5 DataCenter System Administrator's Guide, VERITAS

Also, assume that you are going to restore the 12/04/2001 version of the /home/abc/doc/ directory.

◆ If you do a regular restore, the restored directory has all files and directories that ever existed in /home/abc/doc/ from 12/01/2001 (last full backup) through 12/04/2001:

```
file1
file2
dirA/fileA
dirB/fileB
file3
dirC/fileC
file4
```

◆ If you do a true image restore of the 12/04/2001 backup, the restored directory has only the files and directories that existed at the time of the incremental backup on 12/04/2001:

```
file1
file2
file4
```

NetBackup does not restore *any* of the files deleted prior to the 12/04/2001 incremental backup.

The restored directory does not include the dirA and dirC subdirectories, even though they were backed up on 12/04/2001 with a user backup. NetBackup did not restore these directories because they did not exist at the time of the incremental backup, which was the reference for the true image restore.

Frequency of Backups

Once you understand the general backup requirements for all of the data and the business and legal requirements, you should have a pretty good idea of how much data needs to be backed up and at least a minimum requirement for the frequency. The trick in establishing the ideal frequency policy is to come up with a schedule that gives you adequate protection with minimal media usage. You don't want to back up any more often than needed to get the necessary level of protection, since "more often" means more tapes, more data being moved, and more administration. When in doubt, however, go with more media.

Establishing the best frequency and retention policy for data that is not covered by business and legal requirements also involves knowing why the data is being backed up and what recovery requirements are. In general, truly static data or static systems should not need very frequent backups. They might be backed up as infrequently as once a week or even once a month. As far as the number of copies required, a normal practice is to keep between two and four copies of the backups.

Data that is more dynamic requires more frequent backups and probably needs one of the incremental types. The decision between differential incremental and cumulative incremental is based on recovery requirements versus media usage. Weekly full backups and daily differential incremental backups could require up to six tapes to restore a directory, filesystem, or database in a worst-case scenario. Each of the incremental backup images might be small, but each day's changes could be on a separate tape, or at least different images on the same tape. If you did the same backup sequence with cumulative incremental backups, no recovery would take more than two images that could reside on two tapes; however, if there were enough changes to the data, the cumulative incremental backups could approach a full backup in size. You must decide whether it is better to use fewer tapes with differential backups but run the risk of having to mount more tapes on a restore or potentially use more tapes on the backups but only have to restore two images to restore an entire backup.

Obviously, another piece of this equation is the anticipated type of recovery activity. If the data is being backed up for DR protection or to protect against hardware failures, the question of differential versus cumulative is important. If the data is being backed up to protect against user deletion or error, you should stay with differential backups. The recovery requirement also comes into play. By using the information you gathered during the interview process with the data owners, you can realistically plan based on the expectations you set during your discovery. If the absolute speed of recovery is important, the use of cumulative incremental backups is desired. The incremental type generally comes into play when you are working with filesystem backups. With databases, you generally work with the application tools that are integrated with the backup application, and this will dictate much of what you do.

Retention of Backups

A very common mistake people make is to retain their backups for too long. This increases the cost of backups, since you will need more media. You need to make sure you understand all the legal and business requirements for keeping copies of the backups and ensure you meet them. For normal operations, you want to make sure you have a retention level that at least exceeds the frequency. If you do a particular backup weekly, the retention level must be at least one week or you will be unprotected. A general practice is to keep at least two cycles of each type of backup. This way you will always have two copies of the data on tape when doing the next backup. This method allows you to recover from a crash that might occur on the day/time for the next backup, plus it provides an extra copy in case there is a problem with one of the tapes. Another common practice is to assign off-site tapes a different retention level than tapes kept on-site. The reasons people do this vary, but in most cases, it is driven by the business. For instance, perhaps the business requires that the backup images be kept on-site for 30 days for recovery purposes, while off-site images must be kept for 180 days.

Give this entire issue some careful thought, and don't just say you are going to keep everything forever. If this describes your particular situation, you do have an uphill battle ahead of you, but it's not the end of the world. The best thing to do from this point on is to make sure you can classify your data properly, then redesign your backup policies so you are only backing up and keeping the data you need for the periods of time you require.

Security of Backups

Security of the backups is something else that must be taken into consideration. Your business might require encrypted backups so that the data on the tapes cannot be recovered without the proper key or password. Many backup and recovery applications offer this kind of backup, but there is a performance penalty associated with encrypted backups. The data will be encrypted on the client system before being sent across the network, so this will require CPU cycles on the client and will also slow down the rate of data being presented to the network for backup. The data is very secure, since it is encrypted before it is sent across the network and is still encrypted when written to tape. This also requires the key be known in order to do a restore. Most people rely on keeping the media secure rather than implementing data security by using encryption.

Off-Site Storage Requirements

Most people today realize the need to implement a true data protection strategy of which backup is an integral part. One of the components of this strategy is management of off-site media. You should always select a backup product such as VERITAS NetBackup that offers an automated vaulting or off-site storage solution so you have the management tools for tracking the media that is off-site. The questions that you are addressing for an off-site or vault solution are as follows:

- What images need to be sent off-site?
- How many copies of the images need to be kept off-site?
- How long should each image or type of image be kept off-site?
- Do we have enough tape media on hand to allow for two or more copies?

You must determine which systems need to have off-site copies of their data and if all or only part of that system needs to be sent off-site. Sending a backup tape of the operating system off-site is typically not necessary and not cost-effective. You will need to know if incremental backup images as well as full backups are required for off-site. This requirement can be different for each type or class of system. It also depends on the existence of a DR site and legal requirements.

How Many Copies?

The next question is how many copies of each backup image should be kept off-site. This usually depends on why the data is being stored off-site. If there are legal requirements, then these requirements usually stipulate how many copies. If it is being done for pure DR, one or two copies might be adequate. This decision is usually based on either specific legal and business requirements or on your overall DR strategy. In cases where an off-site storage facility is used, you might only need one copy. If there are multiple sites, it is common to send copies to a sister site that can act as a DR site. In these cases, you might want two off-site copies so one can be kept locally and the other at the remote site. What you really need to do is keep an open mind and take a look at all the possibilities and requirements.

How Long Should They Be Kept Off-Site?

If there are legal or business requirements, these must be met. A common legal requirement is that all data related to any financial trades must be retained for seven years. The other considerations are how many potentially different copies of an image do you want to store off-site and how many tape cartridges are you willing to maintain out of production? Again, it may be up to the business unit managers as to how long they want their data stored off-site. In most companies, the IT department views the business units as their customers; as such, there are costs involved in the services you are providing to your customers. Similarly, when the business unit manager requests that his or her data remain off-site for two years, you must present the costs associated with the management of this data. There will be the cartridge cost, pickup/delivery costs, and storage costs. Even if you are not charging this back to the managers, it is a good idea to document this for your management. Once you are able to present people with the facts, reality sets in and you are able to help them reasonably determine the proper length of time for off-site storage given their business requirements.

Differences between Business Units

Sometimes data must be segregated between business units. There are several ways to do this. The most secure way is to have multiple tape libraries and do the different business unit backups to different physical libraries. Sometimes this is not possible or practical. If this is the case, there are other ways to accomplish this. With a tool such as VERITAS Software's Net-Backup, you can establish unique volume pools and assign media to a specific volume pool. You then assign specific backups to specific volume pools. This allows you to logically segregate the data within a single tape library. We discuss this in more detail later when we look at installing and configuring a backup product. One word of caution: Just because your software solution supports it doesn't mean you have to implement it. In other words, if you do not have a compelling reason to implement multiple volume pools, then by all means do not add a level of complexity to your environment simply because you can. Backup products like VERITAS NetBackup are quite scalable and easily modified should that be a requirement down the road.

Other differences between business units may potentially affect how you architect your backup strategy. Often these will result in unique backup and recovery requirements for some systems. With most backup products, you can set up backup policies for similar clients with similar requirements and separate the clients that have unique needs. You must always be aware of any of these unique requirements before putting your strategy together.

REAL-WORLD CUSTOMER CASE STUDY: PROBLEMS AND SOLUTIONS FOR ENTERPRISE BACKUP AT GLOBAL COMPANIES

Thus far, we have discussed architecting a backup and recovery system. Most of the points I have addressed are based on my experiences helping enterprise users put together their systems. I would like to share my experiences with one such organization that I visited. This was at the height of the e-business explosion. The company was just getting started and was planning to go global. They were starting with a data center on the East Coast, then another on the West Coast, to be followed closely by one in England. I went to their main office with the local sales team to help evaluate their recovery needs and to see if we would be able to help them achieve their objectives.

When we arrived for the first meeting, it was obvious they were very concerned. After brief introductions, they launched into a description of their environment with interjected comments about their situation being just about hopeless. One of the first statements was "You have no idea how much data we already have, and we are just getting started. With our projected growth, I don't see how we can possibly back up all our data." They went on to list all of the existing servers with the amount of storage on each and a grand total. They also summarized their network configuration, the backup-related hardware they had already purchased, and last but not least, their growth projections. The amount of data was impressive. After looking over all this information, my first question caught everyone by surprise: "Why are you backing up this data?"

"Why? Why, we have to. One of our competitors just experienced some type of outage and did not have proper backups. It was a total disaster for them. What do you mean, why?"

I had to rephrase my question so they could understand what I actually was looking for: "How many of your systems have active users with volatile data that might result in files being regularly restored because someone deleted a file or wanted to revert to an older version?" After a few minutes of discussion, they decided this would probably only involve a small number of their total

(continued)

REAL-WORLD CUSTOMER CASE STUDY: PROBLEMS AND SOLUTIONS FOR ENTERPRISE BACKUP AT GLOBAL COMPANIES *(continued)*

systems. "How many of your systems are you backing up just to protect against hardware failure or some type of system crash? How many of your systems are pretty static as far as the data? How many of your systems are running a critical application that you want to ensure are protected from system crashes, hardware failures, and application errors?" We discussed all the different things they wanted to protect the different systems from, and they started to build a different list. By using common sense and actually looking at each system, they were able to determine that their backup challenge was not as bad as they originally thought. They even discovered that a lot of their interface systems were really just replicated systems, so they only needed one copy of the data, not 50.

In subsequent meetings we started to look at their planned environment in more detail and were able to make suggestions in all areas of their backup and recovery strategy. What we were really doing was getting them to look at the backup strategy from the other end, the recovery requirements. You will always be more successful if you approach it this way.

Summary

We have looked at some of the ways business requirements can affect the way you architect your backup and recovery strategy. As mentioned, there are pitfalls along the way as well, such as the business unit manager who wants to keep his or her backup data off-site for a year even though there isn't a real solid business case for it. Backup can become a dumping ground, and if we do not present the business with the costs involved in managing and maintaining this data, it will continue to grow. Just like a laptop with a 30-GB hard drive that only has 4 GB left. Is there really a good reason to keep all that data? No, not really, but I have the space and it's paid for by someone else. Now if this had to come out of my own pocket, or budget, perhaps I would think differently about it. It is always a good idea to look at these requirements and help the business units stay focused on the ultimate goal at each step during this process. Following are the different elements we have discussed:

- Types of backups
- Frequency of backups
- Security of backups
- Off-site storage requirements
- Differences between business units

By evaluating all these requirements and being aware of how they affect you, you will be able to better develop a backup and recovery strategy that meets your business needs. Business prioritization sets the criteria for success.

In the next chapter, we start looking at actually doing something with the information laid out in the first two chapters. We will use VERITAS NetBackup DataCenter as the backup application. We first give you an introduction to this application and then get into the details of deploying it in an enterprise.

## CHAPTER 3

An Introduction to NetBackup

Many commercial backup products are available on the market today. The leader amongst them on UNIX platforms is VERITAS Software's NetBackup DataCenter. We will use this product, which we refer to as just NetBackup, in our explanations and examples of setting up a backup domain. We start with an introduction to NetBackup, including an explanation of the unique architecture of the product, and then we define the terms that it uses. Most of the examples use the latest release, 4.5, but we will mention when there is a significant difference with older releases.

NetBackup Tiered Architecture

NetBackup uses a four-tiered architecture for backup domains, as shown in Figure 3.1.

The tiers are as follows:

Client.   Any system that contains data that needs to be backed up.

Media server.   Any system that has physically connected storage devices to be used for backups. These can be robotic devices, stand-alone tape drives, or optical storage devices.

Master.   The NetBackup server that provides administration and control for backups and restores for all clients and servers. It is also the system that contains all the catalog information for the backup domain.

Global Data Manager. A master of masters that can monitor and facilitate management of multiple master servers and multiple backup domains.

All systems within a NetBackup domain fall within at least one of these tiers and can actually fit into more than one. The first three tiers are always found, even if on the same system. The fourth tier, the Global Data Manager tier, is usually found when there are multiple NetBackup domains that are monitored and administered from a single location. This tiered architecture is one of the things that make NetBackup so scalable and flexible. As you start out, you can have a single master server that gives you a single point of administration, and at the same time, you can have as many media servers as are needed to support your configuration. As you grow, you can add more tape devices and just add more media servers without having a great impact on your overall configuration. If your enterprise continues to grow, you can simply add another master server with media servers as needed. At this point, you might add the fourth tier. The first tier, clients, can be added or deleted easily, since the configuration is kept on the master server.

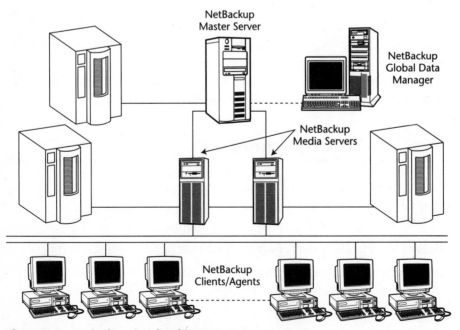

Figure 3.1 NetBackup tiered architecture.

Explanation of Specific NetBackup Concepts

The NetBackup product can be thought of as being made up of two major components: netbackup and media manager. The netbackup component is responsible for the who, what, when, where, and how aspects of the backup jobs:

- Who needs to be backed up? The client.
- What needs to be backed up? The file or file list.
- When do the backups run? The schedule.
- Where should they be stored? The logical storage unit.
- How should this policy be handled? Specific attributes of the backup policy.

It also tracks and manages all the backups and all of the backup images.

The media manager component is responsible for managing all the physical media and all the devices. In general, the netbackup component deals with logical devices, and the media manager deals with physical devices.

The netbackup component tracks and manages all the data that is backed up by using the unique backup identifier assigned to each backup image when it is created. It also manages the overall catalog and the scheduling of new tasks. It selects the appropriate media server to match each backup job.

The media manager component manages all the physical storage devices and the physical media. It is through the media manager that the physical tape libraries and drives are configured, and the volume database is populated. The media manager controls the tape libraries and maintains the inventory of all the volumes.

Layout NetBackup Domain

Now the fun begins. You have gathered tons of data and know more about your enterprise than you ever thought was possible. It is time to put all of this knowledge to use. If this is the first time an actual backup and recovery strategy has been implemented, you will be able to tailor the backup domain. If this is an upgrade or application change, you will probably have to work within the confines of the existing layout, making changes as required.

Using NetBackup as the application in this domain, you first want to list all the systems that will be backed up as clients. This will give you an idea of the number of systems that need to be backed up and the distribution of data. Any systems that have a large amount of data, over 100 GB for example, should be noted, as you might want to make them media servers. The other important thing to track with the clients is their network connectivity. If it looks like there are a lot of network-based clients on slow networks, you should consider installing a high-speed backup network. This gives you increased backup and recovery performance, as well as keeping backup and recovery traffic off the production network. It is now common to install a 100Base-T or Gigabit Ethernet network just as a backup and recovery network.

A NetBackup domain requires at least one master server. In most situations, there will be only one; however, in a later chapter we discuss some reasons to have more than one master. The system that you choose for the master will depend on the size of your enterprise—the number of clients, the total number of files being backed up, and the number of storage units you will need. In a smaller environment, the master server can be a system that is already being used for other work or could be a combined master and media server if it is attached to a backup device. Figure 3.2 shows an example of a configuration where the master server is also a media server and all the client backups are basically LAN-based backups.

In larger environments, the master server is usually a dedicated Net-Backup server, although it could still be a media server. This server must have enough disk capacity to handle the NetBackup catalogs and, potentially, the debug logs. Most of the debug logs are located in /usr/openv/ netbackup/logs. If this directory is not located in a separate partition, you must make sure you do not allow the logs to grow and fill the disk. The largest part of the catalog is the image database, which is located in /usr/ openv/netbackup/db/images. It is not uncommon for this directory to be a separate partition. All of the meta data for all the backups are sent to the master and stored in this image database portion of the catalog. The maximum amount of disk space that NetBackup requires at any given time varies according to the following factors:

- Number of files that you are backing up
- Frequency of full and incremental backups
- Number of user backups and archives
- Retention period of backups
- Average length of full pathname of files
- File information (such as owner permissions)
- Average amount of error log information existing at any given time
- Whether you have enabled the master catalog compression option

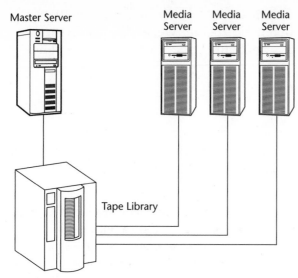

Figure 3.2 LAN-based backup.

To estimate the disk space required for the image database portion of the NetBackup catalog:

1. Estimate the maximum number of files that each schedule for each policy backs up during a single backup of all its clients.

2. Determine the frequency and retention period of the full and incremental backups for each policy.

3. Use the information from Steps 1 and 2 to calculate the maximum number of files that exist at any given time.

> Assume you schedule full backups every seven days with a retention period of four weeks and differential incremental backups daily with a retention period of one week. The number of file paths you must allow space for is four times the number of files in a full backup plus one week's worth of incrementals.
>
> The following formula expresses the maximum number of files that can exist at any given time for each type of backup (daily, weekly, etc.):
>
> Files per Backup × Backups per Retention Period = Maximum Number of Files
>
> If a daily differential incremental schedule backs up 1200 files for all its clients and the retention period is seven days, the maximum number of files resulting from these incrementals that can exist at one time are as follows:
>
> 1200×7 days $= 8400$

If a weekly full backup schedule backs up 3000 files for all its clients and the retention period is four weeks, the maximum number of files due to weekly full backups that can exist at one time are as follows:

3000 × 4 weeks = 12,000

Obtain the total for a server by adding the maximum files for all the schedules together. The maximum number of files that can exist at one time due to the preceding two schedules is the sum of the two totals, which is 20,400.

NOTE For policies that collect true image restore information, an incremental backup collects catalog information on all files (as if it were a full backup). This changes the preceding calculation for the incremental from 1200 × 7 = 8400 to 3000 × 7 = 21,000. After adding 12,000 for the fulls, the total for the two schedules is 33,000, rather than 20,400.

4. Obtain the number of bytes by multiplying the number of files by the average length of the file's full pathnames and file information.

    a. Determining the space required for binary catalogs:

        If you are unsure of the average length of a file's full pathname, use 100. Using the results from the examples in Step 3 yields the following:

        (8400 × 100) + (12,000 × 100) = 1992 KB (1024 bytes in a kilobyte)

    b. Determining the space required for ASCII catalogs:

        If you are unsure of the average length of a file's full pathname, use 150. (Averages from 100 to 150 are common.) Using the results from the examples in Step 3 yields the following:

        (8400 × 150) + (12,000 × 150) = 2988 KB (1024 bytes in a kilobyte)

NOTE If you have ASCII catalogs and use catalog indexing, multiply the number in Step 4 by 1.5 percent.

5. If you are running with debug logging, add 10 to 15 MB to the total calculated in Step 4. This is the average space for the error logs. Increase the value if you anticipate problems.

6. Allocate space so all this data remains in a single partition.

You must take many factors into account when determining what kind of system to use for the master server. It can be any type of system, any UNIX system or Windows system from the supported systems list. If the master is a dedicated system, you will need enough computing power to support the network adapters plus the NetBackup processes, as well as enough memory to support each. If the system is also a media server, the system resource requirements are higher. With NetBackup, it is not uncommon to share a tape library among multiple media servers. In many of these cases, the robotic control is handled by the master, while media servers share the tape drives, either directly connected or truly shared in a storage area network (SAN). (We look at using the Shared Storage Option in a SAN in a later chapter.) The following tables provide information about the number of CPUs and the amount of memory needed to support several hardware and software components, as well as the I/O adapter performance numbers. You should use the numbers listed in Tables 3.1 through 3.3 to design your master and media servers.

Table 3.1 CPUs Needed per Backup Server Component

COMPONENT	NUMBER OF CPUS PER COMPONENT
Network cards	1 per 2–3 100Base-T cards
	1 per 5–7 10Base-T cards
	1 per 2–3 FDDI cards
	1 per ATM card
	1 per 1–2 Gb Ethernet card
	(preferably 1)
Tape drives	1 per 2–3 DLT 8000 drives
	1 per 2–3 DLT 7000 drives
	1 per 3–4 DLT 4000 drives
	1 per 2–4 8mm and 4mm drives
OS + NetBackup	1

Table 3.2   Memory Needed per Backup Server Component

COMPONENT	MEMORY NEEDED PER COMPONENT
Network cards	16 MB per network card
Tape drives	128 MB per DLT 8000 drives
	128 MB per DLT 7000 drives
	64 MB per DLT 4000 drives
	32 MB per 8mm and 4mm drives
OS + NetBackup	256 MB
OS + NetBackup + GDM	512 MB
NetBackup multiplexing	2 MB × no. of streams × no. of drives

Figure 3.3 shows an example of a typical shared library configuration where there is a single master server and two media servers, each with two drives from a shared four-drive library. This would be a good option if the media servers either had a large amount of data or if you wanted to share the workload of backing up network clients.

If the amount of data is small enough, the drives could be directly connected to the master, making it the master and media server. When determining if you need a media server or multiple media servers, you should consider the following:

- Amount of data
- Location of data
- Speed of networks
- Backup window

Let's look at these in more detail.

Table 3.3   Drive Controller Data Transfer Rates

DRIVE CONTROLLER	THEORETICAL MB/SEC	THEORETICAL GB/HR
SCSI	5	18
Narrow SCSI-2	10	36
Wide SCSI-2	20	72
Ultra ATA	33	118.8

Table 3.3   *(continued)*

DRIVE CONTROLLER	THEORETICAL MB/SEC	THEORETICAL GB/HR
Ultra SCSI-3	40	144
Ultra ATA 66	66	237.6
Ultra2 SCSI-3	80	288
Fibre Channel	100	360

Amount of Data

The total amount of data that must be backed up when full backups are done is a good estimate for the maximum data that would be required to be managed. It is also very important to determine how much data is to be backed up on a daily basis. This is usually an estimation based on the amount of user or application data and the daily rate of change. If a filesystem contains 100 GB of data but only has a rate of change of 2 percent, you only have to worry about 2 GB of data for your daily backups. These two numbers, total data and changed data, are also used to determine how many tape drives are needed and are part of the media requirements formula.

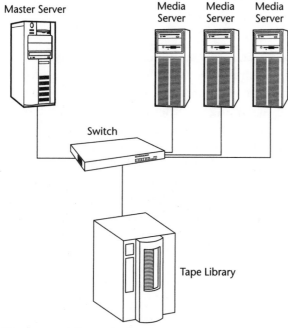

Figure 3.3   Library sharing.

Location of Data

If all the data is located on a couple of large file servers, you should make them media servers by physically connecting them to tape drives and maybe have one more to handle all the network-based clients. If the data is spread throughout your enterprise, you must decide how you want to configure the backup domain. You can configure a dedicated media server or servers and back up all the data over the LAN, or you can distribute media servers closer to the clients. The restriction here will be the SCSI cable length restrictions from the media servers to the libraries.

Speed of Networks

If a significant amount of data resides on clients on a slow network, you should consider either installing a high-speed backup network or, if there is enough data, making one of these clients a media server. The other consideration is the amount of traffic the backup and recovery requirements will add to the existing networks. If possible, you should put the backup and recovery traffic on a dedicated network. If this is not possible, you might have to throttle large backup clients on slow networks or they will dominate the network. Table 3.4 will help you determine how different networks will affect the overall backup performance.

Backup Window

The backup window can also come into play when you are determining media server requirements. Some straightforward formulas are used to calculate how many tape drives are required to back up a known amount of data in a fixed amount of time, assuming no other bottlenecks. We discuss these in the next chapter. If the amount of data to be backed up and the amount of time available result in too many drives required for a single media server, this would indicate another media server is needed. You must always stay within the system constraints when configuring media servers. It does no good to put more tape devices on a server than it has the I/O bandwidth to handle. You do not want to create any unnecessary bottlenecks.

Table 3.4   Network Data Transfer Rates

NETWORK TECHNOLOGY	THEORETICAL GB/HR
10Base-T	3.6
100Base-T	36
FDDI	36
Gigabit GbE	360
Quad FastEthernet QFE Trunked	144

EXAMPLE OF SIZING METHODOLOGY

1. Determine how much data needs to be backed up on a full schedule.

2. Determine the Window for the backups. How much time are you willing to allow for the backups to complete, for instance, 1 hour, 6 hours, 12 hours, and so on—"a weekend" is too nebulous. This needs to be a concrete number from start to finish to make this work out.

3. Once you have determined the amount of data and the window, you can easily determine how many drives are required to physically meet this challenge. This is all about simple numbers. A DLT 7000 drive can write about 8 MB/sec of data on average, so four DLT 7000 drives can write about 32 MB/sec. Therefore, 2 TB of data in a six-hour window will require 11.5 drives – (8 MB/sec × 60 seconds = 480 MB per minute × 60 = 28.8 GB per hour × 6 hours = 172.8 GB per drive per 6 hours. 2 TB / 172.8 GB per hour per drive = 11.57 drives to back up 2 TB in six hours to DLT 7000 tape drives). Drive selection is discussed more in the next chapter.

4. Now it's time to figure out how to provide enough bandwidth to the drives from the media server; a single F/W Diff SCSI card can write only 20 MB/sec, so each port on a card can handle only the bandwidth for two drives.

5. After you have determined the media server physical bandwidth, you need to determine LAN bandwidth to that media server, depending on how many drives it will be attached to. At 32 MB/sec, at least a Trunked QFE at 50 MB/sec or a GbE at 125 MB/sec will be needed. A media server backing up LAN traffic *must* be configured with something other than a 100-Mb network interface card (NIC).

6. So now that you have determined 4 and 5, you need to choose a media server that has the robustness to handle 4 and 5. A Sun Ultra 10 cannot have Quad FastEthernet (QFE) cards and won't handle a GbE; it is all about the numbers and is pure physics. Find out what you need to move across the copper/glass, and then build a system to accommodate this.

Summary

In this chapter, we looked at the first steps of setting up a backup and recovery strategy using a backup product. We selected NetBackup from VERITAS Software. We first looked at the specific architecture used by NetBackup:

- Client
- Media server
- Master server
- Global Data Manager

With this background, we could look at some of the specific system requirements for backup servers. This involved looking at the following:

- CPU requirement guidelines
- Memory requirement guidelines
- I/O adapter specifications

This information coupled with the following considerations gave us enough information to move to the next phase of design—determining media requirements:

- Amount of data
- Location of data
- Speed of networks
- Backup window

In the next chapter, we look at how we evaluate storage requirements, including tape drives and libraries.

Backup Product Tutorial

Evaluating Storage
Media Requirements

The next step in developing a backup and recovery strategy is to determine the storage media requirements. Based on the information you have already gathered, you should have a pretty good idea of how much data is going to be backed up, how many copies you will need to keep, and how long you will keep them. All of this information figures into the total storage media requirements. If this is a new backup domain, you can use this information to determine what type of tape drives and media will work best. If this is an existing domain, you can determine if you have enough drive and library capacity.

As you no doubt have already figured out, this is not an exact science. Every piece is interrelated. The size of the servers is dependent on the number of drives. The number of drives is dependent on the amount of data being backed up and the backup window. The backup window is related to the number of drives and the speed of the drives. The ability to use the bandwidth of the drives is related to the network speed and layout. That is why we picked a starting point of analyzing the data and moved forward from there. You will need all the data gathered using the guidelines in the first three chapters before proceeding.

As you move forward with evaluating storage media, you need to consider the selection of a suitable drive technology. The number of different drive types and the number of different libraries that support the different drives complicate this decision. You should gather enough information to make an informed decision. One place that can provide a comparison of all the different types is www.storagemountain.com/hardware-drives.html. This Web site shows all the different technologies and gives speeds, capacities, and load/unload times, as well as access times. All these figure into the final decision. If backup speed is the primary concern, a fast drive with a high-density cartridge might be the best solution. If recovery speed is more important, you might want to look at a fast drive with fast access, but high-density may not suit your requirements. If you want to recover a single file from the end of a tape, it would be faster to find it on a 20-GB tape than a 120-GB tape.

Backup Window and Amount of Data

One of the most critical steps in evaluating the storage media requirements is determining the actual backup window. This must be the actual amount of time you are allowed to have backups running, while at the same time, controlling the backup hardware, using a major part of the network, and using the resources on the systems being backed up. The size of your backup window is becoming a much harder measurement to define. You must be able to determine the number of hours in a day and in a week that can be dedicated to backups, as this is an integral part of the equation to determine media requirements.

Based on the data we collected in the earlier chapters, you should now have a very good idea of how much data needs to be backed up each day and each week. You need to know how much data needs to be backed up during each window. Generally, the largest backups will be the full backups. In the past, most administrators performed daily incremental backups and did all their full backups over the weekend when most people were not working. This concept is changing. It is very common now for a percentage of the systems, say, one-fifth, to have full backups done each day and the remaining systems to have incremental backups each day. The weekends are saved to do maintenance or to catch up. If this is closer to your model, then your window would be the time each day when backups are performed, and the amount of data would be the average sum of the total data that would be backed up, roughly a fifth of your total data. If you do not have specific operational information on the amount of data that will make up your incremental backups, you can estimate using a percentage of change to calculate the amount of data. It is common to use 20 percent, unless you have a more accurate measurement. The goal here is to try to get as close as possible to your actual environment.

Drives

Now that we have the amount of data and the number of hours needed to store that data, all we have left to do is some basic math. Just take the total amount of data that has to be backed up daily and divide by the duration of the daily backup window:

Ideal data transfer rate = Amount of data to back up ÷ Backup window

If you have 100 GB of data and an 8-hour window, your ideal data transfer rate would be 12.5 GB/hr.

After you have an idea of the ideal data transfer rate, you can then look at the different drive types to see which might offer the best fit for your needs. Not surprisingly, this is a little more complicated than just looking at the base numbers, though. With potential drive technology, you must consider both performance and capacity. In larger enterprise environments, one size usually does not fit all. As mentioned several times, you need to look at the recovery requirements first and work back. This might mean you will need two different types of drives, some that are very high performance but with less capacity and some that offer higher capacity with lower performance. Data that is being kept for long retention periods, especially to fulfill legal requirements, might be better suited for the lower-performance but higher-capacity media. Data that might be required for immediate restores where time is money might be better suited for the high-performance media. It is not uncommon to have backups done to high-performance drives and media and then the images vaulted to high-capacity drives and media for off-site storage.

A sample of tape drive transfer rates, capacities, and access times is given in Table 4.1. This information can be very helpful in determining which drive technology you need, but never forget these are all theoretical numbers and are given without taking into account the internal drive compression. Drive manufacturers advertise compression rates for the different drive technologies. These vary depending on the drive but are also theoretical numbers. These specifications can change with new firmware levels or versions of the drives. To get the most accurate numbers, contact the drive vendor or go to their Web site, where you'll find up-to-date specification sheets.

Table 4.1 Tape Drive Data Transfer Rates and Capacities

DRIVE	THEORETICAL TRANSFER RATE GB/HR (NO COMPRESSION)	THEORETICAL CAPACITIES GB (NO COMPRESSION)	ACCESS TIME EXCLUDING LOAD TIME	COMPRESSION
4mm (HP DDS-2)	1.8	4		
4mm (HP DDS-3)	3.6	12		
Mammoth	11	20	60 sec	2:1
Mammoth-2	42.4	60	60 sec	2:1
DLT 4000	5.4	20	68 sec	2:1
DLT 7000	18	35	60 sec	2:1
DLT 8000	21.5	40	60 sec	2:1
SDLT	39.6	110	70 sec	2:1
9840	36	20	11 sec	2.5:1
9940	36	60	41 sec	3.5:1
LTO	52.7	100	25 sec	2:1
AIT-2	21.1	50	27 sec	2.6:1
AIT-3	42	100	27 sec	2.6:1

When you start actually figuring how many of which kind of drive you will need, we recommend using the native transfer rates and capacities without compression. It is very difficult to estimate what kind of compression rate you will experience, as it is totally dependent on the makeup of your data. Some data is very compressible, while other data will yield very little compression. If you do your architecture based on no compression, the only surprises you should experience should be good ones; you will have plenty of capacity with room for growth.

Capacity

After selecting the appropriate drive technology that provides the performance and cartridge capacity you need, you next want to look at how many cartridges you will need to have available. This involves all the elements we have looked at so far. The number of cartridges required depends on the amount of data that you are backing up, the frequency of your backups, your retention periods, and the capacity of the media used to store your backups. A simple formula that can be used is as follows:

Number of tapes = (Total data to back up × Frequency of backups × Retention period)/Tape capacity

Following is an example:

- Total amount of data = 100 GB
- Full backups per month = 4
- Retention period for full backups = 6 months
- Incremental backups per month = 30
- Retention period for incremental backups = 1 month

Preliminary calculations:

- Size of full backups = 100 GB × 4 per month × 6 months = 2.4 TB
- Size of incremental backups = (20 percent of 100 GB) × 30 × 1 month = 600 GB
- Total data stored = 2.4 TB + 600 GB = 3 TB

Solution:

- Tape drive = DLT 7000
- Tape capacity without compression = 31.5 GB
- Total tapes needed for full backups = 2.4 TB / 31.5 GB = 76.2 = 77
- Total tapes needed for incremental backups = 600 GB / 31.5 GB = 19.1 = 20
- Total tapes needed = 77 + 20 = 97

By looking at this example, you would expect to have a minimum of 97 active cartridges at any given time. This also assumes that all the cartridges will be filled to capacity and there will be no unused tape. These calculations are based on no compression. This does give you an idea of the steps necessary to plan for an appropriately sized tape library. We would never recommend implementing an enterprise backup strategy that does not include a robotic tape library with a barcode reader. Without these, the management can become overwhelming and very susceptible to human error. It is much better to turn over media management to an enterprise backup application.

When figuring out how many slots are required to support your environment, do not forget to include some slots for cleaning tapes and at least two for the catalog backups. Actually, you will want to reserve twice as many slots for catalog backups as are needed so you can keep a copy of the catalog. If you are including an off-site storage solution of some type (vaulting) as part of your backup strategy, you need to include this in your total capacity calculations, since creating duplicate copies requires additional tapes.

Library?

As stated in the previous section, most enterprise backup strategies will include some type of robotic tape library. There are several library manufacturers, each with an entire line of libraries from small to very large. Part of this decision will be based on the drive technology you select, as some libraries support only certain drives. The considerations for selecting a library are as follows:

- Does it handle the desired drive type?
- Will it handle the required number of drives?
- Does it support the needed number of slots?
- Does it have expansion capability?
- What type of connection, SCSI or Fiber?
- Does it support barcode labels?

As you look at the different libraries available, you should also consider if your strategy is best served by one large library that contains all the drives and media or by smaller libraries that are distributed throughout your enterprise. We will discuss some of the reasons for picking one or the other in a later chapter, but part of this decision is whether you plan to implement a SAN or distributed media servers (or both). Generally, it is cheaper to buy one large library than two smaller libraries that equal the same capacity in drives and slots.

A sample of the library vendors are ADIC, ATL, Compaq, Exabyte, Fujitsu, HP, IBM, NEC, Sony, Spectra Logic, and StorageTek. Each of these companies has a Web site that contains all the information for their entire line of libraries. This would be an excellent place to go for information.

Summary

In this chapter, we started looking at the actual storage requirements for the backup. First, we determined the required backup window and calculated the amount of data we need to store each day. With this information, we looked at some of the tape drive technologies and how to determine how many drives might be needed to support the backup bandwidth. This led to a discussion on calculating how many active tape cartridges you would need to support. We recommend selecting an appropriate robotic library that will support the required number of drives and cartridges.

Next, we will look at actually putting this all together in a configuration.

## CHAPTER 5

General Discussion on Configuration

Our next step in our discussion of backup and recovery in the enterprise is to take all the data collected and manipulated in the previous chapters and actually configure a backup domain. We will use VERITAS Software's NetBackup application for this discussion. In this chapter, we go through the unique terms and concepts that apply to NetBackup so you can follow the examples more easily. We look at the elements that go into the selection of a master server, to determine if separate media servers are required, and at the actual steps involved in configuring the storage devices for use by NetBackup, as well as configuring a policy to back up clients. We also examine the internal catalog used by NetBackup and configure the automated backup of this catalog. As part of the configuration discussion, we look at the different methods that you can use to perform the configuration.

Specific NetBackup Configuration Elements

Each backup application uses its own terminology and NetBackup is no different. We have provided a glossary of the specific terms that are used when configuring NetBackup. To configure a NetBackup domain, you start with the selection of a master server. This server contains all the information about the policies that are configured for NetBackup. A policy contains the list of clients to be backed up, the file list, the attributes controlling the backup and all of the schedules. It also contains the information used to determine where the data will be sent for storage. This configuration information is called *storage units* and gives NetBackup a logical representation of the physical storage devices. Each media server contains the actual device configuration information. The master server also maintains and manages the database of all the media that is known to the NetBackup domain. This information is kept in the volume database (volDB). In addition to the actual volume information, the master has a database for the volume pool information (poolDB).

Master Server

Obviously, a good place to start is selecting a system to be the master server. When using an application such as VERITAS Software's NetBackup, your choice is not restricted by the application. You can use just about any UNIX or Windows system that has enough resources. Many people select the type of system that their administrative staff is already familiar with to eliminate the need to learn another operating system. It is very common in an enterprise for the backup master server to be a standalone system. This frees up all the system resources to the backup and recovery requirements of the enterprise and makes the master server independent of other applications. The master server can also be the robotic control host for the tape libraries, especially if it is a dedicated backup server. It is also common to make the master highly available. In some cases, depending on the overall backup workload, the master can also serve as a media server. In Chapter 3 we talked about some of the issues involved in selecting a server.

Here are several considerations when determining the master server:

Number of clients to be backed up.   The total number of clients to be backed up by a master is important primarily for two reasons. First, this has a direct relationship to the total number of jobs. Second, the number of clients affects the overall size of the catalog and the number of directories within the catalog.

Total number of backup jobs.   The total number of backup jobs scheduled daily and weekly is related to the number of clients and the number of schedules that are run for each client. Database agent backups also affect this number, since it is common for a single database backup to generate multiple jobs.

Number and type of networks.   Network interfaces require system resources—especially high-speed networks like GbE networks.

Total number of media expected to be tracked.   The management of the volDB requires system resources. As the expected size of the volDB grows, the system resources must be available to manage it.

Will the master be a media server?   If the master server will also function as a media server, you must select a system that has adequate I/O capabilities. You must also ensure there is enough memory to accommodate both functions.

There might be more considerations, but this list gives you an idea of what you need to be thinking about when selecting a master server. Remember, this server will be doing all the scheduling for the backups, managing the catalogs for all the backups, keeping track of the status and use of the tape devices, tracking all the active and available media that is known to the system, as well as handling all restores. You should make sure the system you select has enough memory and processor capacity to handle all these functions, as well as enough disk space to hold the catalogs, databases, and logs. Also remember to figure in growth in both disk and memory requirements.

Media Server

Every backup domain must have a media server. This can be the following:

Master server as media server.   As discussed in the previous section, a master server can also function as a media server.

Application server that is also used as a media server.   If an application server has enough data to make LAN backups undesirable, it can have tape drives attached, making it a media server. It can either back just itself up or be used to back up other LAN clients.

Dedicated media server.   A system or systems can be dedicated as media servers used just to move data from clients to tape or to read data back in the case of a restore.

Special SAN media server.   The SAN media server is special in that it can only be used to back itself up and cannot be used to back up other LAN clients.

We discussed some of the factors that affect the decision on media servers in Chapter 3. In a larger enterprise, it is common to have dedicated media servers to handle the LAN clients and have the larger application servers also be media servers, used primarily to do LAN-free backups of their data. If there is a SAN, these will probably be SAN media servers. Since the task of a media server is to move the data from a client to tape, it should have good I/O capabilities and adequate memory. The media server can be either a UNIX or Windows system. The most important considerations on selecting systems to be media servers are as follows:

- I/O capability
- Memory
- Network connectivity

Clients

As discussed, any system that has data that will be backed up is a Net-Backup client. This includes the master server, all the media servers, all the application servers, and any other systems that need to have their data protected. As you make your list of clients to be backed up, you should group them by common attributes. This can either be by function, business unit, architecture, or configuration. When you configure your backup policies, you should group clients with similar backup characteristics.

Devices and Storage Units

When you configure any backup and recovery application, you need to configure the specific hardware devices that will be used by the application. With NetBackup, you configure the physical storage devices on the media servers. These devices are first configured with the operating system and then with NetBackup. This allows NetBackup Media Manager to access the devices. NetBackup actually allocates and accesses the physical devices via the storage unit definitions on the master server. This configuration is also required. The order for configuring devices is as follows:

1. Configure the operating system to see and have access to all physical devices. This includes ensuring the proper device files are created.

2. Configure NetBackup Media Manager on the media servers to have access to all the system devices.

3. Configure storage units on the master server to allow access to the physical devices.

Installation

The normal procedure when setting up a backup domain is to install Net-Backup on the master server first and then install the media servers if applicable. The clients are usually pushed from the master, as long as they are similar in that we can push UNIX clients from a UNIX master server and Windows clients from a Windows master server. The actual installation steps are different for UNIX and Windows servers.

UNIX Master Server

NetBackup supports many different UNIX platforms. To simplify the installation procedure, an installation script is provided that interfaces with the specific operating system. This script will work with all the supported UNIX servers for both the master server and media server installation. The easiest way to install the software on a master server is to load the CD-ROM containing the NetBackup release software for the appropriate operating system in the local CD-ROM drive. You then change your working directory to the CD-ROM. A list of the files on the CD-ROM will look like the following for a Sun , HP, or Linux system:

```
# ls
Doc        NB-Java    NBClients  hp-ux    install    linux      solaris
```

It is not necessary to change directory to the different subdirectories at this point, since the install script that is provided will control all this. If you are installing from the other UNIX CD-ROM, the list will look like the following:

```
# ls
Doc        NB-Java    NBClients  alpha    install    ncr rs6000
sequent sgi
```

The installation CD-ROM contains the client software for all the UNIX clients, as well as all the released documentation. The install script determines the type of platform on which you are installing and selects the appropriate binaries to support that operating system.

After locating the proper install script, your next step is to execute the script. The following is the menu that results from executing the script on a Sun system:

UNIX Install Script

```
#  cd /cdrom/cdrom0
#  ./install


VERITAS Installation Script
Copyright 1993 - 2002 VERITAS Software Corporation, All Rights Reserved.

       Installation Options

     1 NetBackup
     2 NetBackup Client Software
     3 NetBackup Client Java Software

     q To quit from this script
Choose an option [default: q]:
```

To install the master server software, you select 1. The script then checks to see if this is a new installation or an upgrade. If it is a new installation, you are prompted to provide the location where you want the software to be installed. NetBackup must always have an origin from the /usr directory, so if you elect to have the software loaded to another location, a symbolic link will be created in /usr for a directory, openv, that will point to the location you selected. On Sun systems, applications are not normally allowed to be loaded in the /usr directory. Therefore, you will be prompted to install the package in /opt/openv, but a link will still be created as /usr/openv that points to /opt/openv. If it is an upgrade, the binaries for the old version are moved and the new version replaces them in the same location. In the case of an upgrade, the install script also checks for processes that are running that must be stopped to allow for a clean upgrade process. If there are NetBackup processes running, the script terminates them. You will also be prompted to provide a list of other UNIX platform types besides the master server that will be clients. This allows all of the appropriate client binaries to be loaded onto the master. Following is how that script looks:

NOTE It is a good practice when installing any new software application to read the release notes. Here you may find information that may not have made it to the documentation, special considerations, and so on.

```
       The Solaris clients will be loaded.

       Do you want to load any other NetBackup
       clients onto the server? (y) [y,n,?] y


       Choose the Platform Client types you wish to install
```

```
by selecting the platform type one at a time
or select ALL client platforms.

Platform Client Options
-----------------------
 1. Alpha
 2. DataGeneral
 3. HP9000
 4. INTEL (FreeBSD)
 5. Linux (RedHat)
 6. MACINTOSH (MacOSX and MacOSXS1.2)
 7. NCR
 8. IBM RS6000
 9. SCO
10. SGI
11. Sequent
12. Solaris
13. ALL client platforms
 q Quit client selection


    Enter Choice (Default is 13)   [1-13,?,q]
```

After you have provided the needed information, the requested client binaries are loaded in a client directory on the master server to be used when you install NetBackup on the clients within this NetBackup domain. The binaries are pushed from the master to the clients. The install script eventually prompts you to enter a license key. You must have either a permanent license key for all the options and features you have purchased or an evaluation key that will turn on all the features for an evaluation period. This prompt looks like this:

```
Installation of <VRTSnetbp> was successful.
Running /usr/openv/netbackup/bin/install_bp


A NetBackup BusinesServer or DataCenter license key is needed
for installation to continue.

Enter license key: xxxx-xxxx-xxxx-xxxx-xxxx-xxxx-xxxx-xx
        NetBackup DataCenter Base product with the following features
enabled:
        Open Transaction Manager
        Intelligent Disaster Recovery
    has been registered.


All additional keys should be added at this time.
Do you want to add additional license keys now? (y/n) [y]
```

If you want to add additional license keys for additional features, you would answer yes. The following prompt appears:

```
License Key Utility
-------------------

A) Add a License Key
D) Delete a License Key
F) List Active License Keys
L) List Registered License Keys
H) Help
q) Quit License Key Utility


Enter a letter:
```

When you are finished entering license keys, this question appears:

```
Installing NetBackup DataCenter version: 4.5GA

Is t-sparc1 the master server? (y/n) [y]
```

This is where you decide if you are installing a master server or a media server. Since this is a master server installation, you would answer yes, which allows the script to continue. This allows the script to set up the system configuration files to support a master server installation. The script also extracts and installs the NetBackup Java software to allow use of the Java interfaces. You are then prompted to supply a host name to store and manage the global device database:

```
In order for device discovery and auto-configuration to work properly in
a DataCenter environment, particularly where peripherals are connected
to multiple servers, one host must serve as the repository for global
device configuration information.

Enter which host will store global device information.
(default: t-sparc1):
```

In almost all cases, this will also be the master server, and that is the default supplied by NetBackup. As the script finishes the installation procedure, you are asked if you want to create example templates and if you want to start the NetBackup processes so you can continue with the installation and configuration. If this is your first experience with the product, having the templates to use as examples is worthwhile. If you are a seasoned user, you might want to save a little time and space and skip these. This basically finishes the software installation for the master server. After you have installed any media servers, you are ready to go to the configuration step.

UNIX Media Server

Installation on a media server is very similar to installation on a master server. The primary difference is in the answer to the prompt, "Is this server the master?" By answering no, you are prompted to supply the master server name and any other media server names. This results in the correct server software being installed, as well as the configuration file being updated to reflect the other known servers in your backup domain. Following is the prompt difference for a media server:

```
Installing NetBackup DataCenter version: 4.5GA

Is t-sparc1 the master server? (y/n) [y] n

What is the fully qualified name of the master server?
```

UNIX Client

Two basic methods are used to push the initial client software out to UNIX clients from a UNIX master server. You can either use the remote shell method, which requires a .rhost file on each client, or you can use the File Transfer Protocol (FTP) method, which uses FTP to move the client software out to each configured client. Once the client software has been installed, the .rhost files can be removed, as the NetBackup processes will handle any future updates.

Windows Master Server

The installation of the NetBackup server software on a Windows server is a simple process. You load the Windows server CD-ROM in the CD-ROM drive, and an install shield should start. Figure 5.1 shows the initial window.

By selecting NetBackup Installation, you are presented with three options: Check VERITAS Web Site for Product Alerts, Start NetBackup Server Installation, and Start NetBackup Client Installation. For a master server installation, you select Start NetBackup Server Installation. After you have been prompted through a few steps of preinstallation checks, the screen shown in Figure 5.2 appears.

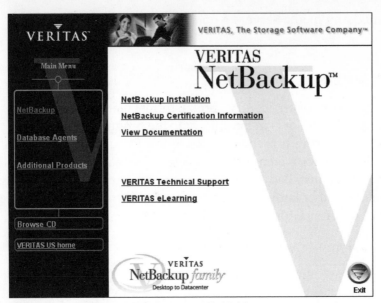

Figure 5.1   NetBackup Windows install shield.

At this point, you must either enter a valid license key, which allows you to continue with the master server or media server installation, or you can install another option, the NetBackup Remote Administration Console. This tool allows you to administer the servers within your NetBackup domain from a Windows system.

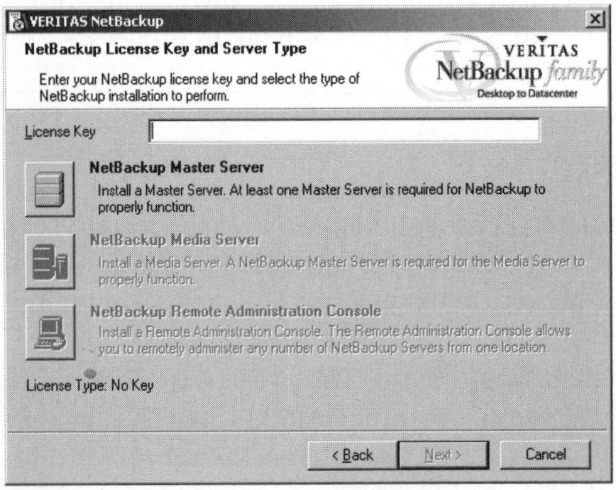

Figure 5.2   NetBackup License Key screen.

Windows Media Server

As seen in the last section, the media server installation is very similar to the master server installation. During the media server installation, you provide the name of the master server and any other media servers. This allows NetBackup to set up all the configuration files to properly reflect your backup domain.

Windows Clients

Windows client software can be pushed from a Windows master server or can be locally installed using the NetBackup release CD-ROM.

Configuring NetBackup

In this section, we go through the steps for the configuring NetBackup. The steps include configuring the physical devices—tape or optical—as well as configuring the storage units, which may again be tape, optical, or even disk, and then finishing up by configuring a policy. Remember, the policy is the who, what, when, where, and how of the NetBackup configuration. It is best to truly think about the implementation of the policies—how the backup policies should be configured, how schedules should be executed, and so on. Too often, when we are asked to perform NetBackup site assessments, it's the policy structure that people want us to spend most of our time focusing on. Unfortunately very little time is given to the overall structure and task of creating the backup policies, and it's the one that can cause the most pain later on down the road.

Devices

After the server software is installed on the master and any media servers, the next step is to configure the backup devices. During the installation, you should have supplied the name of the master server and any media servers. This allows the install process to build the basic server configuration file. All of the physical devices must be visible to the operating system on the media server, and the appropriate device files must exist. VERITAS Software supplies a document titled *VERITAS NetBackup DataCenter 4.5 Media Manager Device Configuration Guide* to assist in the process. This document guides you in configuring the operating system-specific device files needed to access the physical devices.

After ensuring the operating system has access to the physical storage devices, you can now configure the backup application to use these devices. With most server platforms and with most robotic libraries, the device configuration can be completed using the Device Discovery and Configuration Wizard. At the end of the installation process, you were prompted to start all the daemon processes. If you selected not to start the processes, you will need to start them before continuing with the configuration process. There are a couple of ways to start all the processes. If you are on a UNIX master, you can execute the rc script, S77netbackup. You can also accomplish this by executing `/usr/openv/netbackup/bin/initbprd` and `/usr/openv/volmgr/bin/ltid`. This should start all the necessary daemons. On a Windows master, you can use Start, Control Panel, Administrative Tools, Services to start the NetBackup processes.

With the daemon processes running, you can start the administrative interface by issuing the following command on a UNIX system: `/usr/openv/netbackup/bin/jnbSA`. This starts the Java GUI. The first thing you need to do is to log in as either root or a designated non-root administrator on the login screen.

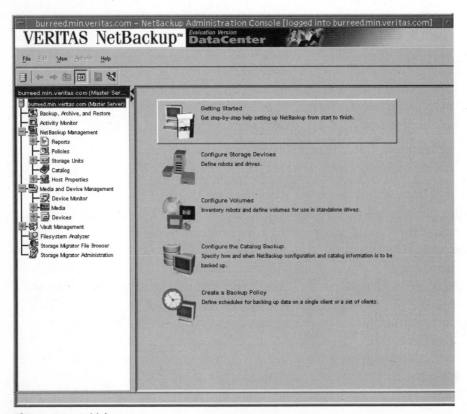

Figure 5.3   Initial screen.

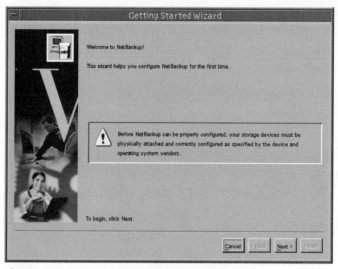

Figure 5.4   Getting Started Wizard welcome screen.

After you log in, the initial Administration Console window, shown in Figure 5.3, appears. Figures 5.4 and 5.5 show the Getting Started Wizard. You just follow the logical prompts until you reach the first window of the Device Configuration Wizard, shown in Figure 5.6.

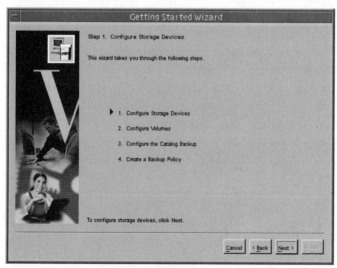

Figure 5.5   Getting Started Wizard: Step 1.

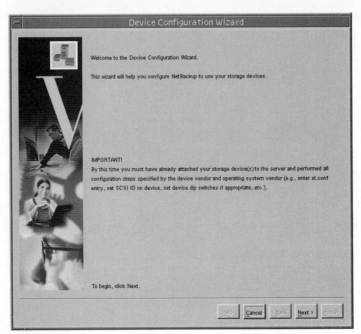

Figure 5.6 Device Configuration Wizard welcome screen.

Clicking Next on the opening screen for the Device Configuration Wizard takes you to the screen shown in Figure 5.7, where you define your media server environment. Here, you can enter the names of all the device hosts, which will generally be all the media servers, in this NetBackup domain.

The master server name will already be present on this screen. If the master is not a device host—that is, not a media server—you can uncheck it and then click on the Add button. This allows you to enter the names of all the media servers. After you have entered all the server names, you click on Next, which will start the actual device detection on each of the servers listed. The results of the auto-discovery process are shown in the Device Configuration Wizard window. When the process is complete, the window shown in Figure 5.8 appears.

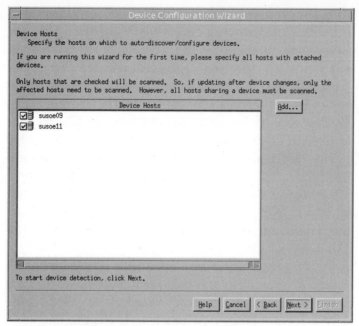

Figure 5.7   Device Configuration Wizard: Device Hosts.

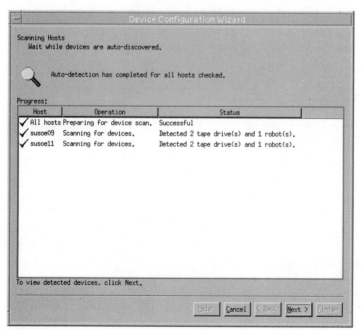

Figure 5.8   Device Configuration Wizard: Scanning Hosts.

You can view all the discovered devices by clicking on Next. Doing so shows the details of the device discovery on each of the device hosts, as you can see in Figure 5.9. You can compare this with the hardware configuration as you know it. Hopefully, they will agree, and you can continue. If there is a problem with discovery on a particular host, you will probably want to go to that host and see if there is a problem with the operating system accessing the devices. One of the most critical fields on this screen is the field labeled Serialized. If any of the tape drives or libraries have a No in this field, the Device Configuration Wizard cannot successfully complete the configuration. When this occurs, you need to contact your hardware provider and determine if the devices you are using support device serialization. If they do not, you can still use the devices and configure them with NetBackup; you just cannot rely on the auto-discovery feature of the Device Configuration Wizard.

In some cases, the drives support serialization and the library does not. If the drives are dedicated to a single host, you can manually finish the configuration started by the Device Configuration Wizard. Select Next on the detailed screen, and the screen in Figure 5.10 appears, indicating there is a library with no drives and there are two drives that are not in a library.

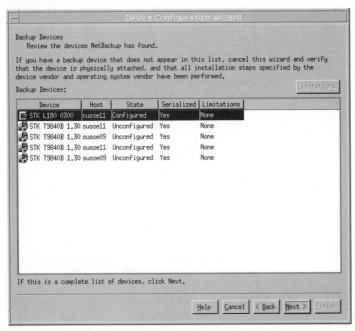

Figure 5.9 Device Configuration Wizard: Backup Devices.

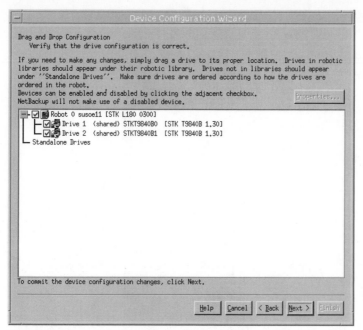

Figure 5.10   Device Configuration Wizard: Drag and Drop Configuration #1.

This is because the drives reported their own serial numbers, but the library did not report the drives' serial numbers. In this case, if you know the physical configuration of the drives within the library, you can drag and drop the drives to the library. If all the devices support serialization, the screen in Figure 5.11 appears. If this is the case, you will not need to do the drag-and-drop configuration and the screen in Figure 5.12 appears.

You first select the drive and then drag it to the Drive 1 location in the library. Then you repeat the step for the second drive. If you are unsure which drive is which, you can select Properties. Doing so gives all the detailed information for the selected device. After ensuring all the devices appear to be correctly configured, select Next to commit the changes. The resulting dialog box gives you one last opportunity to either cancel the changes or continue. Select continue to actually commit the changes and update the configuration database.

In our single device host, single library example, this would result in the screen shown in Figure 5.13.

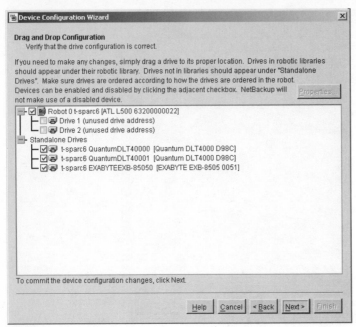

Figure 5.11 Device Configuration Wizard with full serialization Drag and Drop Configuration.

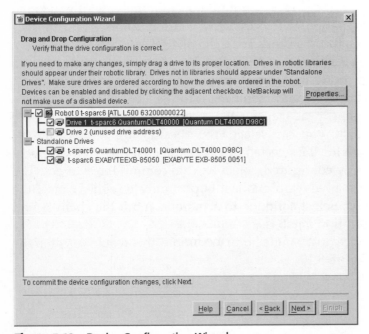

Figure 5.12 Device Configuration Wizard.

Figure 5.13 Device Configuration Wizard: Updating Device Configuration.

Storage Units

You have now completed the configuration of the physical devices within NetBackup. This makes the devices accessible. The wizard now prompts you to continue with the logical configuration of NetBackup. As stated earlier, NetBackup actually uses storage units to access the physical devices. This is the logical representation of the physical devices that NetBackup uses when assigning devices to jobs. The next wizard screen is the storage unit screen, shown in Figure 5.14.

This screen lists all the configured libraries and prompts you to make a storage unit for each one. As you create them, make sure you give each one appropriate attributes. The first characteristic you need to select is the storage unit type—whether it is a media manager storage unit, removable media, or a disk storage unit. This is done from the screen shown in Figure 5.15.

If you select Disk, the default behavior is for the storage unit to be *on demand only*. That means the storage unit cannot be used by NetBackup as a destination for backups unless specifically named by the job. This is not a requirement. On the other hand, if you select Media Manager, on demand only behavior is not the default, but you may select it if desired.

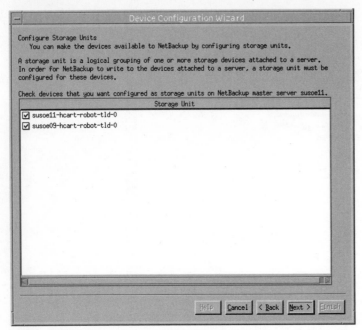

Figure 5.14   Device Configuration Wizard: Configure Storage Units.

The Storage Unit Type Properties are specific to the type of storage unit you select. If you select Media Manager, the properties screen that appears will be specific to that type, as shown in Figure 5.16.

Figure 5.15   Select storage unit type.

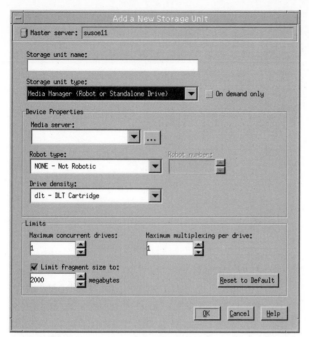

Figure 5.16 Storage unit configuration: Media Manager.

As you can see, you need to supply the media server name, the robot type, and the robot number from the pull-down lists. You also must make sure the density selected in the storage unit matches the density of the robot you created.

There are other properties associated with the Storage Units which further control their behavior:

Maximum concurrent drives. This is a way to throttle the use of drives within a library. If you have a library with 10 drives, but you want a particular family of jobs to only use a maximum of six, you could create a special storage unit with a maximum concurrent drives parameter set to six. This would ensure this family of jobs could never take all 10 drives for backups.

Maximum fragment size. This parameter is used to control how much data NetBackup will write as a single image without a break. With maximum fragment size of 0, a backup is written as a single image unless end of tape is encountered. If a maximum fragment size of 2000 is used, a backup image is broken into 2-GB fragments, each with its own header.

Maximum multiplexing per drive. This allows you to configure how many different streams of data can be multiplexed together on a single drive within this storage unit.

Figure 5.17   Storage unit configuration: Disk.

For a disk type storage unit, you will see the screen in Figure 5.17.

As you see, there are not as many fields to configure, just the hostname, the absolute pathname to the directory that will hold the backup images, maximum concurrent jobs, which allows you to limit how many jobs can write to this disk at the same time, and the maximum fragment size. This has the same use as on the Media Manager storage unit but defaults to 2000 MB, since some operating systems will not allow a single file larger than this.

With the latest version of NetBackup 4.5, there is a slightly different screen for adding storage units. All of the information remains the same; just the screen layout is different. The newest screen is shown in Figure 5.18.

Figure 5.18   Newest storage unit configuration screen for NetBackup 4.5 FP3.

Volumes

Now that we have configured the physical devices, we need to define some storage media to be used for the backups. The physical cartridges are called tapes, media, or volumes. When we discuss them within NetBackup Media Manager, they are referred to as volumes. These are the actual tapes that will be used to hold the data that is being backed up. Once you have configured one or more robotic devices, you can use the Volume Configuration Wizard. An easy way to proceed, at least for the first time, is to use this tool and to inventory the robotic libraries. If you are not using a library or have media without barcodes, you can use the Volume Configuration Wizard, but you would use the "Create new volumes for use in standalone drives" option.

As shown in Figure 5.19, any robots you have defined will show up in the screen, and you can select the one you want to inventory.

Once you have made your selection, the wizard returns the list of actions that are required. This can include new volumes that were found in the library and need to be added to the database, volumes that the database shows as being in the library but that the robot indicates are not present, and volumes that are in different slots. When you select Next, the volume database is updated to match the robot inventory. This is shown in Figure 5.20.

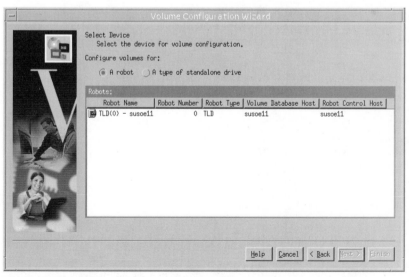

Figure 5.19   Volume Configuration Wizard.

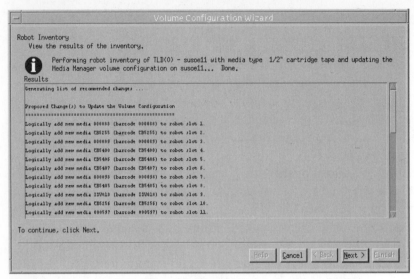

Figure 5.20   Volume Configuration Wizard: Updated volume database.

You are even given the opportunity to identify cleaning volumes that might be in the library, as shown in Figure 5.21.

Slot	Media ID	Barcode	Media Type	Created	Time Assigned
1	000088	000088	HCART	12/09/2002 11:51:58	
2	CB5255	CB5255	HCART	12/09/2002 11:51:58	
3	000089	000089	HCART	12/09/2002 11:51:58	
4	CB5400	CB5400	HCART	12/09/2002 11:51:58	
5	CB5406	CB5406	HCART	12/09/2002 11:51:58	
6	CB5407	CB5407	HCART	12/09/2002 11:51:58	
7	000098	000098	HCART	12/09/2002 11:51:58	
8	CB5405	CB5405	HCART	12/09/2002 11:51:58	
9	ISV018	ISV018	HCART	12/09/2002 11:51:58	
10	CB5256	CB5256	HCART	12/09/2002 11:51:58	
11	000597	000597	HCART	12/09/2002 11:51:58	
14	DGCLN	DGCLN	HCART	12/09/2002 11:51:58	
15	DG001	DG001	HCART	12/09/2002 11:51:58	

Figure 5.21   Volume Configuration Wizard: Identify Cleaning Media.

As you add volumes, either manually or via the wizard, you should ensure that the media type for the volumes matches the media type for the drives. Note that there are three different DLT designations, since a single library could contain a mix of DLT 4000, DLT 7000, and DLT 8000 drives. The different specifications for each of the DLT drive types are listed in Chapter 4. You must be able to differentiate between the volumes for each of these drives. This is done by using DLT, DLT 2, and DLT 3 designations for the drive and media types. The other method used to differentiate between volumes is volume pools.

Volume Pools

As you build your backup environment, you will find that you need to be able to control the flow or keep backup data separate. One mechanism to do this is to use volume pools. A *volume pool* identifies a logical set of volumes by usage. You can create pools that span libraries. It is common practice to have long-retention full backups, such as the monthly full backups, to have a unique pool. If you are duplicating volumes, you should always have the duplicate copies in a different pool than the original copy. It is best if you configure your volume pools before you start adding volumes, since you cannot put volumes in a pool that does not already exist. You can also use the concept of a scratch pool whereby you can define all your pools but you put all the volumes in a scratch pool. NetBackup would then automatically move a volume from the scratch pool to a designated pool as required.

Policy

After configuring physical devices and creating storage units to use these devices, you need to create policies to actually back up data from clients and write it to the appropriate storage devices. There is a wizard that can walk you through the creation of a policy, and it might be helpful to use this initially. After a few policies, however, you will probably go straight to the Policy tab and create your own. One note here: policy is a NetBackup 4.5 term. In previous releases this was called class.

If you decide to use the wizard, the first thing you will be asked is to provide a name and policy type. The policy name should be something meaningful to you. The type is dependent on the type of client you are backing up and the type of backups you are doing on the client. All of the clients within a single policy must use the same policy type. Most of the special policy types, such as the different database backups or Network Data Management Protocol (NDMP) backups, are separately priced options and will

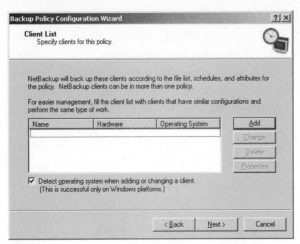

Figure 5.22 Backup Policy Configuration Wizard—Windows.

not show up as possible types without the appropriate license key. After selecting the appropriate policy type you add the specific clients that will be backed up by this policy. The wizard brings up the Backup Policy Configuration Wizard. On a Windows master, the screen looks like Figure 5.22.

Figure 5.23 shows a similar screen on a UNIX master.

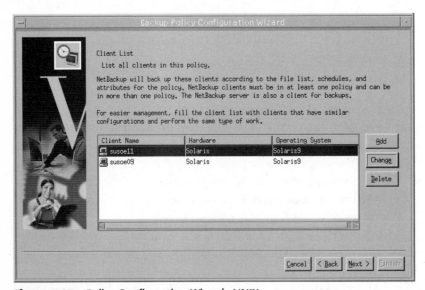

Figure 5.23 Policy Configuration Wizard—UNIX.

After entering all the clients that you want backed up by the policy, you are next prompted to enter a file list or set of directives to select what data to back up. At this point, you can select specific files, directories, filesystems, or raw devices, or you can give directives such as All Local Drives, which tells NetBackup that you want to back up everything. To further control how the backup is performed, you can use this directive with another attribute, Allow multiple data streams. We will go into all these directives when we get to the policy attributes screen.

Following the file screen in the policy wizard is the Backup Type screen, shown in Figure 5.24, where you can select what kind of backup you will be performing. (We discussed the different backup types in Chapter 2.)

As shown, you can select full, incremental differential, incremental cumulative, or user backup. Generally, at this point you would only select one type, since the next screen, entitled Rotation and shown in Figure 5.25, is used to set up the backup schedule for the backup type you have selected.

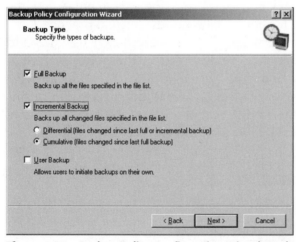

Figure 5.24   Backup Policy Configuration Wizard: Backup Type.

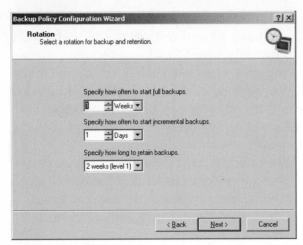

Figure 5.25   Backup Policy Configuration Wizard: Rotation.

If you selected both the full and incremental backup types, you could indicate different frequencies for the full and the incremental, but the retention would be the same for both; this is not the normal practice. Generally, you will keep full backups longer than incremental backups and perform the backup less often. The final screen in the policy wizard is where you set the actual time of day for the backups to start and the length of time the backup window will be open. The Windows version of this screen, shown in Figure 5.26, is different than the UNIX Java version, shown Figure 5.27, but the end results are the same.

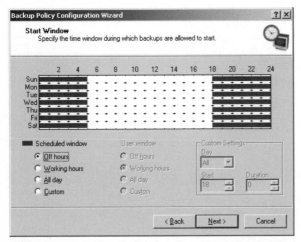

Figure 5.26   Backup Policy Configuration Wizard—Windows.

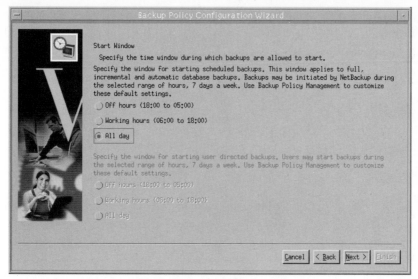

Figure 5.27   Backup Policy Configuration Wizard—UNIX.

At this point, the wizard is finished. You are given the option of saving, canceling, or going back. If you save the policy, you will see it in the policies section of the administration console. You can now take a closer look at the actual attributes of the policy and see if this matches your requirements or if it needs to be modified. The policy attributes screen is shown in Figure 5.28.

As you can see from the policy attributes screen, there are several potential selections that you were not prompted about during the wizard setup of the policy. In the following list, we highlight them and give a brief description for each. The items that are grayed out in the figure are not selectable either because of the policy type, because it is part of a feature that requires a license, or because it depends on another selection. The product documentation goes into every one of these items in detail, so if you have further questions, the appropriate system administrator's guide would be an excellent place to look.

Offhost backup method.   This option defines what will be moving the data for this policy. For normal backups, this will always be Local Host.

Limit jobs per policy.   This defaults to 999 and is a method to throttle a single policy to ensure it does not use all the resources.

Active. Go into effect at.   For a policy to be used, it must be active. You can preconfigure a policy and then give a time for it to become active.

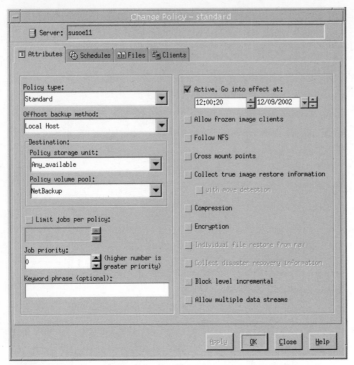

Figure 5.28   Backup Policy Configuration Wizard: Attributes.

Allow frozen image clients.   This field defines if any client in this policy will be using frozen images. This is discussed in more detail in Chapter 7.

Follow NFS.   If selected, this option causes NetBackup to back up data from any NFS-mounted filesystems that are found in the file list.

Cross mount points.   This option controls whether NetBackup will cross filesystem boundaries during a backup or archive on UNIX clients or whether NetBackup enters volume mount points during a backup or archive on Windows clients.

Collect true image restore information (with move detection).   If this option is selected, NetBackup will collect the information to allow a directory to be restored to the exact image that existed at a specific backup. Deleted files and directories are not restored. If move detection is also selected, files or directories that are renamed or moved will be backed up and therefore restored to the correct location.

Compression. This enables software compression on the client. This selection can reduce the amount of actual data moved across the network on a backup; however, it does increase the computing overhead on the client.

Allow multiple data streams. This option specifies that, depending on directives in the file list, NetBackup can divide automatic backups for each client into multiple jobs, with each job backing up only a part of the file list. The jobs are in separate data streams and can occur concurrently.

After selecting the specific attributes need for a specific policy, you can also further refine the scheduling. If you select the Schedules tab from the Change Policy screen, you will see the schedules that you have already created. This window is slightly different for the Windows GUI, shown in Figure 5.29, and the UNIX Java GUI, shown in Figure 5.30.

To add a new schedule using the UNIX Java GUI, you click on New. The screen shown in Figure 5.31 appears.

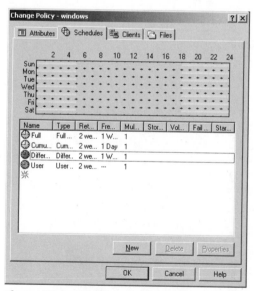

Figure 5.29 Windows Policy Configuration Wizard: Schedules.

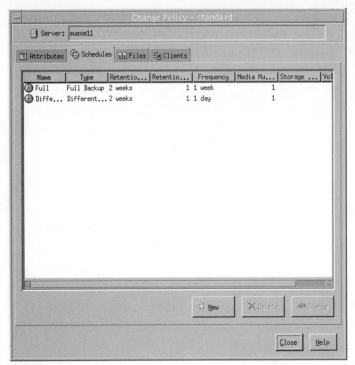

Figure 5.30 UNIX Policy Configuration Wizard: Schedules.

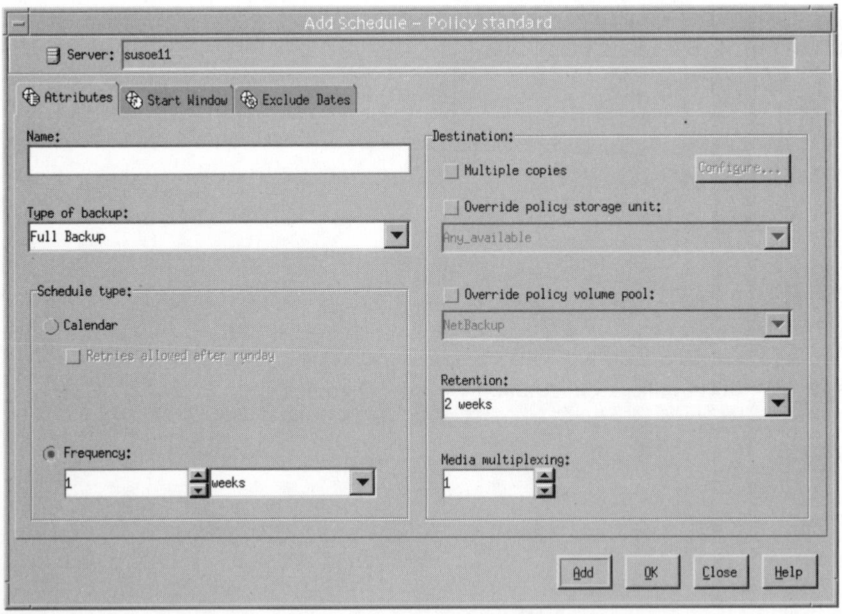

Figure 5.31 UNIX Policy Configuration Wizard: Adding a schedule.

This screen shows additional configuration points to consider:

Schedule type.   Calendar-based scheduling or frequency-based scheduling.

Destination:

- *Multiple copies*. If the vault option is installed, you can select up to four different destinations for the backup.

- *Override policy storage unit*. When the policy is created, you specify that the backups will either go to a specific storage unit, a group of storage units, or to any available storage unit. This allows you to change that selection on a per schedule basis.

- *Override policy volume pool*. This is similar to the storage unit selection but for volume pools.

Retention.   Here you specify how long you want to keep the backups created by this schedule.

Media multiplexing.   This allows you to send data from multiple data sources to a single tape.

After getting all the schedules configured, click on OK if you are finished making changes to the policy; if you want to add more clients or change the file list, select Add, and then the Clients tab or the Files tab, as appropriate. On the Files tab, you can select to add directives. These work together with the attribute of "Allow multiple data streams" to control how many jobs are actually started when a policy begins and how many data streams are sent from a specific client. On a Windows policy type and standard policy type, the directives are the same, with the exception of System_State, which is only applicable for Windows. In the list that follows, we provide brief explanations of the common directives, but we strongly suggest reading the entire section on file directives in the system administrator's guide.

ALL_LOCAL_DRIVES.   If the file list contains the ALL_LOCAL_DRIVES directive, NetBackup backs up the entire client but splits each drive volume (Windows NT) or filesystem (UNIX) into its own backup stream.

NEW_STREAM.   If this directive is the first entry in the file list, each occurrence of this directive results in a new backup job being initiated to back up the files following the directive in a separate stream.

SYSTEM_STATE.   This is used to back up registry information.

UNSET and UNSET_ALL. These directives are used to control policy-specific directives such as set. An example would be if you had a policy type that supported the set command and you wanted the set command passed to the first two streams but not the last, an UNSET or UNSET_ALL can be used at the beginning of the third stream to prevent it from being passed to the last stream.

```
NEW_STREAM
set destpath=/etc/home
/tmp
/use
NEW_STREAM
/export
NEW_STREAM
UNSET_ALL
/var
```

Auto-discovery streaming mode is enabled if "Allow multiple data streams" is selected and ALL_LOCAL_DRIVES is in the file list and NEW_STREAM is not the first line in the file list. If this is the case, the file list is sent to the client, which preprocesses the list and splits the backup into streams.

Catalog Backup

The installation and configuration is almost complete. All that really remains is to configure the application to back up its own database. The Getting Started Wizard walks you through the process, or you can do it directly from the Administrative Console. It is important to complete this step so you can protect your backup environment. The wizard prompts you for the information needed to set up this protection. You are asked to provide the media server where the catalog backup will be performed, the paths to all the critical data on the master, the names of all the media servers, and the paths to their data. Figure 5.32 shows the NetBackup Catalog Backup Wizard.

The critical data paths that should always be included for the master server are as follows:

- /usr/openv/netbackup/db. Automatically created for master during installation

- /usr/openv/volmgr/database. Automatically created for master during installation

- /usr/openv/var. Automatically created for master during installation
- /usr/openv/db. Must be manually added

You will also want to include the catalog paths for all media servers. These must be added manually.

- media_server_name:/usr/openv/netbackup/db/media
- media_server_name:/usr/openv/volmgr/database
- media_server_name:/usr/openv/var

After setting up the file paths to ensure all the data will be backed up, you need to configure the destination for these backups. You can either have the catalog backups sent to tape or disk or both. NetBackup can use two different destinations and will rotate between the two on each backup. If you select Disk, you need to identify an absolute path to be used to store the backup of the catalog. If you select Tape, you must select one or two specific volumes. Once a catalog backup has been sent to tape, that tape cannot be used for normal backups without being manually relabeled. You can configure NetBackup to use a tape for one destination and a disk path for the other. In this situation, every other backup would go to tape and every other would go to disk. The catalog backups do not append to tape. The tape is rewound, and the previous image is overwritten. The last decision for the catalog backup is the schedule.

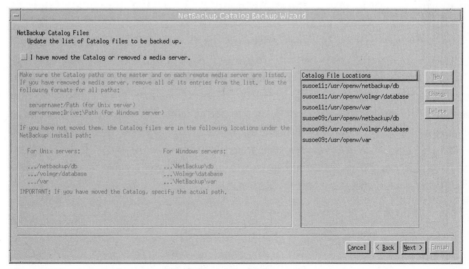

Figure 5.32 NetBackup Catalog Backup Wizard.

The choices are to back up the catalog

After each session of scheduled, user, or manual backups.   Backs up the catalogs after any session that results in the creation of at least one successful backup or archive. This includes automatic, manual, and user backups.

After each session of scheduled backups.   Backs up the catalogs after any automatic backup session that results in at least one successful backup of a client. A backup *does not* occur after a manual backup or a user backup or archive.

Only when manually initiated.   Does not automatically back up the catalogs. If you elect to back up catalogs manually, select Master Server, Catalog, right-click on Catalog, and select Back Up Net-Backup Catalog.

What User Interface to Use?

There are a couple of different ways to configure any application, and Net-Backup is no different. A lot of work goes into making the graphic interfaces easier to use. A growing emphasis has been placed on wizards to make the initial configuration much easier and more intuitive. Does that mean you must have a graphic console to install and configure the software? And what if you happen to be remote and want to tweak the configuration? You could encounter a problem trying to display back a GUI via dial-up.

Well, there are other options, and they also work quite well, although we would recommend them for the more experienced user. Just about everything that can be done from the UNIX Java GUI can also be done from the command-line interface (CLI). Many of the CLIs are documented in the manual, as well as in the release documentation. With many of the commands, you can also get usage information by executing the command with −help. The CLIs can be very useful when you are working remotely or from a nongraphic terminal or workstation. There are also the following character-based, menu-driven interfaces:

bp.   A backup, archive, and restore utility for users on NetBackup UNIX clients. It has a character-based menu interface.

bpadm.   An administrator utility that runs on NetBackup UNIX servers. It has a character-based menu interface.

vmadm.   A Media Manager administrator utility for managing volumes. It runs on UNIX and has a character-based menu interface.

These interfaces are easier to use than the CLI but can still be used over a dial-up or from a terminal without X graphic capabilities. Here are some examples of bpadm:

```
NetBackup Server:  wormwood.min.veritas.com
NetBackup Administration
-----------------------
s)   Storage Unit Management...
t)   Storage Unit Group Management...
p)   Policy Management...
g)   Global Configuration...
r)   Reports...
m)   Manual Backups...
x)   Special Actions...
u)   User Backup/Restore...
e)   Media Management...
h)   Help
q)   Quit


ENTER CHOICE: p
                Policy:  <ALL>
               Clients:  <ALL>
             Schedules:  <ALL>
Output Destination:  SCREEN


Policy Management
-----------------
a)   Add Policy...
m)   Modify Policy Attributes...
d)   Delete Policy
s)   Schedule Management...
c)   Client List Management...
f)   File List Management...


b)   Browse Policies Forward
r)   Browse Policies Reverse
e)   Enter Policy
l)   List/Display Policies
o)   Output Destination  (SCREEN or FILE)
h)   Help
q)   Quit Menu


ENTER CHOICE: b
                Policy:  test
               Clients:  wormwood
             Schedules:  FULL
Output Destination:  SCREEN

Policy Management
```

```
    -----------------
a)  Add Policy...
m)  Modify Policy Attributes...
d)  Delete Policy
s)  Schedule Management...
c)  Client List Management...
f)  File List Management...

b)  Browse Policies Forward
r)  Browse Policies Reverse
e)  Enter Policy
l)  List/Display Policies
o)  Output Destination   (SCREEN or FILE)
h)  Help
q)  Quit Menu

ENTER CHOICE:
```

As you can see, this interface allows you to manage the configuration without using a GUI. On Windows systems, this is not as much a concern, since you should always be able to use the Windows GUI. There is no character-based interface for the Windows systems, but many of the CLIs are still supported.

Summary

In this chapter, we looked at what is needed to actually start the installation and configuration of a backup application. We then went through the individual installation and configuration steps required to complete a basic installation of VERITAS Software's NetBackup. We touched on all the steps and also looked at the different interfaces. This should give you an idea of what is involved in setting up your basic backup application. In the next chapter, we look at how to monitor your backups.

Monitoring the Backup Process

Now that you have successfully installed and configured your backup domain, you are ready to sit back and take it easy. But wait, someone knocking on your door wants to know the status of their backup or restore. I guess you will have to start monitoring the backup and restore processes. While we are at it, we might as well look at monitoring some of the other elements in the backup domain that might need our attention. In this chapter, we go through some of the tools available to monitor the activities of our example backup and restore application, VERITAS NetBackup.

Using the Activity Monitor

The most common tool for monitoring the backup and restore activity is the Activity Monitor. This is available on both the UNIX Java GUI and the Windows GUI. Selecting the Activity Monitor on the Administration Console, as shown in Figure 6.1, results in the screen shown in Figure 6.2.

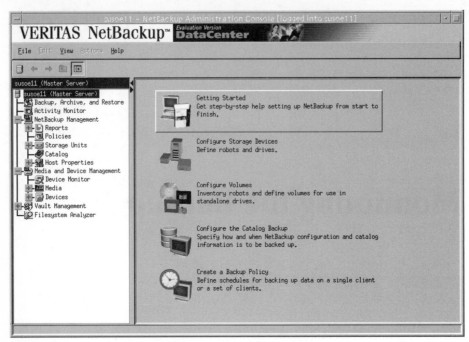

Figure 6.1   Administration Console.

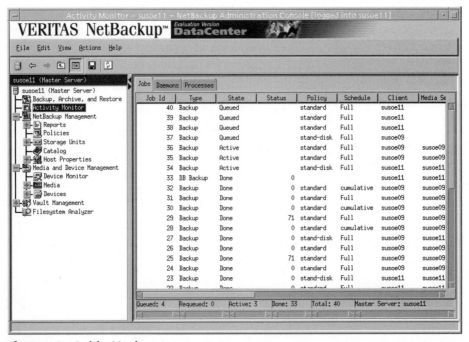

Figure 6.2   Activity Monitor.

This screen lists all the jobs that are currently being tracked by Net-Backup, including jobs that are queued, active, and finished. You can also see the summary information that includes all the jobs in each of these categories, plus the sum total of all jobs and the master server name. From the Activity Monitor, you can cancel individual jobs or cancel all running jobs. This is done from the Actions menu at the top of the screen.

Fields in Activity Monitor

The following list details the information contained within the Activity Monitor window:

Job ID.   This field displays the identifier that is assigned by Net-Backup to each job.

Type.   This shows the type of job activity, which can include any of the following job types:

- *Backup*. All backup jobs, no matter how they are initiated.
- *Restore*. All restore jobs, no matter how they are initiated.
- *Archive*. User-directed archive.
- *Catalog Backup*. All catalog backup jobs, no matter how they are initiated.
- *Duplication*. Image duplication jobs used to create a copy of an existing image.
- *Import*. Image import jobs used to build a catalog entry to allow restore from an image that is unknown to the master.
- *Verify*. Image verify jobs that are used to verify the contents of a tape.
- *Vault*. Jobs that are running as part of the vault process.

State.   The Activity Monitor also gives the current state of all the jobs. Following are the states:

- *Queued*. Jobs in the NetBackup scheduler queue waiting to run. A queued restore job is one for which NetBackup is still determining which files are needed.
- *Active*. Currently active jobs.
- *Re-Queued*. Jobs that are placed back in the scheduler queue as retries because the previous attempt was unsuccessful.
- *Done*. Completed jobs.

Status.   This field shows the status of each job. The status is shown when the job completes. A status of 0 indicates that the job completed successfully. Any other status indicates that there was some problem with the job.

> **NOTE** A backup job that completes with a status of 1 is considered partially successful but the image is written to tape and the image header file is updated in the catalog and marked as a complete backup. This indicates that the image will be kept for the normal retention period.

There are additional fields that give information about each job, including the actual policy name and schedule for backups, start time, elapsed time, media server name, client name, end time, number of this attempt, and others. These are all detailed in both the UNIX and NT versions of the System Administrator's Guide.

Detailed View

You can also highlight a job and select a detailed view that provides more information about the selected job. Figures 6.3 and 6.4 show what the job's detailed view looks like.

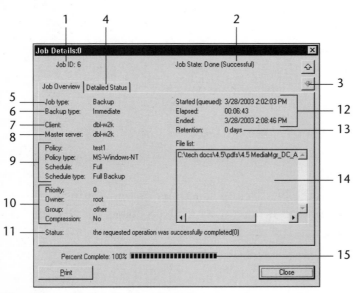

Figure 6.3   Job Details: Overview tab.

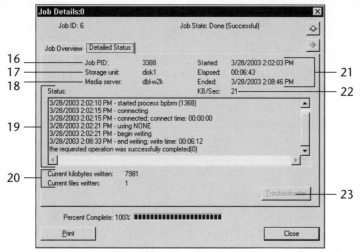

Figure 6.4 Job Details: Details Status tab.

Following are the fields in the screen shown in Figure 6.3:

1. Unique Job ID for the job in the queue.

2. The current State of the job.

3. Navigation buttons to scroll through the Activity Monitor.

4. Job Details Tabs.

5. Job Type, whether Archive, Backup, Restore, Catalog, or Duplication.

6. A description of how the job was submitted, either Immediate, or manually submitted, or Scheduled.

7. The client this job is currently working with.

8. The master server.

9. Backup policy information.

10. Specific attributes associated with the backup policy.

11. Completion status.

12. Job submission information, such as time it was submitted to the queue, the time that has elapse since the backup became active, and the time when the job ended.

13. Retention level for this particular job.

14. Files and directories configured in the backup policy.

15. Status bar.

Following are the fields in the screen shown in Figure 6.4:

16. Job process ID assigned by the operating system that corresponds to the NetBackup scheduler process (bpsched).

17. Storage unit, the logical storage device.

18. Media server.

19. Detailed job status information.

20. Kilobytes and number of files written.

21. Job times.

22. Performance data.

23. Troubleshooter to help identify problems and possible resolutions if the job completes with anything but a status of 0.

You can get to the Job Details screen by selecting a job from the Activity Monitor and double-clicking on it, by highlighting a job, right-clicking, and selecting Details from the menu, or by highlighting a job and then clicking on Actions at the top of the window. Doing so results in a pull-down menu with Details as a selection. The Jobs Details screen contains two tabs: Job Overview and Detailed Status. These screens can give you a very good idea of what is going on with a specific job. Also, if a job has a nonzero status, you can select the Troubleshooter button. This wizard provides an explanation of the specific status code and can be very helpful in discovering what might have caused a job to end with a nonzero status code.

Figures 6.5, 6.6, and 6.7 show an example of a nonzero backup job that has completed, as well as how to enter the Troubleshooter.

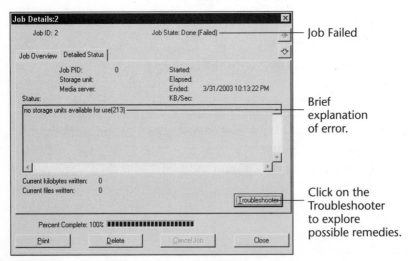

Figure 6.5   Job Details: Non-zero job details.

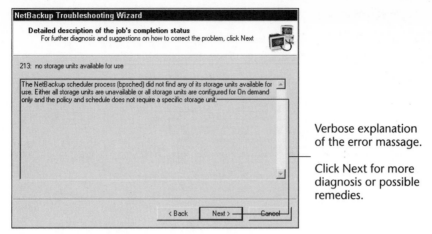

Verbose explanation
of the error massage.

Click Next for more
diagnosis or possible
remedies.

Figure 6.6   Troubleshooter: Problem description.

Figure 6.8 shows the equivalent to the GUI but this time from the command line.

The `bperror` command is a very useful tool that can be used in a variety of scripts for reporting on backup status, throughput statistics, and so on. You will see its value as we look into the reporting later in this chapter. For reference, the `bperror` command may be found in the following directories per your installed system for NT/2000 and UNIX, respectively.

```
<install_path>\Veritas\NetBackup\bin\bperror.exe
/usr/openv/netbackup/bin/bperror
```

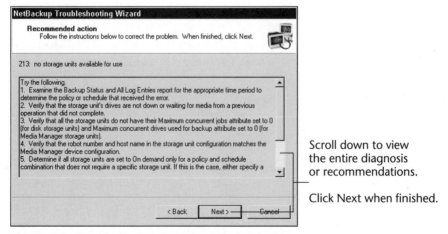

Scroll down to view
the entire diagnosis
or recommendations.

Click Next when finished.

Figure 6.7   Troubleshooter: Recommended actions.

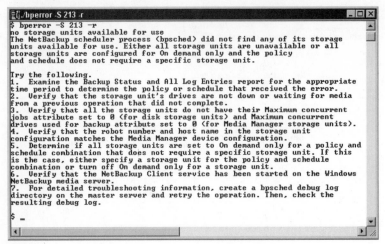

```
./bperror -S 213 -r                                              _ □ X
$ bperror -S 213 -r
no storage units available for use
The NetBackup scheduler process (bpsched) did not find any of its storage
units available for use. Either all storage units are unavailable or all
storage units are configured for On demand only and the policy
and schedule does not require a specific storage unit.

Try the following.
1.   Examine the Backup Status and All Log Entries report for the appropriate
time period to determine the policy or schedule that received the error.
2.   Verify that the storage unit's drives are not down or waiting for media
from a previous operation that did not complete.
3.   Verify that all the storage units do not have their Maximum concurrent
jobs attribute set to 0 (for disk storage units) and Maximum concurrent
drives used for backup attribute set to 0 (for Media Manager storage units).
4.   Verify that the robot number and host name in the storage unit
configuration matches the Media Manager device configuration.
5.   Determine if all storage units are set to On demand only for a policy and
schedule combination that does not require a specific storage unit. If this
is the case, either specify a storage unit for the policy and schedule
combination or turn off On demand only for a storage unit.
6.   Verify that the NetBackup Client service has been started on the Windows
NetBackup media server.
7.   For detailed troubleshooting information, create a bpsched debug log
directory on the master server and retry the operation. Then, check the
resulting debug log.

$ _
```

Figure 6.8 Troubleshooter from the command line.

Daemons/Services

The Activity Monitor window also has two other tabs on the UNIX Java
monitor and three other tabs on the Windows Activity Monitor. There is a
Daemons tab on the Java GUI, a Services tab on Windows, a Processes tab
on both system types, and a Drives tab on Windows. The Daemons/
Services tab allows you to see all the NetBackup and Media Manager
daemons or services that are running on the system. It also gives you the
ability to stop and start them. The Services tab is shown in Figure 6.9. The
UNIX Daemons tab is shown in Figure 6.10.

The Processes tab on both GUIs displays all the NetBackup and Media
Manager related processes that are running. The Windows GUI has a third
tab for drives that gives another view of the physical drives. The Windows
GUI also has a topology view that is currently not available as part of the
Activity Monitor with the Java GUI.

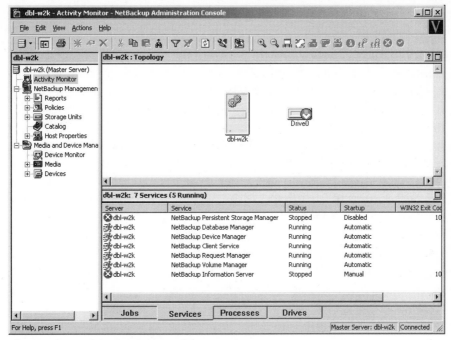

Figure 6.9 Activity Monitor: Services.

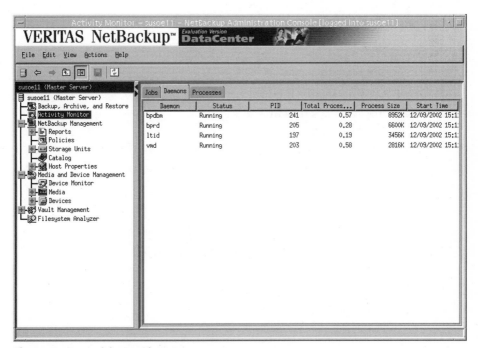

Figure 6.10 Activity Monitor: Daemons.

Monitoring without the GUI

At times, you may want to know the status of the backups or other jobs and you don't have access to a graphic terminal or are working remotely. You can still get information and monitor both the jobs activity and the device status. You can monitor the jobs by using the command-line interface (CLI) `/usr/openv/netbackup/bin/admincmd/bpdbjobs` on a UNIX system or C:\Program Files\VERITAS\NetBackup\bin\admincmd\bpdb-jobs.exe on a Windows system. This command allows you to see what is going on in the job queue. You can either issue the CLI without options, or you can add options to further refine the output. The output on a Windows system is shown in Figure 6.11.

You can also find out what daemons are running on your UNIX master by issuing this command: `/usr/openv/netbackup/bin/bpps -a`. This returns a list of all the NetBackup and Media Manager daemons and processes that are running on the system. A typical output is shown in Figure 6.12.

If you want to know the status of the physical devices without using a GUI, you could use the following for UNIX and NT/2000, respectively:

```
/usr/openv/volmgr/bin/vmoprcmd -d
C:\Program Files\VERITAS\Volmgr\bin\vmoprcmd
```

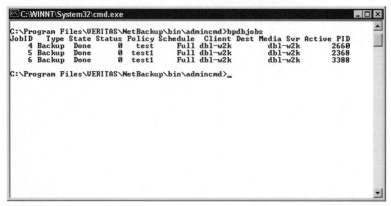

Figure 6.11 Monitoring jobs from the command-line interface on a Windows system.

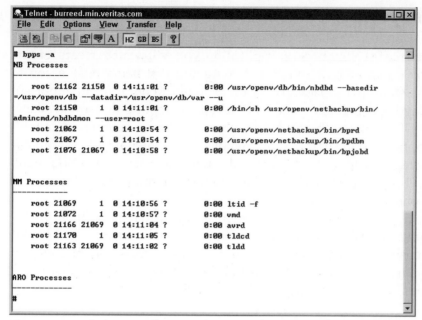

Figure 6.12 Display UNIX daemons from command-line interface.

This will give you an output similar to that shown in Figure 6.13.

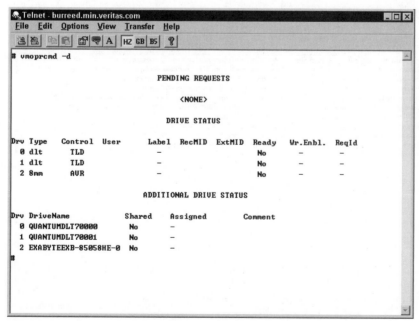

Figure 6.13 Drive status output from the command-line interface.

What Reports Are Available and What Do They Tell?

As you start to use your backup application, you will want to create reports that help you know how things are going and that better enable you to update the status of the backup domain to others. Reports are an important part of any backup application. NetBackup has reports that are available from the GUI. Most of these are actually created by executing a CLI with specific options. Many of these commands are documented, so you can use them to create custom reports if you do not find exactly what you want. Figure 6.14 shows the list of reports available from the Windows Administration Console.

Following is a list of the "canned" reports, but keep in mind there are literally endless possibilities for reporting if you care to dive into the CLI and create a custom reporting script. Several of these scripts may be found at www.BackupScripts.com, a Web community devoted to the sharing of scripts, tips, and traps associated with NetBackup.

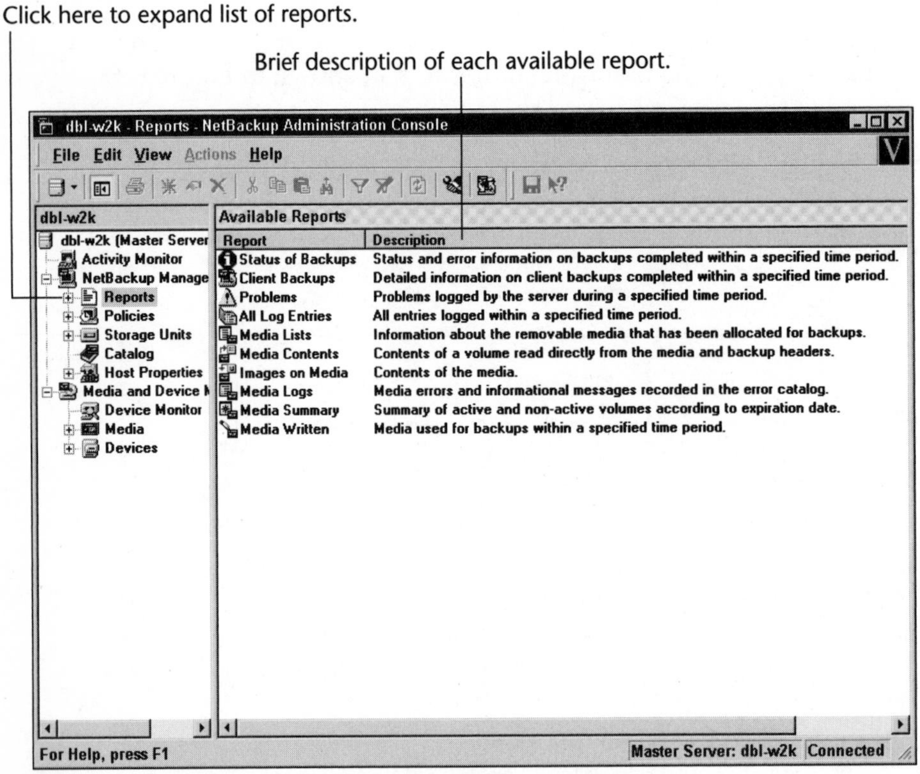

Click here to expand list of reports.

Brief description of each available report.

Figure 6.14   Reports from Windows Administration Console.

- Status of Backups
- Client Backups
- Problems
- All Log Entries
- Media Lists
- Media Contents (Caution: This will mount a tape and read its contents. This could potentially take a considerable amount of time depending on the size of the backup image you are reading.)
- Images on Media
- Media Logs
- Media Summary
- Media Written

If you are using a UNIX master and want to see the reports without using the CLI or GUI, you can use the character-based menu interface bpadm. This also gives you access to all the reports. Figure 6.15 lists the available backup reports and the media report category available to run. This interface may be a bit difficult at first to navigate, especially if you are used to using only a GUI, but after a few times, it should become quite easy and much faster for remote management requirements.

The two interfaces are very similar in that they both allow you to run the exact same reports, but the character-based interface presents their selections a bit differently from the GUI. As you can see in Figure 6.15, the following backup reports are listed:

- Backup Status
- List Client Backups
- Problems
- All Log Entries

While this interface may not be your first choice, it is an excellent tool to help you understand the NetBackup architecture. The reports in the preceding list are purely NetBackup reports, relying completely on the NetBackup logs, /usr/openv/netbackup/db/error on UNIX or c:\Program Files\Veritas\NetBackup\db\error on Windows NT/2000.

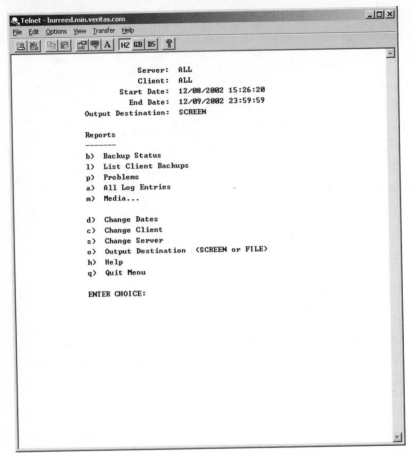

Figure 6.15   Character-based interface bpadm.

There are two general types of reports: backup reports and media reports. Backup reports report on the jobs and errors. Media reports give you the ability to look at the catalog information from the perspective of the media and from the perspective of the image. As mentioned earlier, these are the canned reports that are available to run the following (see Figure 6.16):

■ Media summary report.

■ Images on media.

■ Media log entries.

■ Media written report.

■ Media contents report. We mentioned this before, but it is worth repeating. When this report is run, it will actually mount the requested tape, read the contents of the tape, and compare the headers on the tape against the information stored in the NetBackup catalog.

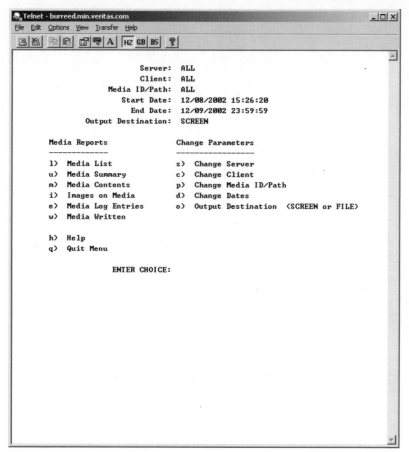

Figure 6.16 Media Manager reports.

To provide you with a greater understanding of what NetBackup and Media Manager are doing, we have included the command-line equivalents for each of the reports below and a brief description of what processes are used and databases that are touched.

To run the media list report through the command line, you may issue the following command from either your NT/2000 or UNIX server:

```
/usr/openv/netbackup/bin/admincmd/bpmedialist -U -h <MEDIA SERVER>
c:\Program Files\Veritas\NetBackup\bin\admincmd\bpmedialist.exe -U -h
<MEDIA SERVER>
```

If you run this command from the master server without specifying a media server, the master will report on all available media servers in your report. These CLIs will always report to STDOUT, so if you would want to keep this report, you should redirect STDOUT somewhere else, such as a file, printer, or mail recipient. Typically, a UNIX term, STDOUT, or standard output, refers to the screen or monitor. Similarly, STDIN, or standard input, refers to the keyboard. When we talk about redirecting STDOUT, it means that you will change the typical output device using the redirect symbol on the command line. Following is an example of STDOUT being redirected to a file:

```
/usr/openv/netbackup/bin/admincmd/bin/bpmedialist -U -h SRVR > report.txt
c:\Program Files\Veritas\NetBackup\bin\admincmd\bpmedialist.exe -U -h
SRVR > report.txt
```

We expand on the use of STDOUT and STDIN in Appendix A, "Command-Line Interface Guide."

Some important information to note in this report are the images and vimages columns. These indicate the total number of images, as shown in Figure 6.17.

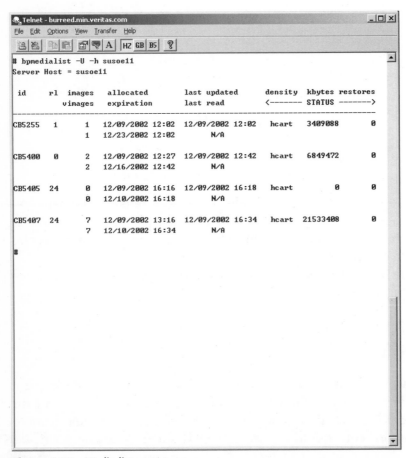

Figure 6.17 Media list report.

This report is useful to identify the number of tapes used and their particular *states*. A tape can be in one of five states, as shown in the figure:

ACTIVE. An assigned piece of media with active backups, available for use until the End of Tape (EOT) marker is reached.

FULL. A tape that has reached its EOT and is marked FULL; it is no longer available to be written to but will be available for reads until the last image on the tape has expired.

SUSPENDED. A tape that has been suspended is no longer available to be written to but will be available for reads until the last image on the tape has expired. When all the images on a suspended tape expire, the tape will be made available again. Tapes can be suspended tapes as a result of media errors or operation intervention.

FROZEN. A tape that has been frozen due to hard errors during a backup will no longer be available to be written to until the tape has been manually unfrozen by an administrator. The tape will, however, be available for reads until the last image has expired.

IMPORTED. A tape that has been expired previously or brought into this NetBackup domain from another one and has now been imported in order to facilitate recovery of some files. An imported tape will never be available for writes, but it will naturally be available for reads.

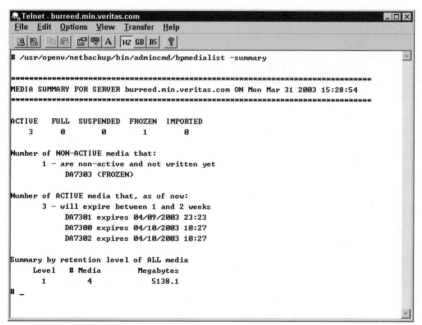

Figure 6.18 Media summary report.

The CLI for running this report is as follows for UNIX and NT/2000, respectively:

```
/usr/openv/netbackup/bin/admincmd/bpmedialist -summary
C:\Program Files\Veritas\NetBackup\bin\admincmd\bpmedialist.exe -summary
```

While the report, shown in Figure 6.18, may not be the most attractive from the command line, or for that matter, the GUI, it is rich with information about your images written to the media managed by your NetBackup servers. As one of our clients found out, this report helped to track down a questionable tape drive in their environment that was causing extended restore times because of this hardware failure. In the figure, DWO stands for Drive Written On; this column indicates the drive index number of the physical drive used to write the image fragment you are looking at in this report on the host listed in the report. So, in Figure 6.19, the DWO was 0 for the first image and the host that wrote it was "susoe09." This particular client found that one of the drives had a calibration problem when writing its tracks to the tape. This problem would not manifest itself during backup, but rather during the restore when the original DWO was not used for this read process. When mounted in a properly calibrated drive, the tracks written by this original DWO were just far enough off to cause soft errors that are recoverable through the drive error correction algorithms; however, when you are error correcting the entire length of the tape, it adds considerable overhead and extends the normal duration of a restore exponentially. The information from this report was very helpful in identifying the root cause.

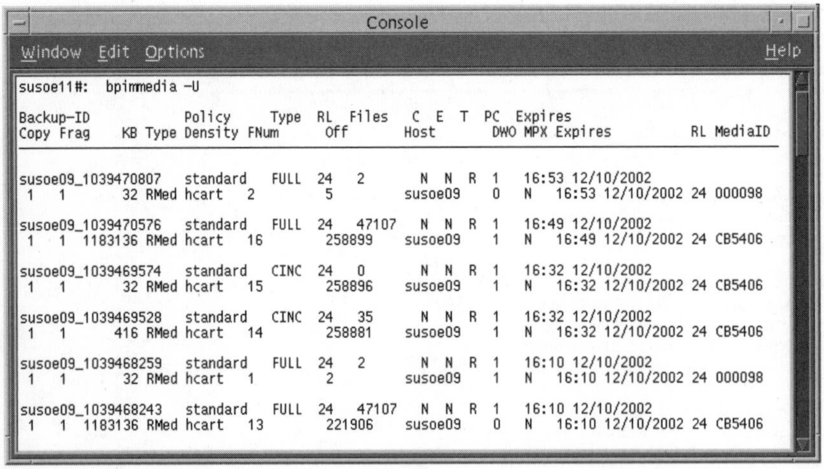

Figure 6.19 Images on the media report.

The commands are listed for UNIX and NT/2000, respectively.

```
/usr/openv/netbackup/bin/admincmd/bpimmedia -U
C:\Program Files\Veritas\NetBackup\bin\admincmd\bpimmedia.exe -U
```

When you are interested in the activity that has been logged regarding the media, the Media log entries report, shown in Figure 6.20, is the report to look at. You will see when media IDs are expired, frozen, suspended, or even removed.

The commands are listed for UNIX and NT/2000, respectively.

```
/usr/openv/netbackup/bin/admincmd/bperror -U -media -d <date> -e <date>
-server SRVR

C:\Program Files\Veritas\NetBackup\bin\admincmd\bperror -U -media -d
<date> -e <date> -server <SRVR>
```

Some customers use the media written report, shown in Figure 6.21, to identify the tapes that were used for backup during the previous night's backup so they may send off these originals to their off-site data recovery site. While it isn't our recommendation to send off original single copies, it does offer that as an option through this report.

The commands are listed for UNIX and NT/2000, respectively.

```
/usr/openv/netbackup/bin/admincmd/bpimagelist -A -media -d <date> -e
<date>

C:\Program Files\Veritas\NetBackup\bin\admincmd\bpimagelist -A -media -d
<date> -e <date>
```

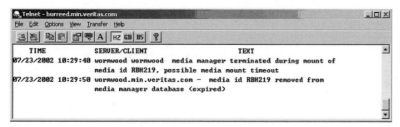

Figure 6.20   Media log entries report.

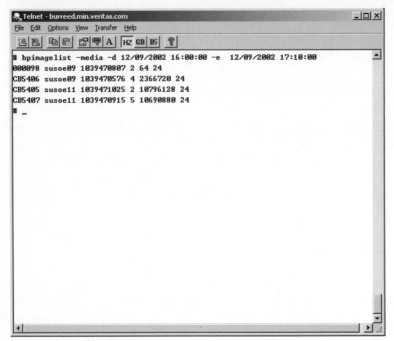

Figure 6.21   Media written report.

If you need detailed information about the contents of a specific piece of media, the media contents report shown in Figure 6.22 gives you this capability.

The commands are listed for UNIX and NT/2000, respectively.

```
/usr/openv/netbackup/bin/admincmd/bpmedialist -U -mcontents -ev
<MediaID>  -h <SRVR>

C:\Program Files\Veritas\NetBackup\bin\admincmd\bpmedialist -U
-mcontents -ev <MediaID> -h <SRVR>
```

Advanced Reporting

As we have seen, there are reports for jobs, media, and images. These reports can provide you with most, if not all, of the information you need to manage your backup domain. Unfortunately, there are other reporting needs. Sometimes it is nice to be able to produce graphical reports and to have reports on other parts of the overall backup domain. These advanced

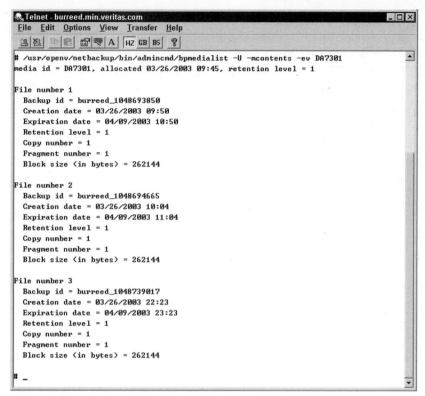

Figure 6.22   Media contents report.

reports may be produced in various ways. VERITAS Software offers an option product, NetBackup Advanced Reporter (NBAR), with over 30 different reports. You can also write your own custom Perl scripts that can interface with the program interface in NBAR to produce your own reports. This is a Web-based tool. The available reports help you analyze your NetBackup environment by presenting NetBackup data from four broad viewpoints:

- High-level summaries, which allow you to drill down to the specific trouble spots

- Detailed operational views, including a consolidated error log

- Historical perspective for trend analysis and event/time correlation

- Performance indicators, such as data throughput

Many of these reports can be tailored to provide exactly the information you need. NBAR also includes an online version of the *NetBackup Troubleshooting Guide*. NBAR gives you a tool that allows you to use the information provided in the NetBackup debug logs without having to manually analyze the text log files. NBAR passively scans the VERITAS NetBackup logs for specific information about each client and copies that information to its own database. It then uses that data to generate reports on NetBackup backup and restore activities, catalog operations, and media usage. Maintaining a separate database allows Advanced Reporter to retain a record of NetBackup activities long after the NetBackup administrator has purged expired backup information from the NetBackup logs.

NBAR consists of the following components:

- A client delivery system that distributes the Java applet GUI to individual browsers
- The Java applet GUI that is started from a browser
- A database server for the NBAR database
- A data collection service
- A configuration utility

NBAR is installed on a NetBackup Data Center master server. The NBAR database server resides on this master server, as do the configuration utility and the client delivery component. NBAR gathers information about the NetBackup environment by running NetBackup commands. NBAR then loads the information gathered into its database. NBAR can be installed and configured on Sun, HP, and Windows master servers. It is also fully integrated with the NetBackup Global Data Manager (GDM), which we discuss in a later chapter. By using NBAR with GDM, you can actually roll up reports from multiple masters to a single global master.

Summary

Several tools are available that allow you to monitor your backup domain. You can monitor many different elements of the total domain:

- Job activity
- Media usage
- Image status

- Device status and configuration
- Errors
- Daemon and process status

By using the different reports, you should be able to get a good idea of the status of the status of your backup domain, including the jobs and devices.

Now we will look at some of the other backup features and options that you might be interested in using. These can give you the capabilities to handle the backup and recovery requirements that go beyond the standard filesystems.

Evaluating Other Backup-Related Features and Options

We have discussed architecting a backup and recovery solution using traditional backup methods. We have looked at some of the things that must be considered in selecting the systems that will function as the master and possibly the media servers within the backup domain. In many cases, this will allow you to successfully perform necessary backups and restores, but in some situations, you need to look at other features and options. In this chapter, we discuss several of those features and options, some of which require additional software or a new license, and we provide guidance as to the situations where you might want to use them.

Backing Up and Restoring in a SAN Environment

It is becoming more common to find storage in the enterprise located on a storage area network. This allows more servers to have better access to more disks and makes it possible to have better overall utilization of the disk resources. It is also possible, and in some cases very desirable, to use the SAN for backup and recovery. There are a couple of reasons why we should do this. The most obvious is to have the ability to move the backup data from the client disk to the tape drive without going over the local area network. There are other ways to do LAN-free backup without implementing a SAN backup solution. The primary way is to use library sharing as discussed in Chapter 3. In this case, multiple media servers are directly connected to tape drives in a library via SCSI cables, with one of the media servers having robotic control. A specific media server now owns one or more of the drives through this direct connection and is able to do LAN-free backups. The downside of this solution is that the drives are only accessible by the media server directly connected to it. When that media server is finished with its own backup, the drive or drives either sit idle or that media server must start doing backups of clients on the LAN. This is shown in Figure 7.1.

Another option for LAN-free backups is to use a SAN solution. Servers that have too much data to be effectively backed up over the LAN can be connected to a fiber switch or director that also has tape drives connected to it. Now instead of each media server being directly connected to a drive or drives, all the media servers in the SAN can access all the drives connected to the SAN. This allows each media server to use as many drives as needed to finish its backup. When it is finished, the drives are reassigned to another media server. As long as there is data to be backed up, the drives will remain busy. This allows you to get much better utilization of your tape drive resources. The drives can either be located in a robotic library or standalone drives, as long as they are connected to the SAN. This gives you a way to share standalone drives that is not possible in a standard backup environment. The assignment of the drive resources is arbitrated by the backup application.

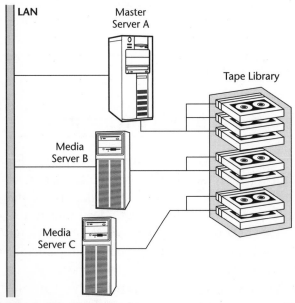

Figure 7.1   Library sharing.

BACKUP AND THE SAN

One example of SAN backups involved a customer who had been doing standard backups with NetBackup for a couple of years. Their environment had grown to the point that, even after adding media servers, tape libraries, and drives, backups were just about exceeding their window, taking 18 to 19 hours to finish each day. They finally decided that more hardware just wasn't the answer and implemented a backup SAN. This more effective use of their existing hardware enabled their backups to finish in eight hours.

VERITAS Software offers this feature with NetBackup Shared Storage Option (SSO), shown in Figure 7.2. With this feature, the backup and recovery data moves across the SAN, not the LAN. It also means the drives are connected to the media server via Fibre Channel instead of SCSI Channel. This eliminates the SCSI cable restrictions for connecting the drives.

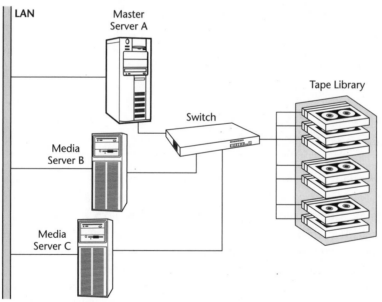

Figure 7.2 NetBackup Shared Storage Option (SSO).

Database Agents

Many vendors offer a variety of methods for backing up the databases, most with "agents" that talk directly to the database in order to back it up "hot"—that is, without shutting down the database. VERITAS NetBackup, for instance, supports the hot backup of Oracle, Informix, MS Exchange, MS SQL Server, and Sybase. They are very efficient and highly reliable once they are configured and put into production.

One "nonbackup" software company called FalconStor offers the administrator the ability to back up databases using its TimeMark technology to back up data independent of the database agents offered by most of the backup vendors today. TimeMark enables FalconStor's IPStor (a storage virtualization tool) to create periodic, scheduled, point-in-time copies of data volumes. A tool such as this provides near instantaneous recovery of single files or an entire volume back to a known-good-point in time. Coupled with their Zero-Impact Backup Enabler, which allows third-party backup software from BakBone and VERITAS to perform full, incremental, and differential backup/restore at the block level, it allows online, incremental backups of databases to be performed with transactional integrity when used with IPStor's database-aware Snapshot Agents.

Block Level Database Backups
Using Database Editions

While database agents are very helpful in the backup process, sometimes they are just not enough. For backups of an Oracle database, VERITAS Software offers an alternative. By combining the VERITAS Database Edition for Oracle with NetBackup for Oracle Advanced BLI Agent, you can do true block-level incremental backups of your Oracle database. The VxFS Storage Checkpoint facility keeps track of data blocks modified by the database since the last backup. This is a copy-on-write snapshot facility, which we discuss in detail later in the chapter. NetBackup with BLI Backup leverages this facility to back up only changed blocks, not the entire database, for an incremental backup. A database BLI Backup is done at the filesystem block level, which means only changed blocks, *not* the changed files, are backed up. Because the VxFS Storage Checkpoint facility identifies changed blocks in real time, BLI Backup does not need to search the entire database for the modified blocks. BLI Backup saves time, decreases the amount of backup media required, and significantly reduces CPU and network overhead during backups. In addition, this allows more frequent backups, making backup images more up-to-date. BLI Backup supports full, as well as block-level, incremental backups of Oracle databases. When restoring Oracle database files, NetBackup restores an appropriate full backup and then applies the changed blocks from the incremental backups. This restore process is performed automatically by NetBackup and is completely transparent. In addition, BLI Backup supports both cold (offline) backup and hot (online) backup to meet database availability and performance needs.

The Advanced BLI Agent interfaces with RMAN (Recovery Manager) via the Proxy copy feature. Proxy copy requires System Backup to Tape (SBT) API 2.0, which was introduced with Oracle 8.1.5. There are two types of Storage Checkpoints: Nodata and Fulldata. The Advanced BLI Agent uses Nodata Storage Checkpoints for Proxy copy BLI backups. Nodata Storage Checkpoints will track changed VxFS filesystem blocks with a bitmap. With Nodata Storage Checkpoints, the tablespaces are kept in hot backup mode for the duration of the backup. An added benefit of using the RMAN Proxy copy feature is that backup and restore operations are managed and controlled via RMAN, thus reducing administration complexity.

If you choose not to use RMAN, the NetBackup for Oracle Advanced BLI Agent offers a script-based alternative. The script method uses both the Nodata Storage Checkpoint (described previously), as well as the Fulldata Storage Checkpoint. The Fulldata Storage Checkpoint differs from the Nodata in two ways. First, a copy of the changed filesystem block will be copied into the Storage Checkpoint before the first write change is made to the block. Second, the tablespaces are left in hot backup mode only for the amount of time it takes to create the Storage Checkpoint.

Frozen Image Backups

The administrator faces many challenges today with backups, but one of the largest is determining how to finish the backup within the allotted backup window. One of the constraints on the backup window is the requirement to keep the database or filesystem fully available as much as possible. As we have just seen, the database agents make it possible to do hot database backups, but there is still a performance impact. Another way to address the requirement to backup data, especially data that resides in active volumes or databases with a minimal impact on the application, is to use some type of frozen image backup. A *frozen image* can best be defined as a stable disk copy of the client's data made prior to backup. Such a copy is important on active filesystems and databases, where updates to files or tables can occur at any time. In such cases, making a stable, consistent copy (frozen image) is a prerequisite to making a correct backup. A frozen image is created very rapidly, causing minimal impact on other applications. There are two basic types: copy-on-write snapshot and mirror.

Copy-on-Write Snapshot

A *copy-on-write snapshot* is a detailed account of data as it existed at a certain moment. Unlike a mirror, which we discuss next, it is not really a copy of the data, but a particular "record" of it. The copy-on-write snapshot process works as follows:

1. When a frozen image is required, any unfinished transactions or changes to the source data are allowed to complete, but new changes are temporarily stalled.

2. The source is momentarily idled (made quiescent), and a snapshot driver is injected into the host operating system.

3. Once the snapshot driver is activated, new transactions or changes (writes) to the source data are allowed to take place. However, the snapshot driver briefly intercepts or holds the write requests. While holding those requests, it copies to cache any blocks that will be affected by those writes and keeps a record of the cached blocks.

In other words, the snapshot driver reads each source block that is about to change, copies the block's current data to cache, and records the location and identity of the cached blocks. Then the intercepted writes are allowed to take place in the source blocks. The immediate results of the snapshot are as follows:

- A cached copy of those portions of the source that were about to change at a certain moment
- A record of where those cached portions (blocks) are stored

The copy-on-write snapshot does not produce a copy of the source; it creates cached copies of the blocks that have changed and a record of their location. The backup process refers to the source data or cached copy of the data as directed by the snapshot driver. An accurate backup image is obtained by combining the unchanged portions of the data with the snapshot cache. When a backup of the snapshot frozen image begins, the backup application copies the source data until it comes to a block that changed after the snapshot driver was activated. The snapshot driver tells the backup process to skip that changed block and read in its place the cached (original) copy. The backup application continues copying source data until it comes to another changed block. Cache is read again as the snapshot driver dictates. The backup, when finished, is an exact copy of the source as it existed the moment the snapshot driver was activated.

Different kinds of snapshot backups are available. VERITAS Software's NetBackup offers a copy-on-write snapshot using a proprietary snapshot driver called nbu_snap that works with either Sun Solaris UFS filesystem or VERITAS Software's VxFS filesystem. It also supports filesystem clones, which is a feature of VxFS.

Another backup challenge that can be helped with snapshot backups is the backup of a filesystem that contains hundreds of thousands or millions of small files. Doing a standard backup of such a filesystem using the standard operating system commands is very time-consuming. Just to traverse the filesystem building a list of all the files takes a lot of time. The best way to back it up without using snapshot technology is to do the following:

1. Unmount the filesystem.
2. Perform a raw backup of the filesystem.
3. Remount the filesystem.

There are some disadvantages to doing this kind of backup:

- The filesystem is not available during the entire time of the backup.
- All backups are full backups.
- All restores are full filesystem restores. Single file restores are not possible.

The better option for backing up this kind of data is to use a snapshot backup. An example is the NetBackup FlashBackup option. With this technology, you have the advantages of the raw backup without the penalties. This is a copy-on-write snapshot technology using a proprietary snapshot driver. This feature is available for the following filesystem types: Sun Solaris UFS, VERITAS Software's VxFS on Solaris or HP-UX, and Online JFS on HP-UX. For backups, FlashBackup creates consistent, point-in-time backups at the file level. In the event of a restore, it uses file mapping created during the snapshot to restore single files or directories. It also enables administrators with millions of files to conduct backup and restore operations by using a combination of file mapping and snapshot technologies.

The advantages of using a technology such as FlashBackup over standard filesystem or raw backups are as follows:

- It provides increased performance, especially if the filesystem contains a very large number of files and most of the filesystem blocks are allocated.
- It allows individual file restores.
- The volume or filesystem remains mounted.
- It supports multiple data streams.
- It supports full and incremental backups.

Mirror

A *mirror* is a complete data copy on a separate disk, physically independent of the source. Every change or write to the source data on the primary disk is also made to the copy on the secondary disk. This creates a mirror image of the source data. As with a copy-on-write snapshot, when a frozen image is required, transactions are allowed to finish and new I/O on the primary disk is briefly halted. When the mirror image is brought up-to-date with the source (made identical to it), the mirror is split from the primary, meaning that new changes can be made to the primary but not to the mirror. At this point, the mirror can be backed up.

Since mirroring requires an exact, complete copy of the primary image, it consumes more disk space than a copy-on-write snapshot. The data can exist in a disk management software mirror, such as VERITAS Software's VxVM mirrors, or it can exist on a disk array controlled by the array-specific

---

BACKING UP THE MAIL

No doubt there are many examples of customers using frozen image backups to handle applications such as mail. We know of one in particular that was using a UNIX system and had the challenge of backing up 4.2 TB of data that was across several filesystems and contained 82 million files. A standard filesystem backup of this data was taking 27 hours. After implementing NetBackup FlashBackup, they could finish their backups in 8 hours. In another case where the backup was for Netscape mail, the standard backups were taking 48 to 60 hours for full backups, and incremental backups were taking 24 to 36 hours. After FlashBackup was implemented, the full backups were completed in 15 to 20 hours, and the incremental backups were in the 9- to 12-hour range.

mirroring software, such as EMC TimeFinder, Hitachi Data Systems Shad-owImage, HP-UX BusinessCopy, IBM FlashCopy, and others. At the end of the backup, the split mirror is rejoined with the primary mirror and the mir-rors are resynchronized. Some backup applications, such as NetBackup, allow you to run with the mirrors split and resynchronize the mirrors just prior to backing up the data. This is a plus for those people who like to syn-chronize the mirrors once a day and then run with the mirrors split.

Offhost Backups

As the challenges of backup continue to grow, everyone is looking for new ways to meet these challenges. One of the new backup methods is some-times referred to as serverless or server-free backup. The more correct name is *offhost backup*. This backup method uses a separate backup agent located on either a media server or a third-party copy (3PC) device to actu-ally move the data from the client disk to storage.

Figure 7.3 shows an example of an implementation of offhost backup using NetBackup. The backup agent in this case could be either a media server or a third-party copy (3PC) device that implements SCSI Extended Copy commands. Many types of 3PC devices can act as backup agents, such as

- Bridge
- Router
- Robotic library
- Disk array

One of the key elements for offhost backups is that the backup must be done from a frozen image. Any of the frozen image types listed in the sec-tion can be used. Sometimes this feature is confused with the LAN-free backup feature such as the NetBackup SSO feature. If the requirement is to keep the backup data off the LAN or to do a frozen image backup so that the application can continue to be available, either SSO or frozen image backups will fulfill the need. If the problem is that the backup overhead is too much for the application server to handle, offhost backup is the solu-tion. By using offhost backup, you are moving the disk reads and the tape writes to a separate backup agent who will actually perform this work.

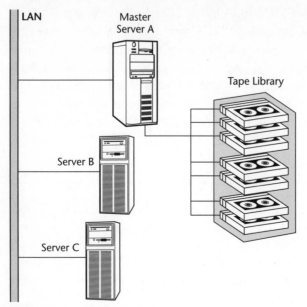

Figure 7.3   Offhost backup.

Managing a Large Environment Using Global Data Manager (GDM)

Many people are finding that a single backup domain is no longer an option. This can be due to physical reasons (domains in different geographic locations), business reasons (different domains for business units), or size (too big for a single domain). Finding yourself with multiple backup domains can make the administration much more complicated. In situations like this it is nice to find a feature such as Global Data Manager (GDM) from VERITAS Software. This feature is a fourth tier in the Net-Backup architecture. It is a master of masters that provides a single console that allows you to see and manage all of your backup domains. This type of feature makes it much easier to administer distributed backup domains by using a dashboard that gives you, at a glance, the real-time status and health of all your domains.

Figure 7.4 shows a typical GDM layout. As you can see, each of the master servers gathers data about its own domain and either rolls the data up to the master of masters or stores it in a local database where it is available to the master of masters should it be needed. Figure 7.5 is a sample of the dashboard used by GDM.

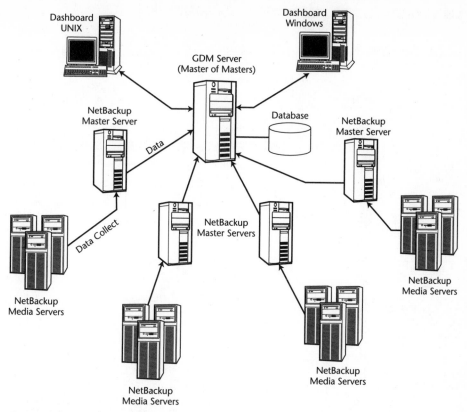

Figure 7.4 Global Data Manager.

Vault Solutions

While backup is a very important part of any enterprise data protection strategy, it alone does not provide for true disaster recovery. Any enterprise DR strategy should include an off-site backup management system such as VERITAS Software's NetBackup Vault or Gray House Solutions' Duplication Suite. A vault product is one that enables you to make multiple copies of your backup images, gives you the tools to eject the desired tapes from the robotic library, and provides the reports to track the movement of the tapes while outside the library. The tapes that are outside the library are generally stored at an off-site location. The vault product provides tracking of the tapes in the off-site location, and it notifies you when the images on the off-site tapes have expired and the tapes should be returned to the library for reuse. This is done so if there is a disaster at the primary site, the data will still be available from the off-site tapes.

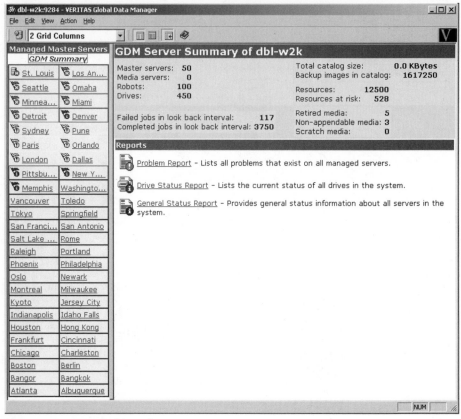

Figure 7.5   GDM dashboard.

The requirements for an off-site backup management system are as follows:

- A schedule for sending media off-site
- A method to determine what data to send off-site
- A mechanism to automate the creation of duplicate media (images)
- A mechanism to duplicate the catalog
- A way to determine which media to retrieve from off-site storage for reuse
- A system for tracking both the data and the media while stored at the off-site location
- A method for reporting on media shipments
- Efficient use of resources

Since this is the cornerstone in any enterprise DR strategy, the selection of the product to fulfill these requirements is very important. Make sure you select a product that gives you all the functionality you need, along with flexibility and ease of use. Vault is generally considered a three-step process:

1. Duplication of backups.
2. Backup of the catalog.
3. Ejecting of media and reporting.

Depending on your individual requirements, you can perform any or all of these steps. With some of the vault products like NetBackup Vault, you can configure the backup session to write to multiple tapes, creating multiple copies of the backups without having to duplicate them. This would fulfill the requirements for the first step. At the end of the backup session, and the duplication session if required, Vault needs to make a tape copy of the catalog to accompany the media as it goes off-site. When it is time to transport the media to an off-site location, Vault should eject the appropriate media and generate the necessary reports to track the media. A part of the reporting is the recall of expired media to be reused.

Another option within the NetBackup Vault feature is disk staging, which is discussed in the next section on disk-based storage units.

Disk-Based Storage Units

What's the best way to increase performance of your tape backup solution? Take the tape out of your backup and replace it with disk. Disk-based backup methods are becoming quite popular, with the cost of disks dropping dramatically in recent years. Before we get into the implementations of the disk-based methods, let's look at some of what is on the market today. First are disk-based solutions like Quantum DX-30 and Alacritus Software's Securitus Disk-Based Virtual Tape Library Appliance that front-end the disk to the backup software with what looks like a tape library. Then there are the filer-based solutions like Maxtor's MaxAttach, Network Appliance's NearStore, and even LeftHand Network's solution. Large independent software vendors (ISVs) like Legato and VERITAS offer disk-based backup solutions within their applications, as does one of the smaller ISVs, BakBone Software's NetVault. Like IBM's Tivoli Storage Management (TSM), they can use disks as a cache area during backup to stream the tape drives on the back end. At this point, you might be saying, "But disks are a finite storage device." That is true, so in order to implement a solution like this, you need to do some planning and maybe even some scripting, depending on the backup tool you have selected. We will use VERITAS NetBackup for any specific examples, but we believe the concepts can carry over to any other solution that supports disk-based backup.

Implementing Disk-Based Storage

Since disk-based storage is finite, you really need to take into consideration how you will manage it once your backups are on this device. More importantly, you need to determine which clients you want to back up to it. You surely cannot select *all* of the clients. That would require an equal amount of disk-based backup storage as online storage. So, practically speaking, it is best to determine ahead of time which clients you will be backing up to the device.

Once you have decided which clients will be backed up to the disk-based storage device, you need to do some math to figure out how long you can keep the backup images stored there. It is best to keep the backup there as long as you possibly can to facilitate faster restores should the need arise. For illustration purposes, let's say that you only have enough space for 72 hours before you will effectively run out of space. Now what? Well, you can migrate them manually by doing a copy, or duplication to a tape device. You can also implement a hierarchical storage management (HSM) solution, like VERITAS Storage Migrator, that will manage the filesystem for you automatically by migrating the "data" to a secondary or tertiary storage device. Or you could use the plug-in module Watermark for Duplication Suite by Gray House Solutions, which will monitor the filesystem of the disk storage unit for growth and make a duplicate of the stored images on tape when the user-definable watermark is met, or it will expire backup images that already have more than one copy, freeing up valuable disk space. Another solution is to use NetBackup Vault to duplicate stored images through *disk staging*. Disk staging allows you to back up to disk and then schedule a duplication of the disk-based image to one or more tapes. The tape or tapes can have different retention periods both from the disk-based image and each other. You can also configure Vault to delete the disk image as soon as the duplication process successfully finishes.

The bottom line is that disk-based storage devices are inexpensive, fast, and typically highly reliable. The first rule of thumb when performance tuning is to address all of your bottlenecks—and tape may be one of those in your environment.

Storage Migration Products and Backup

Full backups must by definition back up all the files within a filesystem. By adding an HSM software package such as VERITAS Storage Migrator to your NetBackup environment, you can drastically reduce the amount of data that needs to be backed up while still protecting all your data.

HSM manages filesystems for both optimizing space and reducing the management time. Optimizing space involves copying inactive files from the primary storage medium (hard drive) to another medium, like tape, optical, or a less expensive disk drive. Once the inactive data is secured within another medium, the data blocks on the primary don't need to be backed up anymore to safeguard the data.

An intelligent backup product like NetBackup recognizes that the HSM has safeguarded at least one copy of the data to another medium, so Net-Backup only needs to back up the meta data (inode or placeholder information) for that file. So instead of backing up all the data blocks for all the static files in a filesystem during a full backup, it only needs to back up the active (nonmigrated) data and the placeholders for the migrated data. Real-world testing has shown that a backup of 3.5 hours can be reduced to about an hour by simply adding an HSM to your environment.

The primary reason that backups are ever done is for insurance; you need to be able to recover your company's data if, for some reason, it's gone. For the most part, you generally do backups in a leisurely manner (relatively speaking), but you almost always restore in a panic. Since using HSM technology can help speed up your backups by reducing the amount of data backed up, it can also increase your speed when restoring a filesystem. By doing your backups more intelligently by incorporating an HSM, you can not only decrease your backup window, but also your recovery window. With NetBackup and Storage Migrator, a full restore of a filesystem works exactly the same as a "normal" restore, except that you only physically restore the "active" nonmigrated files and all the placeholders for migrated files. All of the migrated files are readily available; just access the placeholders like any normal file, and Storage Migrator will cache the data blocks back to the filesystem, all automatically. Meanwhile, you're back in business, since your active data is back. You can start processing data faster than if you had to wait for all the active and inactive files to be restored. For safeguarding your data, it's highly recommended that you let the HSM make two copies of all your migrated data and that your second copy be taken off-site, along with your full and incremental tapes. This provides a disaster recovery set of tapes should you ever need them.

Starting with NetBackup 3.4 for UNIX, there is a tool called the File System Analyzer that analyzes a filesystem and reports back the usage patterns, size, and number of files within a filesystem. It provides a what-if scenario that you can change to see how many files you back up on *every* full backup that haven't changed in a long time. Most customers are very surprised at how much of their data isn't used very often. The analyzer can be very helpful in determining if a particular system or particular filesystem/volume within a system is a good candidate for an HSM product.

Another way you can utilize Storage Migrator with NetBackup is as a repository for backup images. It is not uncommon to have slow clients, and even with multiplexing, you can't always keep a tape drive streaming. Once a tape drive can't be kept streaming, the tape drive's performance is greatly reduced. A way to address this problem is to back up to a disk storage unit. Storage Migrator can then manage the disk storage unit. As NetBackup backs up these slow systems (or fast systems on slow networks), it creates backup image fragments. These fragments together are one NetBackup image. Storage Migrator then can migrate these fragments to secondary storage. By doing this, each client is creating its own backup images at whatever its speed without having a tape drive shoe-shining its tape head (shoe-shining, as we discuss in Chapter 9, means that the drive is not streaming and must wait to receive data then reposition the tape before writing continues). Once the backups are done, Storage Migrator can efficiently copy the images to tape. Now, as most system administrators know, most restores are done within a few days of the backup. If you have adequate disk space, the images could still be on disk. Your restores would then be from disk instead of tape. If the image had been purged (the data blocks freed from disk for disk space considerations), when the restore accesses the placeholder, Storage Migrator will automatically retrieve the backup images from tape and the backup will continue as normal.

Summary

As we have seen, many features and options are available to help you enhance a standard backup and recovery architecture. Some of these may be necessary from the beginning, while others might be added as your enterprise grows and changes. To highlight, the features and options are as follows:

- SAN backup and recovery
- Database agents

- Database editions
- Frozen image backups
- Offhost backups
- Managing a diverse environment with GDM
- Vault solutions
- Disk-based storage units
- Storage Migrator and Backup

You want to always keep up-to-date on the additional features and options available. This should allow you to address your backup and recovery needs as your enterprise changes. In the next chapter, we look at some hints and tips on troubleshooting your backup and recovery environment.

## CHAPTER 8

General Troubleshooting Tips

After all the work and planning for your new backup and recovery system, you finally get it installed and configured. You start running backups. Life is good. But wait, someone just called and said there was a problem. How could there be a problem? You have been so careful and thorough. This can't be happening! Well, it really does happen. In fact, if you look at your backup and recovery architecture, you will notice that a simple NetBackup backup of a client touches a significant amount of your enterprise.

This backup starts by having a process run on the master server that determines if it is the proper time to do a backup. Then there are communications between the master server and the media server, followed by communications between the media server and the client. The media server communicates with a robotic library and requests a specific tape be loaded into a specific drive. The client starts a process to read the data from its disk and starts sending the data across the network to the media server. The media server receives this data and passes it through shared memory to a tape drive while passing the meta data back to the master server, where it is stored in a catalog on a disk on the master server. When the backup is finished, the media server closes the tape and asks the library to take the tape from the drive and put it back in a specific slot.

We have exercised disks on a couple of different systems, exercised the network, used a robotic library, written to a drive—we've really exercised a good portion of the total enterprise. This makes backup and recovery one of the best enterprise-wide diagnostic tools. It also makes troubleshooting backup and recovery problems all that more important and difficult, since you could be troubleshooting network issues, client system issues, hardware issues at several different places, and overall operating system issues, just to mention a few. In this chapter, we give you a basic idea of how to approach these problems and identify some of the tools you will need.

Functional Overview

The most important part of troubleshooting is to understand how your particular application works. Functionally, what services, daemons, or processes are started as a result of a backup job being executed? Backup applications are like avalanches; once the backup job starts, it tends to spawn several other supporting processes to accomplish the task. Therefore, being able to track the relationship of these services, processes, and daemons is the first step in your journey to troubleshooting your environment. If you don't have a good solid understanding of the backup architecture and functional overview, your troubleshooting will be hit-or-miss. We have seen many backup administrators troubleshoot a problem from the entirely wrong direction, thus losing valuable time. If your software vendor hasn't published such an overview, contact them and request it. Ask as many people as you can to get this information, because without it, you won't have all the right tools necessary to maintain your environment properly.

Whatever the case, you should document for yourself how the software is deployed on your environment. If this is an inherited environment, you should have either an outside consultant or internal IT staff perform a site assessment to document your current state. It's always better to do this assessment before you have the trouble looming over your head so you can be prepared and proactive.

First Order of Business: What Problem Are You Troubleshooting?

First things first: We need a problem to troubleshoot. How do you determine what the problem is? You may see a variety of symptoms, but understanding the root problem is key to troubleshooting. Symptoms include the following:

- Performance is slow.

- Backups fail.

- Restores fail.

- You cannot start a backup on client A.

- Backups start out fast, but decline.

And a favorite of every technical support person:

- Nothing has changed, and all of a sudden, all of your backup jobs won't start.

So are these symptoms or the actual problem? The way to determine that is to drill down further and further into the issue with reasonable depth. If it is a performance problem, is it tape drive performance, client performance, network performance, or disk performance? How do we determine where the problem lies? What about failed backups? Could that be bad media or a bad tape drive? In this chapter, we present an outline for troubleshooting that we have found to be very helpful in our years of experience assisting clients with their troubleshooting.

As mentioned, the key is to determine what exactly is the problem. Here is an example from an actual client that had a couple of issues: First, the client saw that their tape usage had increased considerably, but the amount of data they were backing up had not changed, nor had the backup policies changed. The assumption was that the tape drives were having problems and either were not writing to the end of the tape or had firmware problems that would cause the data to be written improperly. Unfortunately, to add fuel to the fire, one of the tape manufacturers whose tape they were using announced that some of their tapes were flawed because of a servo problem at their plant. The servo problem would either fail the backup job with bad media or write the job successfully until the tape was full or failed with media errors. This led the client to the quick conclusion that it was in fact the tape cartridges themselves, along with possibly the drives, that were causing the problems they had detected.

Upon arriving on-site to have a look at the problem, we asked the administrators several questions, such as "What has changed in the last three months on the system?" Naturally, the answer was, "Nothing has changed. It has been fairly static." The key words are "fairly static," which means that something had changed. Because we didn't know exactly what, we began assessing the problem.

The Natural Progression of Troubleshooting

When troubleshooting, always start with the most obvious first, such as network cable, daemons, or filesystem problems (unless, of course, you have ruled out the obvious through your identification process). Usually, the most obvious place to start is also the least time-consuming. This is important to keep in mind, especially if you have certain service level agreements with your customers. You should plan your strategy for troubleshooting, then work that plan to fruition.

Because it seemed appropriate, we started looking at the error logs to determine what was happening internally to the backup application. This is an important exercise. If you do not understand how to read the error logs pertaining to the backup application, it is strongly suggested that you either take the time for some self-education or enroll yourself in the next available training class and be sure to inform the instructor that deciphering the error logs is one of your objectives.

Since our expertise comes from VERITAS NetBackup, we will continue to use it as our method of example when necessary. As we look through the logs, we need to have an idea what we are looking for. Remember, this is a cursory review of the most obvious place to start; therefore, we look for obvious errors, such as media errors from the bperror log or any physical errors that have been logged regarding the drives themselves in /var/adm/messages.

Nothing glaring was uncovered during this discovery, so we completed this cursory review of the logs and began confirming the configuration. Since the problem the client described was not necessarily one pertaining to the configuration of the backup policies, we knew we could avoid that and focus squarely on the physical aspects of the configuration. NetBackup is actually composed of two components: NetBackup and Media Manager. The Media Manager component deals with physical devices and media, so this is a natural place to begin after reviewing the logs. The best way to display the configuration from the command line with NetBackup is to use the following:

```
/usr/openv/volmgr/bin/tpconfig -d
```

or

```
/usr/openv/volmgr/bin/tpconfig -data
```

This displays how the physical drives and robots are configured and is a good first step for your troubleshooting. Since this problem hinged on data storage to tape, it was reasonable to ensure that the correct device files were being used, and since it was a UNIX installation, we wanted to make sure that the compression device file was being used. Once we confirmed that, in fact, it was configured properly, the next step, since this was a Sun server, was to check the st.conf file. The st.conf file, found in /kernel/drv, is the configuration file for all SCSI tape devices that allows you to configure how the device file will interact with the physical device, including how it will handle compression.

When we reviewed the entries for the client's tape devices, we found that the compression settings were at default: no compression. The entire file looked to be at default; none of their custom settings were present. At that point, we asked about that "fairly static" state that the server had been in the past several months. We found that they had installed a Sun jumbo patch to this server about 45 days prior. What the client didn't realize is that the jumbo patch will overwrite the st.conf file during its patching process. The solution was to restore a copy of the st.conf file before the patch and reboot the server. After a few weeks, it was apparent to the client that this was the problem after all.

When you are troubleshooting, you really take on the role of investigator, especially if you are not the primary administrator on the server. When you are asked to help out, you really need to be prepared to ask questions to help you determine the root cause. We recommend starting as though you know nothing of the application, within reason, and begin asking questions. Here's a sample of the questions that were asked in order to begin work troubleshooting the previous example:

1. What exactly is (are) the problem(s) you are seeing?

2. When did you notice the change or the errors?

3. Have there been any changes to the main backup server? Media servers? Backup clients?

4. What, if anything, have you done already to troubleshoot this problem?

5. Do you have any site documentation to look at? Architecture topologies?

6. What are your expectations once the problem has been ratified?

This should give you enough information to begin the troubleshooting.

Once you are done with your initial, cursory review of the site, you should have another set of questions based on what you find. It's always a good idea to document your plan in the event it takes longer than you anticipated so you can provide that to technical support or a consultant whom you may bring in to assist in the troubleshooting phase. Another reason you want to document is the mere fact that should this problem reoccur, this document may be used by another team member to resolve it much more quickly than before.

BACKUP OF 19 GB IN 10 TO 11 HOURS? SOMETHING'S WRONG

Another client example took 18 months to solve, mainly because the consultant on the project was called off to architect another backup solution, only to return to the original project to find that the problem was never remedied. This didn't involve failed backup jobs, crashing servers, or anything else so drastic. This was a simple case of backup speeds. The client assured the consultant that there was a full T3 between their buildings (45 Mb/sec), so there ought to be blazing speeds for backup. (We won't debate why they chose to backup across this T3 as opposed to putting another backup server in the other facility. Let's just say budget was the primary reason.) So it was on the consultant's shoulders to make this work and work well.

The numbers say that a full T3 should push 5.625 MB (that's mega*bytes*) per second, 337.5 MB per minute, and 20 GB per hour. The network that the client had in place for the servers was 100BT, which should push 12.5 MB/second, 750 MB/minute, or 45 GB/hour. As you can see, it definitely looked like our T3 was going to be the bottleneck for our backup jobs. However, as we began testing and tweaking, we found that the backups were taking exceptionally long for the remote servers. We made sure that the servers were configured properly—specifically, that they had their NIC settings to 100 FULL and not AUTO, since we know that some switches and a certain server manufacturer's host-motherboard-Ethernet interface do not play well when set to AUTO-NEGOTIATE.

All of the network issues were worked out on our end; we made sure the administrators at the other location verified all of the network points as well, including server, switch, and router. They assured us everything was A-OK. After running the second test, the same performance numbers were realized. After making sure all of our network connection points were properly configured, we felt it was necessary to take it to the network group to have them look at the link between the buildings—maybe the backup T1 was actually primary and the T3 was secondary.

One thing we ought to mention, though, is that the IT team in the remote facility didn't get along very well with their counterparts in the primary facility. This is never a good thing. Teamwork and intercommunication are key to any successful IT organization.

After the network department assured us that the T3 is primary and wasn't even close to being fully utilized, we turned it back onto our network configurations between buildings. Naturally, the primary building where our consultant was sitting was reviewed a second time to make absolutely sure that it was configured properly. However, the IT team on the remote site didn't feel it was necessary to check their work, since they told us they had already done that.

About this time, our consultant was pulled off to work the architecture job; he had instructed the customer that the problem appeared to be on the remote site, but without having physical access, it was difficult to prove. During the absence of our consultant, the test backup policies went into production and the backup speeds continued to return very poor results. Unfortunately, the customer didn't pursue the issue of speed either, mainly because of personnel resource limitations.

Upon the consultant's return to complete the project, he found that the problem still existed and the client had simply grown accustomed to the performance and just figured that's the way it's going to be. Well, not for our consultant; he insisted that the network group turn a sniffer (network analyzer) on to see exactly what was happening between the main backup server, the switch, router, and backup client. So, at 10:00 P.M. the network administrator found the problem. Everything was connecting perfectly at the primary site, 100 FULL DUPLEX, until we got across the T3. The consultant noted that it was dropping down to 10 Mb/sec after the router, which would explain the performance numbers.

With hard information in our hands, we approached the remote site again and asked them to walk the wire, because somewhere on their end, it was dropping down to 10 Mbps. Fortunately, we found an administrator in the remote site who was more than willing to work with us. He tracked down the problem to the switch. There he found the switch was not set for 100 FULL, but AUTO-NEGOTIATE. Once that was changed, we saw our backup speeds increase from 19 GB in 10 to 11 hours to 19 GB in just a little over 90 minutes.

Sometimes it is not the software configuration, hardware configuration, or the backup administration; it is just an oversight in the network architecture somewhere. This problem was different from the previous one in that the consultant was the de facto backup administrator for the group, so he didn't necessarily have to ask any questions, but he did have to understand where the breakdown was occurring. Having an intimate understanding of how the backup product works is a considerable help when trying to troubleshoot these problems.

NT/2000, 300GB, RAID5, and Home Directories

The next real-life example involves an NT/2000 server backup client and a UNIX backup server. The customer indicated that this particular NT machine was having problems completing its backup job. The backup job was failing with a Network Timeout error. The information our consultant received was that it was an NT/2000 machine whose purpose was serving as a home directory server, it used RAID 5, and it had 300 GB of disk, of which 80 percent was in use. The backup infrastructure for this customer is quite impressive: large STK9310, 9840A, 9840B, and 9940A drives; ACS/LS library software; Sun servers for the backup servers; and GB Ethernet server network—a very nice environment to work in. However, this NT client had a return performance number of ~3 MB/second. Now before you jump to conclusions, this NT server was no slouch; it was nicely configured as well:

- Windows 2000 SP2
- 2-GB RAM
- Two 10/100 Compaq NC3131
- One Gigabit Ethernet Compaq NC6134
- One Compaq Smart Array 431 Controller
- Two Compaq StorageWorks HBA
- Three Intel P3 550 MHz

As mentioned earlier, the storage on this server had a volume of 300 GB with 80 percent utilized, or approximately 240 GB of home directory data.

Before we get into the troubleshooting, let's talk about what we should expect to see out of this client. Gigabit Ethernet theoretically can give you nearly 100 MB/second transfer speeds. The 9840A, the slowest of the three, is rated at 10 MB/second native and 35 MB/second compressed. So as you can see, if we can push data even at 40 percent of the Ethernet rate, we still should be able to keep that drive streaming—the operative word being *should*. However, we were only seeing 3 to 5 MB/second to the tape drive for this particular client. Now, there are several components that we can review here:

- Network
- Client
- Backup server
- Tape hardware
- Tape hardware connectivity to backup server

Any one of these items could be the culprit at our customer site. As troubleshooter, it is your job to narrow your scope in order to bring closure to this issue quickly. One of the ways we do that is by logical deduction.

Here's what we know about the problem:

1. It is not pervasive; in other words, it is not affecting all clients across the board.

2. Other clients are completing successfully to the same tape hardware as the failed client with relatively good performance numbers.

3. Our cursory review did not conclusively pinpoint a particular tape drive as the potential culprit.

4. It appears only to fail on full backup jobs; incremental jobs seem to finish, although they are beginning to fail as well.

5. The NT/2000 servers are on a separate network from the UNIX servers, and while other NT/2000 servers are completing successfully, their performance could be better than what was observed.

So we can eliminate some of the items from the list initially while we plan our strategic troubleshooting procedure. Based on what we know, the backup server seems to be the least likely candidate causing the problem because other client backup jobs are completing successfully and with relatively good performance numbers. The tape hardware and the connectivity seem to be eliminated based on the success rate of the majority of the backup jobs and the fact that there was inconclusive evidence to prove that there was a particular drive having detrimental problems—not to mention the fact that the failing backup client has yet to complete a FULL backup successfully. This leads us to focus our troubleshooting efforts on the network and the NT/2000 client machine. Since the NT/2000 servers are on a separate network from the UNIX servers, which are not having this type of problem, it was reasonable that we would include that in our troubleshooting test plan. And, naturally, since we are looking at network timeout issues, the NT/2000 client machine is a candidate. So, of those two categories, what components will we begin troubleshooting?

- Network
  - Speed from backup server to NT/2000 client machine
  - Speed from NT/2000 client machine to backup server
- Client
  - NIC configuration—GIG/FULL DUPLEX
  - Disk speed
    - Copy
    - Use component of backup software to read disk (i.e., bpbkar with NetBackup)
  - Disk fragmentation
    - ScanDisk
  - Number of directories
  - Number of files

As we review this list, we first need to prioritize what we want to accomplish and make sure that as we move through the troubleshooting process, the previous task leads to the next, when possible. So as we begin, let's prioritize and document what our tasks will involve. Remember, a lot of troubleshooting is based on gut feel, so as you apply this in your environment, keep this in mind: There is no perfect method for troubleshooting, simply various styles. Choose your style and run with it.

Our plan was to focus on the client first and not the network, especially since we knew RAID5 was involved. For those of you who don't know, RAID5 is great for writes but terrible for reads. With backup, we do *lots* of reads and very few writes. Knowing this made our troubleshooting job much easier. Picture, for example, a pebble in a pond. The initial break in the water by the pebble is our NT/2000 client, and each subsequent ripple is another one of our tests, ultimately leading us out to our backup server. A natural progression is a good practice to adhere to when possible.

From the client, our test plan looked something like this:

1. Run ScanDisk, if we can get approval from the admin team for this box.

2. Copy data from disk in question to a *separate* disk, note time started and time finished, size (minimum 1 GB of data).

3. Use utility from backup software if available to read data from the disk in question. Note time started and time finished. Size should be a minimum of 1 GB of data.

4. Investigate number of files/directories.

5. View properties of several directories, note time.

We weren't able to run ScanDisk on the drive because the administration team thought it would take too long and didn't think that was going to be the problem anyway. We skipped to Step 2. Copying data from the command prompt to an entirely separate disk didn't reveal any serious determent; of course, we were transferring only 1 GB of data. Next (Step 3) we used one of the programs that come with the backup software, in this case NetBackup, which actually is responsible for the file collection process to test the speed of the disk. This program is called bpbkar.exe. We started a process that would copy the files to an infinitely fast device, the "bit bucket," eliminating the network and isolating it at the NT/2000 client machine:

```
c:\Veritas\Netbackup\bin\bpbkar32 -nocont c:\ > NUL 2> e:\temp.f
```

temp.f will contain all of the files that bpbkar has collected. This will grow considerably if there is a large filesystem or directory structure you are testing.

WARNING The text file collecting all of the files is going to a separate disk. Do not send it to the same disk you are testing with; otherwise, your testing numbers may be skewed. Be sure to time this as well.

When this was done at the customer site, the results were staggering. It took literally hours for it to simply read the files/directories off of this server. We finally canceled the process and delivered the news to the administration team. However, this didn't mean our work was finished. We still had two other steps in our client plan, as well as our network plan, which we haven't even outlined for you yet. When the administration team saw the results, they reluctantly ran ScanDisk on the drive to see the results. Have you ever seen a ScanDisk report with all red? We did. Defragmentation ran over the weekend and finished Monday morning. We all breathed a sigh of relief when that happened. But our troubleshooting wasn't over yet. While we did see some improvement in the performance, it didn't meet our expectations, so we then followed our network test plan:

1. NIC configuration
2. FTP speed from backup server to backup client
3. FTP speed from backup client to backup server
4. Backup speeds from the backup client to backup server to bit bucket

During our review of the NIC configuration, we found that the NIC was set to AUTO-NEGOTIATE. Apparently, when the admin team applied a Compaq NIC patch, it reset all of their NICs to AUTO-NEGOTIATE. So not only did this server suffer because of it, but several others did as well. After we changed the NIC back to FULL DUPLEX, we tested our backup speeds. As we anticipated, the backup speeds were meeting and in some cases exceeding our expectations.

Now that the problem had been fixed, we really didn't need to complete our network test plan, but in order to maintain consistency, we did so. We performed FTP tests between the servers and found the speeds to be quite acceptable. We even set up a NULL device on the backup server to test the network speed from client to server, isolating it from the tape devices and server back plane. Our goals were met, and these test plans were successful in helping us not only fix the problem but also in documenting it for future administrators who may run into a similar situation.

Incidentally, we did recommend that they address the RAID5 issue and consider some other RAID, such as RAID0 or RAID0+1, but since the customer's expectations were met, they didn't have a compelling reason to make such a drastic change.

Things to Check before Calling Your Dedicated Support Professional

Usually, we think about troubleshooting problems after things have failed. A little planning in the beginning really helps. Most backup applications have the ability to create their own specific logs. You need to know how logging works within your application and be prepared to enable logging. The authors usually enable all logging during the initial installation so we have the appropriate logs if our initial attempts at backups and restores are not successful. After things are looking good, you should reduce or shut down logging. In some instances there can be a performance impact from logging, and in all instances the logs will consume disk space.

You also need to know how each operating system in your environment handles warning, error, and normal messages. You will discover that just about every operating system will handle these a little differently by default. On most UNIX systems you can see how the system will handle logging by looking at the /etc/syslog.conf file. Here is a sample of this file from a Solaris system:

```
#ident  "@(#)syslog.conf      1.5     99/02/03 SMI"   /* SunOS 5.0 */
#
# Copyright (c) 1991-1999 by Sun Microsystems, Inc.
#
# syslog configuration file.
#
# This file is processed by m4 so be careful to quote (`') names
# that match m4 reserved words.  Also, within ifdef's, arguments
# containing commas must be quoted.
#
*.err;kern.notice;auth.notice                   /dev/sysmsg
*.err;kern.debug;daemon.notice;mail.crit        /var/adm/messages

*.alert;kern.err;daemon.err                     operator
*.alert                                         root

*.emerg                                         *

# if a non-loghost machine chooses to have authentication messages
# sent to the loghost machine, un-comment out the following line:
```

```
#auth.notice                    ifdef(`LOGHOST', /var/log/authlog,
@loghost)

mail.debug                      ifdef(`LOGHOST', /var/log/syslog,
@loghost)

#
# non-loghost machines will use the following lines to cause "user"
# log messages to be logged locally.
#
ifdef(`LOGHOST', ,
user.err                                /dev/sysmsg
user.err                                /var/adm/messages
user.alert                              `root, operator'
user.emerg                              *
)
```

As you can see, most of the messages you are interested in are logged to /var/adm/messages. On an HP-UX system you will see something completely different. Here is a sample /etc/syslog.conf file from an HP system:

```
# @(#) $Revision: 74.1 $
#
# syslogd configuration file.
#
# See syslogd(1M) for information about the format of this file.
#
mail.debug              /var/adm/syslog/mail.log
*.info;mail.none        /var/adm/syslog/syslog.log
*.alert                 /dev/console
*.alert                 root
*.emerg                 *
```

You are really looking for two things: the location of the log file and making sure it is not disabled. If there is a hash (#) in the first column, then that line is commented out. By default, some systems have all the logging lines in the /etc/syslog.conf file commented out. You should enable the appropriate lines to ensure logging is turned on. This log is where you would see if the system is reporting problems, along with some of the processes that are running as part of the backup application as they also log to the system log. On Windows systems, the application will usually have its own logs. In addition, you will need to use the event viewer to access the system logs and the application logs. You should also be familiar with network error logging, since the network can play a very large role in backing and recovering systems. The netstat command is commonly used to get a basic idea of the condition of your network. Here is a sample netstat command output on a Solaris system:

```
# netstat -i
Name  Mtu  Net/Dest      Address       Ipkts     Ierrs    Opkts    Oerrs
Collis Queue
lo0       8232 loopback      localhost     434768    0        434768    0
0         0
hme0  1500 burreed       burreed       280473    0        254050    0
546       0
```

Your backup application should also include a troubleshooting manual that will provide helpful information, including a list of error codes and recommended actions. If you have a backup or restore failure, you can look up the specific error code and get an idea of where the problem might lie. If it appears to be network related, you should make sure you have good network connectivity between the systems involved. You could go to each system and see what the network logs show. The troubleshooting manual might also suggest some commands to try. As you investigate, be sure to gather all the logging information as well as configuration information, so when you call the support hotline, you will already have the information that the support person needs to assist you.

How to Gather Information

The different backup applications have their own mechanisms or methods to gather data. With VERITAS Software's NetBackup, a script named "support" is provided with the system in /usr/openv/netbackup/bin/ goodies. On a Windows system, the script is in \Program Files\VERITAS\ NetBackup\bin\goodies. This script can be used to gather system, patch, version, and configuration information. It can also be used to gather information from the application logs. The output of the script is placed in a file that can be sent to the support folks to investigate any problems.

In addition, a newer utility, NCVU, can be used to verify your configuration. For more information about this utility, go to http://seer.support .veritas.com/docs/247698.htm.

Where to Find Information to Assist in Self-Diagnosis

The best source for troubleshooting information is located in the application troubleshooting guide. This information is located online with many of the applications today and is accessible via hot keys. The operating system also contains valuable information to help in diagnosing problems, including the man pages and other online documentation. As you get into some of the more complex configurations, the troubleshooting also gets more complex. If you are using a SAN, there are actual diagnostic tools for the different elements in the SAN, such as the switch, the router, and even the host bus adapter (HBA). Each of these devices has its own set of error codes, logging facility, and monitoring tool. VERITAS also has a log analysis utility that you can download from their support FTP site. This utility is designed to help analyze the debug logs on either backups or restores. You can enter a job ID, and the utility will extract information for all the logs related to the selected job. This utility is available at http://seer.support .veritas.com/docs/248369.htm.

As you consider troubleshooting your backup, remember, it is an application that touches many parts of the system. With this in mind, you should become familiar with some of the assistance commands and support tools available at the operating system level. Your backup application, such as NetBackup, is an application, and as such, it relies on the operating system and its infrastructure to accomplish its mission.

Tools are available with most operating systems that will assist you in gathering additional information produced by the operating system during its normal operation. The first place to look is usually the system's own logs. Many times, errors that seem to occur in the backup application are actually triggered by a lower-level failure that is seen by the operating system. Often, these types of failures are reported to the application and in turn reported as an error code by the application. A case in point is a Status 23 reported by NetBackup. NetBackup describes this as a "Cannot Connect on Socket" error. While this is technically true, the underlying cause is usually found to be a failure in the system networking structure.

Although this section cannot delve into all types of errors and their analysis, we hope that an explanation of how you may go about resolving issues will help you understand the interaction and usage of the operating system tools as a means of troubleshooting and solving problems. We hope that after finishing this chapter, you will begin to automatically think of the interaction of the application, operating systems, mechanical infrastructure, and mechanical infrastructure software found in the switches, routers, and drives that make up an enterprise.

In the next section, we help you include the infrastructure used by the application itself as part of your troubleshooting technique. This will help you to become more efficient in your daily activities.

Some Tools to Become Familiar With

Most systems and devices have some form of commands or interfaces that can be used in troubleshooting. We will take a quick look at a few of them to help you better understand how the use of these additional tools can help resolve problems more rapidly. Many of these commands have equivalent commands on other operating systems.

Following are some of the basic operating system commands:

- `truss(1)` —Trace system calls and signals on Sun Solaris
- `tusc`—Trace system calls and signals on HP systems
- `par`—Trace system calls and signals on Silicon Graphics systems

These commands can be used to determine what is happening within a given process. They can be used when it appears the backup application is hung. By using truss or one of its equivalents, you can determine whether a particular file residing on a filesystem, when accessed by the operating system, could cause the same type of hang to occur. You can then confirm this by reading the file manually using some other type of operating system command. In this case, the use of the system command od could be used to enable you to determine that a file had an incorrect symbolic link to it.

Another situation where the od command is used is to show that accessing a file on a drive would cause the drive not to respond. This type of troubleshooting made clear that the problem was not with the application since it was waiting for the operating system to return the requested data. Therefore, the corrective action must be accomplished within the operating system.

In the second example, the system logs should show a failure as a time-out posted by the drive. However, in the case of the incorrect symbolic link in the first example, there were no errors and the system was happily spending its time trying to determine the endpoint of a circular link, resulting in the application appearing to be hung when trying to back up a particular file. The od command can also be used to manually read the data on a tape to help determine if the backup utility is writing the expected headers and data on the tape.

While rare, it is possible that the backup application can either directly or indirectly cause a system to panic or crash. In some instances, this can be caused by interoperability between the different vendors' hardware or firmware versions. In these cases, analysis by all the vendors involved is required for the problem to be determined. By using commands such as crash, you can sometimes determine if the problem is repetitive, which may signify a coding problem, or if it is random, which might point to some type of hardware problem. It is not our intention to teach you system dump analysis; however, we want to make you aware of some of the tools that are available.

Other areas that you need to become familiar with are the utilities that are incorporated in some peripheral devices, including those that are part of the SAN, such as switches, bridges, and routers. Although the terms bridge and router are sometimes used interchangeably, in the networking world, a fine distinction may be made. A *bridge* allows the change of medium between devices. For example, the Chaparral FS1310 allows connections between SCSI devices and fiber networks. It is a bridge between the two technologies. With a *router*, there may not be a transformation of medium.

No matter what you call the devices involved, failures at this level may result in the backup application reporting backup errors. Keep in mind that the backup application will probably be the first place that there is an opportunity for the error to become visible to the user. Within most devices that are on the SAN or network, there is also what one could consider a small operating system that is responsible for a particular type of activity. In these devices, there is usually a small command set that you can use to help determine the cause of a failure. These command sets can be used to show connections, errors, firmware levels, and so on. In addition, you can sometimes use these command sets to determine status of connections, health of the physical medium, and so on, as well as to determine where a failure may be happening.

Summary

In this chapter, we looked at some things to consider when you run into problems and have to troubleshoot your backup and recovery system. We looked at some of the tools and also provided some real-world examples to give you a better idea of how to approach problems or performance issues.

In the next chapter, we look at ways to handle growth in your enterprise and the accompanying growth in your backup and recovery requirements.

The Expanding Backup System

Once you have designed (or inherited) your backup architecture, experienced a successful rollout, and had an opportunity to monitor the activity, performance, and usage, eventually it will be time to address growth and expansion. Naturally, the best way to address growth is to anticipate through capacity planning; however, most find themselves in the middle of expansion without the lifeboat of preplanning at their disposal. As a result, many of the decisions being made are reactive, based on the person or groups that happen to be, figuratively speaking, threatening the most bodily harm.

In this chapter, we give you the information you need about expanding your backup environment to make your life as a storage administrator as easy as possible. The backup tool you selected for your environment will dictate the practical application of what we will be discussing in this chapter. For purposes of illustration, VERITAS NetBackup is used in most of the examples, but when possible, a more generic approach for capacity planning is used.

React versus Respond

Time is slipping away. Yes, in most environments the amount of time we are given for backup is shrinking. Neither of us has ever been at a client site where we were told that we have been given another three hours for the backup window; that just doesn't happen—at least in our experience. Not only is time slipping away from us, but the data continues to grow, sometimes at an alarming rate. Once, a pristine backup environment would successfully complete every job before the window closed. Now we are struggling to get all jobs done within the window. For the unprepared storage administrator, this happens very slowly, almost unnoticed, until one day you are faced with a report full of failures and begin to *react* as opposed to *respond* to managers, administrators, and users who are at your desk looking for their data to be restored. We will try to illustrate this contrast in the next paragraph, but suffice it to say that we are less likely to be productive when we react as opposed to being able to properly respond. We want to move away from a reactive posture to a responsive posture as storage administrators. When we react we tend to occasionally lose our temper and make irrational decisions. Conversely, with a responsive posture, we tend to start with a goal in mind, and our moves are planned and intentional. This means we need to plan for the eventual growth of our environment, again putting the onus on the people who control the budgets so they too may take a responsive posture within their own job responsibilities.

It's human nature to react when you feel you are being attacked. Within that context we do one of two things: fight or flee. This concept has been around for a long time. In disaster recovery (DR) presentations, the presenter will normally ask how many in the audience actually have a DR plan. Inevitably someone speaks up and says, "Yeah, it's my updated résumé"—in other words, a flee response. Then there are the shouting matches surely you have witnessed between a storage administrator and a business unit manager when data was lost and couldn't be restored. What started out calm turned into a tsunami right before your eyes—a classic fight response. Both of those examples aren't healthy for our professional careers or our physical stature, so instead of the fight or flee reaction, let's be prepared with responsive solutions. You may never be able to avoid some battles, but if you have the right information to back your position up, then you as storage administrator can at least stay calm during the process and still be productive at the end of the day. When you can achieve this kind of harmony within your organization, you will find growing your backup environment to match the expansion of your enterprise is not as daunting as you might have otherwise believed.

Capacity Planning

In a previous chapter we discussed how to plan for your initial backup architecture, including the following considerations:

- What data to back up
- How much data to back up
- The rate of change for that data

Capacity planning is a very similar but easier exercise, since we have most of the information already in our hands. Using the information gathered during your interview of the data owners, you should be able to extrapolate an estimation of how fast the data will grow. Most database administrators that we have talked to have a very good idea of the percentage of growth within their databases. Make sure you ask these questions during your initial interview phase with them to make this part of your capacity planning go as smooth as possible. Here are a few sample questions to ask data owners:

- How large is your data/database?
- What percentage of change happens to your data daily?
- Is there a particular point when the data changes more than usual?
- How much of that change is actual data growth?
- Can you anticipate an annual percentage of growth?
- What are your recovery expectations?

The most important part of capacity planning is determining where your data plateaus during the backup schedules and retentions you have subscribed. It is the plateau that will allow you to properly size your environment. The charts and tables to follow graphically represent the equations we have used to arrive at the results found in our examples. Even though these equations look daunting, trust us, it is only math and we will explain in detail how we are achieving these numbers.

Table 9.1 shows a sample of some of the data we have collected at a client site with regard to growth and capacity planning. To make things easy, we converted frequency and retention levels to days.

Table 9.1   Capacity Planning Chart

SERVER	AMOUNT OF DATA	FULL FREQUENCY (DAYS)	RETENTION (DAYS)
Mammoth	~100 GB	7	28

INCREMENTAL FREQUENCY (DAYS)	RETENTION (DAYS)	PERCENTAGE OF CHANGE	REQUIRED STORAGE
1	14	10%	520 GB

Here we will present to you the formulae used to calculate the required backup storage media need for the server, Mammoth, based on the maximum retention level, or 28 days. The percentage of change comes from our initial interview of the data owners, who may know the estimated percentage of change, or by simply taking a rough estimate, for the sake of example we are going to use 10 percent as our rate of change. While this rate of change may seem high or low, it makes the examples much easier to visualize. If you are using VERITAS NetBackup, you may use their File System Analyzer tool, which may give you a more accurate view.

The chart in Figure 9.1 visually represents the equation used to define the total capacity required for the full backups. While you may not need a chart to understand how much data a full backup will take, this graphic and these equations are a consistent method for which to use in modeling your backups.

Let's take some time to understand the Backup Models. The top portion of the figure is a graph that represents the days along the x-axis (1–33), with the data (D-Amount of data backed up) backed up running along the pos-y-axis and the data changed (pD) along the neg-y-axis. Whenever we use an arrow in the positive direction on the y-axis, it represents a backup that has been run, while an arrow in the negative direction on the y-axis represents changed data (pD, where p is the rate of change and D is the amount of data). Notice the Ff (Full-frequency) between #1 and #2, this represents the number of days between scheduled full backup jobs. Also note none of the changed data (pD) is being backed up. Since this is a Full Backup Model no distinction is made between changed data and unchanged data as with the Incremental Models discussed later.

The Total Backup graph shown directly below it presents a graphical view of how we reach our data plateaus and when. As you can see from the chart, Full Backups performed every 7 days and retained for 28 days means that we will need $4D$ or 4 times the total amount of data backed up with each Full. A much easier way to look at this is the formula. If we keep the fulls for twenty-eight days, then we will have a maximum of four full backups stacked at any one time. Using our example, $4D$ or 400GB will be required for this one client based on the policy requirements subscribed to. The incremental backups become a bit more interesting as you will see in the following charts and graphs.

Now again in Figure 9.2, we have the familiar 33-day graph, with Data (*D*) backed up traveling on the positive y-axis and the changed data (*pD*) traveling on the negative y-axis. Notice once again, *Ff* is the number of days between scheduled full backup jobs and now we have introduced *If* or the number of days between scheduled incremental backup jobs. This time we do show changed data (*pD*) being backed up because this is a Differential Incremental Backup Model.

For the next example we retain the differential incremental backups for 14 days. These numbers are typical of most customer sites we have visited, so it's interesting to view these backup models because it paints a very clear picture of how much tape you actually require for your backup jobs. Day one we have a full, so the bottom graph does not show an incremental backup; however, on day two we backup *pD*, which again is the rate of change × Total Data being backed up. This continues for as long as the Incremental frequency defines itself or until a Full backup is required to run, which you can see happens on day 8 of the bottom graph shown by a dotted line box. Notice our plateau is roughly 3× the amount of data we are backing up.

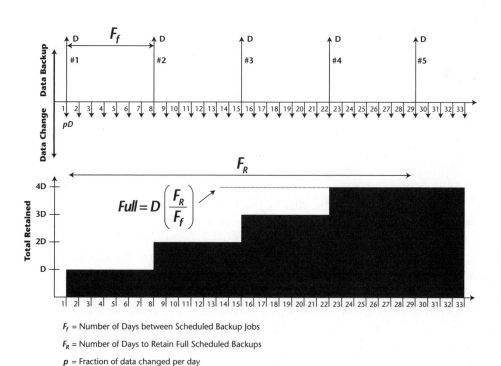

F_f = Number of Days between Scheduled Backup Jobs

F_R = Number of Days to Retain Full Scheduled Backups

p = Fraction of data changed per day

D = Total Amount of Data to be Backed Up

Figure 9.1   Full Backup Model.

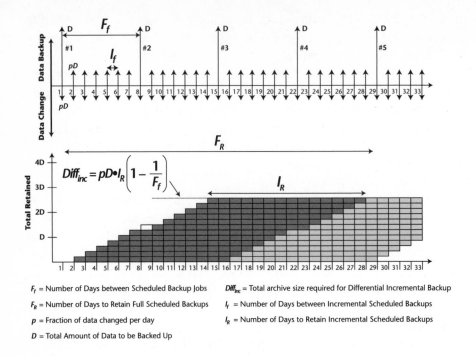

F_f = Number of Days between Scheduled Backup Jobs

F_R = Number of Days to Retain Full Scheduled Backups

p = Fraction of data changed per day

D = Total Amount of Data to be Backed Up

$Diff_{inc}$ = Total archive size required for Differential Incremental Backup

I_f = Number of Days between Incremental Scheduled Backups

I_R = Number of Days to Retain Incremental Scheduled Backups

Figure 9.2   Differential Incremental Backup Model.

Finally a cumulative incremental will backup data changed since the last *full* backup. In our example here we are retaining our cumulative incremental backups for only seven days, not the 14 days as previously used by the differential example. The reason we decided on 7 is due to the sheer volume of data a cumulative would retain. You will quickly appreciate our decision as you look at the graph. Remember, the key here is where does our data plateau. Day one, as shown in the top graph, is our full backup, day 2 is *pD* or rate of change*Data, day 3 is *2pD*, day 4, *3pD* and so on. Since a cumulative incremental adds data changed from the last full, the amount of data required becomes significant. Essentially we are looking for the total data required for a cumulative incremental to be *(p*D)+(2p*D)+(3p*D)+(4p*D)+(5p*D)+(6p*D)*. So you can see from our bottom graph that by the seventh day we are past 2x the total Data being backed up by the full, unlike the Differential Incremental where it took us approximately two weeks to reach that point. With that being said, it may be prudent to perform full backup jobs more often if cumulative incremental is your preferred method, this should greatly reduce the amount of tapes required for your backups. Now if you retain your cumulative backups for 14 days, you simply would *IR/Ff*Cinc* (cumulative incremental).

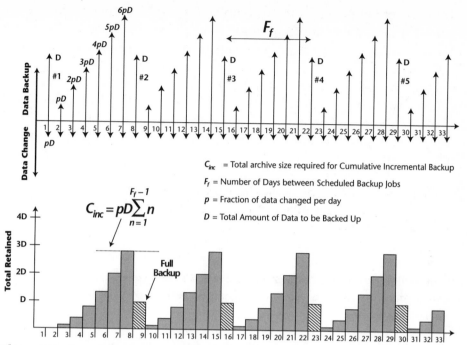

Figure 9.3   Cumulative Incremental Backup Model.

As a matter of practice we have included a proof for the differential incremental equation in Figure 9.4.

Total Number of Incremental Backups = $T_{BU} = \dfrac{I_R}{I_f}$

Number of Days of Full Backups (Differential Not Needed) = $T_F = \dfrac{I_R}{F_f}$

Size of Incremental Backup = $D_{inc} = pD \bullet I_f$

Proof:

Total Archive Size:

$$Diff_{inc} = D_{inc}\,(T_{BU} - T_F)$$

$$Diff_{inc} \quad = \quad D_{inc}\,(T_{BU} - T_F)$$

$$= \quad pD \bullet I_f \left(\frac{I_R}{F_f} - \frac{I_R}{F_f} \right)$$

$$= \quad pD \bullet I_f \bullet I_R \left(\frac{1}{I_f} - \frac{1}{F_f} \right)$$

Figure 9.4   Proof of Differential Archive Size.

Grab a piece of paper and your number 2 pencil and follow along with the proof. Math is a wonderful thing.

So as you can see, capacity planning is made much easier by employing these charts, graphs, and equations. After you set up your favorite spreadsheet application with these formulae you can begin to model your environment based on estimated growth and proactively plan accordingly. Incidentally, since other backup tools allow you to do similar types of backups, you should be able to use these formulae to apply to those environments as well.

NOTE As a reminder, a cumulative incremental backs up all changed files since the last full backup. Differential incremental backs up all changed files since the last backup.

NOTE Using the information gathered during the interview process of the data owners should allow you to extrapolate an estimation of how fast the data will grow.

Using the plateaus as your guide, this client will require approximately 520 GB of storage to sustain the full and differential incremental retentions subscribed to in the policy and 610 GB for the full plus a cumulative incremental. Now if you have schedules that run once a month or once a year, these calculations should work as well, but the real girth of your required storage will be in your weekly full and daily incremental backups. If you are using a solution that employs the incremental-forever paradigm, you should still be able to apply these formulae to help you size your environment.

By taking all of the numbers for all of your clients, which you so masterfully calculated using your favorite spreadsheet, and multiplying them by the percentage of growth that you were able to ascertain from the data owners, you can plan for expansion by extrapolating them out by one year, two years, three years, and so on. Ideally, the data owners have some idea of the percentage of growth; if not, you can track that with a variety of tools—even a rudimentary UNIX shell script for NetBackup will help you track the data growth for a particular client, or some of the more expensive storage resource management (SRM) tools will provide that data to you as well. It seems everyone has an SRM tool today, so you shouldn't be too hard-pressed to find some to evaluate (in fact, you may even find some deployed somewhere in your environment already).

Take the information on the data growth and present that to your management for future budgetary purposes. That way, they will not be shocked when the time comes to either update your tape library, add more disks, or hire additional team members to support the storage infrastructure.

Understanding the dynamics of the environment will help during this phase of your approach. With this in hand, we will be able to better address the next few points in this chapter.

- When do I need to divide into multiple backup server domains?
- Do I need more backup servers in the domain or tape capacity or both?
- Given my data, what does that mean for my network requirements?

The Great Divide

As with most of the backup products on the market, you can add additional backup servers to offset the workload of an overly burdened server. The question is, when and what advantage or disadvantage is there when implementing a solution like this? In this section, we will be using VERITAS NetBackup as the backup tool for the illustrations, but practically speaking, the concepts you discover within this chapter can be applied to most other solutions on the market as well. A word of advice before we jump into this section of the chapter: Unless there is a compelling reason for additional server resources, maintain the existing environment for as long as you can to minimize its complexity.

For example, one of our clients who was using VERITAS NetBackup had a decision to make with regard to their expanding environment. They had two buildings—for the sake of this illustration, let's call them building A and building B—6 miles apart, with a fairly equal amount of data in each data center. Both buildings had a large-capacity tape silo and dark fibre between the buildings—although the dark fibre was yet to be implemented—as well as a 2-GB network pipe currently in use for connectivity. They knew they wanted to expand into building B; the decision before them was whether to add another primary backup server or a secondary server within the current primary domain. The other challenge presenting itself was a request from the business to readdress the architecture to meet their new data requirements.

The business unit managers made it known that they wanted their data secured off-site as close to the completion of the backup jobs as possible. This seemed like an unrealistic expectation given that most off-site vendors typically operate during normal business hours for pickup and delivery, unless you pay a premium. We did some personal research to see what an off-site vendor would charge for that type of service, just in case the client asked for any input on the matter. If memory serves correctly, the expense outweighed the benefit. They decided to look at other options, such as using the two buildings 6 miles apart to move data during backup to an "off-site" staging facility.

One of the options would consist of placing a media server in building B within the domain of the NetBackup master server in building A. The media server in building B would back up the data in the same building, then a copy would be created to be taken off-site.

> **NOTE** A NetBackup master server manages the who, what, where, when, and why of the backup polices. A backup server under the control of a NetBackup master server is called a media server, which is any NetBackup server having management control over physical storage devices, such as tapes, tape drives, optical drives, robotic control, and robotic management. The media server will respond to requests from the NetBackup master server for tape mounts and optical mounts, and it tracks the physical condition and location of all the media.

The architecture of this expansion takes on a new perspective, since this client was using VERITAS NetBackup Version 3.4, which does not support the pooling of the logical storage or storage units (called storage unit groups in Version 4.5).

> **NOTE** Had the client deployed NetBackup Version 4.5, they could have used storage unit groups to contain the data to a geographic location. For example, if all the data in building B had to be backed up to building A, a storage unit group could have been created containing all of building A's storage units. Then all they would have had to do is modify the backup policies to use the storage unit group versus the single storage unit. If you find yourself running into this situation, you should consider an upgrade to Version 4.5.

So this would mean that all backup policies for building B would have to specifically request the storage unit in building B. If building B never grows beyond its current size, this would work out beautifully, but as we know, data grows, so eventually they would have had to expand with yet another media server in building B. Then the complexity of this solution under NetBackup Version 3.4 increases and becomes much more difficult to manage.

In this scenario, the administrator would basically be required to "balance" the backup policies between the storage units. However, this didn't meet the original expectations of the business unit managers, who wanted to have their data off-site as soon after the backup as possible. The idea of a cross-building backup was introduced; again, this would have worked well with NetBackup Version 4.5, using the storage unit groups.

Now we were starting to see the complexity of having to manage 40 or more backup policies and balance them properly among the storage units between buildings, as a result of the limited functionality of pre–4.5 NetBackup. If ever there were a compelling reason to upgrade to the latest version of software, this is one of them. If you choose "Any Available Storage Unit" in your backup policy, NetBackup will, in a round-robin fashion, select any available storage unit *not* defined as demand only (meaning only backup policies that specifically demand this storage unit may use it). If all of the storage units are available for use by the Any Available Storage Unit attribute, it very well means that data we want backed up to the other building might end up locally backed up.

You can start to see more complexity building up now. This is all a part of being a storage architect: planning based on customer expectations and working through all of the possible scenarios to come to a reasonable solution. This particular scenario proved to be the wrong solution for this environment, given the customer's desire to remain at the current version.

The second option explored was creating a completely separate NetBackup master server domain in building B. This would allow cross-building backup and effectively meet the expectations of the business unit managers. The storage units could be created to be used by any backup policy, so no "over-administration" would be required for the backup policies; the backup from building A to building B could happen without issue.

All of the issues that were uncovered when reviewing the additional Media Server would have been addressed by either upgrading to NetBackup Version 4.5 or by continuing with NetBackup 3.4 and deploying the second master server. A higher priority was given to bringing building B online without an upgrade, but an upgrade was planned for some time next year during phase III of the architecture plan.

If you go this route, you have two catalogs to back up and ensure are working properly, two separate client configuration files to maintain, two separate global configuration policies to maintain, two separate backup policies, media databases, and the list goes on. However, this was the best solution given what the customer was interested in doing.

The question of when to divide into multiple backup servers is clearly answered by two words: It depends. It depends on what your environment, the customers, and your business are willing to tolerate. Remember, change for the sake of change only adds potentially unnecessary complexity to our already busy schedules as storage administrators.

TIP Identify those compelling reasons for change, decide if the benefit outweighs the pains of change, then plan your work and work your plan.

Advantages and Disadvantages of the Great Divide

There are advantages and disadvantages in any choices we make. For instance, consider the purchase of a new vehicle. You want more seating capacity—the advantage—but find that a larger vehicle requires more fuel to operate—the disadvantage. Further, the advantage may even become a disadvantage. For instance, now that you have more seating capacity, you find that you have become the de facto chauffeur whenever you have those large group lunch outings.

You can come up with many reasons why or why not to divide your configuration into multiple server domains. In the following, we outline some advantages and disadvantages of using a single backup server or master and multiple backup servers or masters:

Lone-Server Advantages

The benefits of keeping a single master include having a single point of control, configuration, and backup image catalog repository. This doesn't sound like much when you are only talking about two servers, one master and one media. However, if you have one master and 22 media servers, it clearly minimizes the complexity of the environment.

Single Point of Administration

There is one location to manage all of the servers within the domain. This includes all of the policy control, job control, device control, and media control. While additional server resources will add some complexity to your environment, having a single point of administrative control will minimize the management effort.

Central Catalog Repository

The image catalog for VERITAS NetBackup typically will be the largest of all the catalogs that it manages, and it is a very critical piece of the puzzle when recovering client data. Having only one master means there is only one location for the image catalog which means there is only one catalog to back up.

Central Configuration Control

Backup policy changes or global configuration changes are made at one server for all of the backup servers within the domain. Again, if we are speaking of two or three servers, this might not sound that terrible, but when the number reaches 22, you then start to see the benefit of a single primary or master server.

Storage Access

With the additional device servers or media servers, there exist more storage devices to be used during the backup process and a sharing of the backup workload across all backup servers. If the reason for the expansion was performance related, this might help to increase the aggregate throughput of the backup jobs.

Minimize Complexity

Simpler is better. You are less likely to have a misunderstanding with some of the more junior members of the administration staff, or even the more senior members. A single-master approach also minimizes the site documentation that needs to be developed and maintained, which we know can be tedious work.

Scalability

At least with NetBackup, its strength is in its scalability; it can transition from a small to medium-size site with one server acting as both master and media server to an environment with multiple media servers protecting the enterprise and all being controlled by one master server.

Lone-Server Disadvantages

The disadvantage of having a single master server is also one of the advantages we listed previously: central repository of the image catalog and central configuration control. Some people find this to be a disadvantage because it means a single point of failure. If you are running 22 servers and lose the master server, you have lost the control center for all scheduling of backups, whether or not you are using NetBackup's scheduler. Plus you have lost all possibility of restoring any data until you recover this failed resource. Yes, you do have the option of recovering data from the Net-Backup tapes independent of having a NetBackup server, since NetBackup writes in a TAR-compatible format, but in reality, we know of very few people who choose this method of recovery. Therefore, if this backup server is considered critical and must be highly available, perhaps installing clustering software like VERITAS Cluster Server, IBM HACMP, or similar tools would be a benefit.

Single Point of Failure

Once we lose the master server, all backup, restore, and duplication possibilities are lost until this server is recovered and returned to an online status. This adds cost to the total cost of ownership, since we would have to purchase some clustering software to eliminate this disadvantage. Note that if you do elect to use VERITAS Cluster Server (VCS) or some other High Availability (HA) tool, you must not only failover the application if it is a master server, but you must failover the device control if it is also a media server. Figure 9.5 depicts a master server *only*, with no robotic or physical device control whatsoever, with VCS configured in an active-passive role. This, in our opinion, is the best approach when attempting to make NetBackup a highly available service, but also adds a higher cost of ownership.

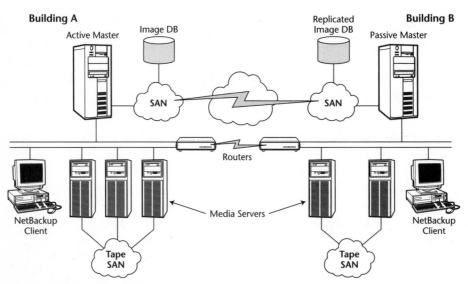

Figure 9.5 Active-passive master server solution.

Central Catalog Repository

Depending on the environment, this may look like a disadvantage. If the intention of the architecture was to protect against facility loss, then having this centrally located for *all* client backups may be a disadvantage if you do not have the additional software necessary to protect you from this facility loss. However, if you are backing up data from building A to building B and lose building A, you still have a master server in building B. If you further set up building A to write its catalog backup to building B, you could restore data for building A clients with some minor configuration changes. It is a bit confusing, but on a white board, it becomes very impressive and shows the power and flexibility of the solution. Figure 9.6 illustrates the architecture. Each building is performing its own local catalog backup to disk; then by design, each server is backing up the opposite building's, A to B and B to A. Therefore, when the backup of master A is done to building B, master A's local catalog backup is protected in the process.

Complexity

The following may add much more complexity to your environment:

- Multiple catalog backups
- Client configuration files
- Backup policies to create and maintain
- Multiple points of monitoring, reporting, troubleshooting, and so on
- Necessity to create and maintain a balance in the distribution of data because of the limitations of the existing product (i.e., NetBackup Version 3.4)

Multiple-Server Advantages

No doubt the format for the information in the next two sections is becoming very evident. Once again, where there are disadvantages in one environment, there are advantages to another. So let's take some time to briefly outline the advantages of having multiple master servers.

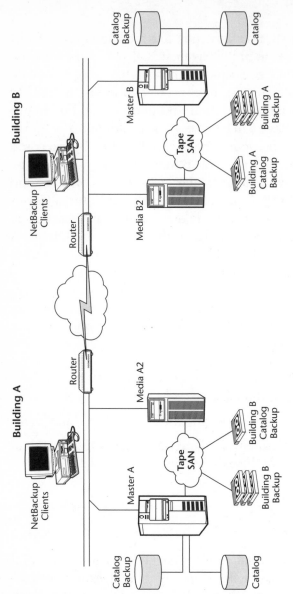

Figure 9.6 Two-master server configuration.

Multiple Points of Recovery

As in the example given, if the master domains are backing up one another's data, as well as backing up the NetBackup Catalog information across buildings, then you potentially have built a much more resilient backup architecture, because you now have multiple points of recovery within your enterprise. If you are in a similar situation as described in this chapter—two buildings roughly 6 miles apart on separate power grids, with one of the buildings being used for an off-site staging area—in the event of a full facility disaster, either of the buildings could be used for a recovery site. For instance, if you lose building A for a considerable amount of time, but building B is still online, what you have lost in the midst of this disaster is the backup service for building B; however, you have all of building A's data at the ready to be restored to any server the administration team requires in order to restore the business. If building B has the necessary hardware, a quick configuration change could be made to the client files in order to successfully back up and protect its own data.

Independent Scalability

As in the previous examples, NetBackup can scale as needed with additional device servers or media servers. Having two masters allows that to happen based on the environments independent of one another. An argument could be made saying that if you had one master, you would still be able to scale the environments independent of one another. That is true, but independent scaling goes beyond just adding more device servers; it also speaks to the ability to globally configure each of the buildings differently as it is required by an SLA or other service-level mechanism that your company may have enacted.

Secured Segregation

What does secured segregation mean? Well, simply put, the two buildings are completely and totally separated, each having its own set of security rights managed by perhaps two completely different management groups. In the examples that have been given thus far, it would not make sense to segregate the rights of the administrators between buildings, but there might be a compelling reason to do so. For instance, you might have two administration teams within your company, a corporate team and a regional team. In some companies that we have consulted with, this definite division exists, so having multiple master servers fulfills the requirement nicely here, since the two groups have completely different data protection strategies, security policies, schedules, and so on.

Multiple-Master Disadvantages

Finally, in this section, we cover the last point of when to divide backup servers. We have read about the advantages and disadvantages of single backup servers and the advantage of multiple backup servers. We have simply listed bullets of the disadvantages of having multiple backup servers here, since most of the advantages and disadvantages are similar whether you are using multiple or single backup servers.

- Twice as much administration
- Multiple points of administration
- Configuration management
- Catalog management
- Much more complexity

Most people design their backup environment with one goal in mind: to back up the data as efficiently and quickly as possible. Others, however, design their backup environments to include the newest technology toys. We're not against the fancy toys, but we are against unnecessary complexity and wasteful resources that eventually lead to an environment that is struggling to meet the service level agreements that your group has made with the business. Backup is a critical service, probably the most important role in the company next to that of the visionaries who create the future for the company. After all, backup protects these visionaries' intellectual property, and without it, we risk losing all of that precious data. Minimize your exposure by architecting a solid backup solution, but do it in a way that makes the management of that environment feasible for everyone who will have any responsibility within the environment.

NOTE Service-level agreements are typically used to define performance expectations for a given service between the customer and the provider. Some companies use this for internal purposes to track performance of the various computing solutions offered to the business units. In this respect, the SLA would be between the IT group or the provider and the business unit or customers. For this reason, it is very important that you properly manage the expectations for backup and recovery from the very beginning.

The bottom line for the customer in the two building illustration: it was best to deploy two masters because of the WAN in the middle. When the WAN goes down, you essentially have lost all communication to the other facility, so if all you had was a media server in building B, you would be effectively down until the WAN was fixed. They too would be in dire straits if the WAN went down, based on their desire to back up between facilities, but it was a risk they were willing to take since they had redundant network links by different providers between buildings.

Determining Your Need for Additional Resources

Now that we have determined some of the advantages and disadvantages of dividing our backup domains, we will look at when we need to add more device hosts or media servers, tape capacity, or perhaps even both.

NOTE VERITAS uses the terms *device host* and *media server* interchangeably to indicate a server that has some control of physical devices for the purposes of backup and restore with regard to VERITAS NetBackup.

When to Add More Device Hosts

Again using the NetBackup illustration, the good news is that adding device hosts or media servers is not as daunting a task as determining whether or not to divide your backup domain. Typically when you find that you aren't meeting your backup window, but you have plenty of capacity in your tape library, it's a sure sign that you need to add a media server. By performing some very basic mathematical formulas, you can determine the approximate amount of data your current environment can actually handle. First, identify any bottlenecks in your backup environment before you decide that you need to invest in more of anything.

As an example, let's look at a master server with one network interface and a 100-Mbps Ethernet on a switched backup network, illustrated in Figure 9.7.

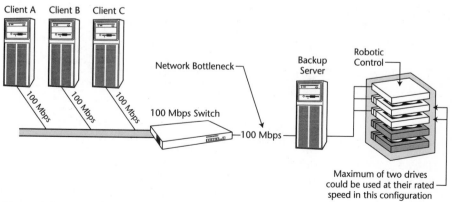

Figure 9.7 100-Mbps network bottleneck.

A single 100-Mbps interface is capable of handling approximately 12.5 MB/second, or roughly two DLT8000 drives at native speeds of 6 MB/second. This definitely looks like a potential bottleneck, and one would more than likely benefit by having an additional media server in place to share the burden.

With a GbE between the backup server and the switch, as illustrated in Figure 9.8, you can drive 125 MB/sec into the backup server, or approximately 20 DLT 8000 tape drives. Naturally, all of this would be dependent on the I/O interface to the tape drives, but assuming you had multiple SCSI interfaces or were using Fiber-connected drives, the numbers would hold fairly true. Would you really want to drive 20 DLT drives from one backup server? Probably not. At that point you would want to expand to another media server or another tape drive type. Table 9.2 shows tape drive statistics that you can use to help decide which drive type might be best.

Either by inheritance, slow growth, or, quite frankly, a very tight budget year, we will one day be faced with a backup environment that hops across networks. When the time comes, and budgets are loosening up, you definitely want to consider introducing a media server into this type of environment. Not only are you backing up another network, but also you are pulling all of that data across the network back to the media server to be written to tape. Wouldn't it be better to have that data remain within the network of its origin and only have to send the meta data back to the master server? We hope you answered yes. If you didn't, you are probably still under very tight budgetary constraints.

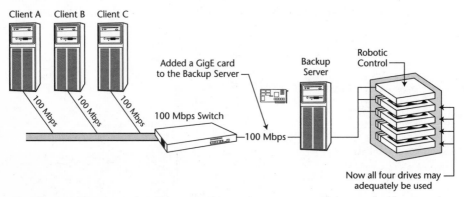

Figure 9.8 GbE network enhancement.

Table 9.2 Drive Types and Speeds

NAME	NATIVE SPEED	CAPACITY	COMPRESSION	CAPACITY MAX
DLT8000	6 MB/sec	40 GB	2:1	80 GB
SDLT220	11MB/sec	110 GB	2:1	220 GB
SDLT320	16MB/sec	160 GB	2:1	320 GB
IBM LTO Ultrium	15 MB/sec	10 GB	2:1	200 GB
STK T9840B	19 MB/sec	20 GB	2:1	40 GB
STK T9940A	10 MB/sec	60 GB	2:1	120 GB

Let's look at an illustration to clarify this. In Figure 9.9, there is 1 TB of data located on clients D, E, and F. If that is true, there would be a significant impact on performance when backing up between networks. Adding a media server would streamline this solution by increasing the aggregate throughput through this division of labor.

As you can see from Figure 9.10, we took into consideration that we had more than enough tape drives for our data requirements, but not enough horsepower. So instead of purchasing more tape drives and another tape library, we were able to connect two of the drives to the new media server and keep two of the drives on the master server. This may not be possible in the event that distance plays a role, in which case it would be prudent to then size the appropriate tape library for the second location and deploy another media server along with it.

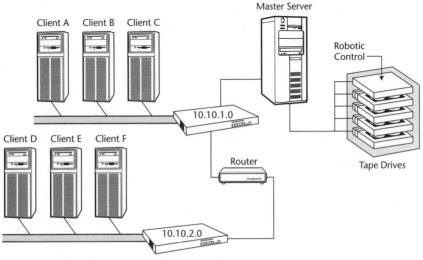

Figure 9.9 Multiple network bottleneck.

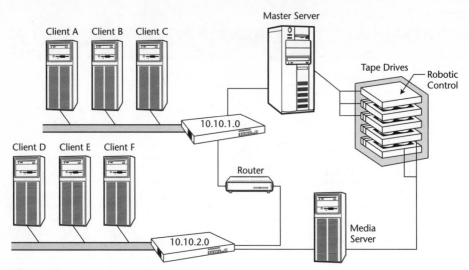

Figure 9.10 Network enhancement.

Another reason to add a media server may be that the amount of data on a particular server has so grossly outgrown even the ability of the network to handle the transfer that it makes good business sense to upgrade that machine to become a media server. For example, let's say that under the best circumstances, it takes a GbE network 23 hours to do a full backup of a server with 1 TB of data that needs to be backed up regularly. That is to say, 43 GB/hour is what our network can handle based on the numbers we charted earlier. We need to carry 1 TB, or 1000 GB, of data to the media server with a full backup, so dividing 1000 GB by 43 GB/hour gives us 22.72 hours. This probably doesn't meet the acceptance criteria for data protection at your facility, so the options are to either break down that server's storage or perform local backups by making this server a media server. Using what you learned in the *Laying Out Your Backup Domain* section in Chapter 3 to determine the memory, I/O, and processor requirements, make sure this new media server will be adequately outfitted with enough power to produce the results you expect.

More Tapes or Tape Drives, or Both?

Again, we cannot stress enough that, in order to get the most out of your current and future investments, you need to find the bottlenecks in your environment before you start spending money. After you have done your due diligence, adding more tape is reasonably simple, especially if you went through the capacity planning section at the beginning of this chapter. If you find that you are getting errors in your backup reports saying backups are incomplete because of unavailable media, you have an issue you need to address. This is done by understanding what is happening to your media. For example, has it had multiple media errors during a previous backup session? If this is the case, has your backup application, in this case NetBackup, marked this media unusable by *freezing* it? In this situation, you should create media reports and view the status of all the media, identify those that have been marked unusable or frozen, and then investigate why this is happening. Alternatively, if your media appears to be just fine except for the fact that most of it is in a *full* condition, you may have to remove some of the full media and replace with scratch media. If that is not an option, consider a larger tape library or an additional tape library.

When should physical tape drives be added? Well, again, it all comes down to math. If you have gathered all of the information related to your clients—tape drives, network speeds, SCSI speeds, fiber speeds—and so on, you are well armed to report whether your current environment will tolerate the amount of data you are looking to protect. See Table 9.3. You want to avoid "shoe-shining" the drives as much as possible. *Shoe-shining* is a term used to describe a situation where a drive is not receiving data fast enough to keep writing and must wait to receive data; therefore, it rewinds a bit to reposition, then begins writing when the data finally arrives.

Now we will lay out some basic planning formulas that may be used in your quest for backup utopia. (By the way, if you ever find backup utopia, please let us know.) First, gather the information needed to perform the math:

- Network speed (10 Mbps, 100 Mbps, 1000 Gbps, etc.)
- I/O speeds to the storage device (SCSI, Fibre, Disk Channel, etc.)
- Output device speeds (we use the native speeds)

Table 9.3 Example of Network Bottleneck and Proposed Resolution

TYPE OF SERVER	NETWORK FEEDS	I/O SPEEDS	NATIVE DRIVE SPEEDS	OBSERVATIONS
Master server	100 MB/sec	40 MB/sec × 2 (2-SCSI)	11MB/sec × 6 (6 SDLT 220s)	Find lowest common denominator
Real numbers	12.5 MB/sec	80 MB/sec	66 MB/sec	Network is a bottleneck

(continued)

Table 9.3 *(continued)*

TYPE OF SERVER	NETWORK FEEDS	I/O SPEEDS	NATIVE DRIVE SPEEDS	OBSERVATIONS
Proposed	Upgrade to GbE	3 –drives / SCSI	Maximum Reached	To achieve maximum throughput
	1000Mbps	40 MB/sec × 2	11 MB/sec × 3 on SCSI A	33 MB/sec
			11 MB/sec × 3 on SCSI B	33 MB/sec
	125 MB/sec	80 MB/sec	Total aggregate 66 MB/sec	
Best practice to avoid shoe-shining	1GbE	40 MB/sec × 3	11 MB/sec × 2 on SCSI A (22 MB/sec)	Headroom for burst speeds on the drives, which may reach 22 MB/sec
	(125 MB/sec)	(120 MB/sec)	11 MB/sec × 2 on SCSI B (22 MB/sec)	
			11 MB/sec × 2 on SCSI B (22 MB/sec)	

Now, assuming of course that you used the recommendations in Chapter 4 for your server component selection, such as memory, processors, and so on, you will be on your way to that utopian land we all strive for. All of the "busy" work may seem a bit mundane, but it is a very worthwhile exercise, especially during budget time. See Table 9.4.

It's very helpful to create charts and spreadsheets like this for each of the servers you plan on using. Not only does it help you with these architectural decisions, but it may be the basis for your own site documentation, a task we all love to do. Furthermore, this exercise applies whether or not you are using NetBackup.

Table 9.4   Example of a Server that Can Support More Tape Drives

TYPE OF SERVER	NETWORK FEEDS	I/O SPEEDS	NATIVE DRIVE SPEEDS	OBSERVATIONS
Master server	1GbE	Fibre Channel (100 MB/sec)	15 MB/sec × 4 (4 LTO Ultrium)	Find lowest common denominator
Real numbers	125 MB/sec	100 MB/sec	60 MB/sec	Room for ~2 – 3 more LTO drives
Best practice	125 MB/sec	Fibre Channel	Add two more LTO drives, bringing aggregate total to ~90 MB/sec	To achieve maximum throughput

What about Tape Technologies?

Many tape technologies are on the market; some were listed earlier in this chapter. How do we answer that question for you in these pages? We really cannot. You will know if you need new tape technology based on your due diligence. Nothing we can write here will tell you definitively that you should change your tape technology (unless, of course, you are using a QIC drive for your backup; in this case, we would feel safe recommending that you at least give it some thought). But even after you have done your due diligence, what if you have a system that cannot push the data any faster than the QIC drive can read? What if we said you should move off of those DLT 8000 drives and get into something faster without first looking at your server, NIC, or I/O to the drives? This would, of course, be ridiculous, and anyone that claims they can tell you different may also have a bridge in backup utopia to sell you too. Do some investigating. Interview the vendors, asking them for real benchmark test results, for the *native* speeds of their drives, not the theoretical numbers. Always look for the disclaimer, "your mileage may vary"—another way of saying results are not typical. Take the time to perform the math calculations and see exactly what you are getting yourself into before you put your name on a proposal that carries a price tag of $1.2 million. Otherwise, you might find yourself surprised.

Alternative Network Solutions

How to continue to meet the expectations of the business and finish your backups within the allotted time continues to stand before us. There are some very good alternatives to the traditional approach; most of what will be covered in this section has become more of the norm rather than the exception. In this section we briefly cover the other network solutions you might want to look into as your backup system needs to expand and keep up with the expectations of the business.

- 10 Mbps, 100 Mbps, 1 GbE
- Dedicated backup network
- Storage area network (SAN)

10 Mbps, 100 Mbps, 1 GbE

As we were evaluating our network looking for bottlenecks, we touched on the subject of moving up from 10 Mbps to 100 Mbps, or even 1GbE (1000 Mbps). The benefit as you slide up the scale is more and more data being moved along the network pipe, and today most people have a switch in their environment for their large servers. If you don't, that might be the first thing you place on the budget proposal for the next fiscal year.

There are several camps on this subject, but the rule of thumb we have always used has been the effective throughput of an Ethernet network is 1.25 MB/second for 10 Mbps, 12.5 MB/second for 100 Mbps, and 125 MB/sec for 1000 Mbps (1GbE), and even then, we tend to round those numbers down. See Table 9.5.

We know some people, ourselves included, who use these numbers and apply an overhead reduction to them of approximately 30 percent. It is a good baseline to start with while you are looking into the possibilities of uplifting your network to a higher-speed technology. With the knowledge of the previous sections in this chapter, you should be much better equipped to size or plan the deployment of your backup solution.

Table 9.5 Ethernet Speeds

10 BT	10 Mbps	1.25 MB/second
100 BT	100 Mbps	12.5 MB/second
Gig Ethernet (1000 Mbps)	1000 Mbps	125 MB/second

Dedicated Backup Network

You may find that even by upgrading your network bandwidth to 100 Mbps or even 1 GbE your primary network is so busy during the evening hours when backup runs that it would still hinder performance. That's when you want to consider implementing a dedicated backup network. These are great if you can afford to put one in. All of the backup data travels across this dedicated backup network and nothing travels across your public network. Many customer sites that we have visited have dedicated backup networks, and the performance benefits are tremendous. A dedicated backup network requires an additional interface in the servers to be hosted on this new network. This also may require some configuration modifications to your backup software in order to ensure you are using the dedicated network versus the public network. One of our customers has two dedicated networks, as shown in Figure 9.11.

Normally, this would be a good time to recommend that you deploy another device host, or media server. However, while on site, we discovered that they had plenty of horsepower in the master server to drive the tapes and receive the data, so it wasn't necessary to install another server in the domain. Instead we opted for another NIC to allow this server to back up the clients on the 10.10.2.0 network. This was a very efficient method and saved the client's budget for other things in the enterprise.

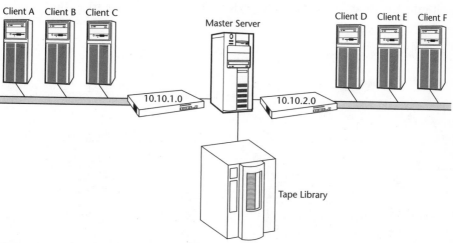

Figure 9.11 Dual networked master.

Another method similar in look and feel is a SAN.

Storage Area Network (SAN)

Sometimes called a TAN, for tape area network (if that's all being hosted on the switches), a SAN usually consists of some kind of fiber or fabric switch, host bus adapters (HBAs) in the servers, and a zoning configuration on the switches to ensure proper routing of devices and information. A SAN is very similar to what you are used to with traditional networking. A LAN, for instance, consists of a switch or even a hub that has servers and other computing devices attached to it for the purposes of sharing resources. Similarly the main purpose of a SAN is to share resources, but instead of a 100-Mbps switch, it is a fiber switch. Not only can servers attach to it but also storage devices, such as disk and tape. A SAN is not as complex as you might think. Really, if you think about it, networking is just plumbing. You have a variety of pipes that connect together in order to deliver something. In a home, it's water; in a data center, it's data. So we have this elaborate piece of plumbing that allows the sharing of resources in a very efficient and surprisingly fast manner.

Figure 9.12 is a basic design of a SAN, two SAN routers for redundancy, a SCSI-to-Fibre bridge in order to bring the tape drives into the SAN, dual HBAs in the servers, and a master server, all connected to the SAN switches. This type of configuration would enable the data to be read from the SAN-attached clients and written to the SAN attached tapes, without having to traverse the public network with large amounts of data.

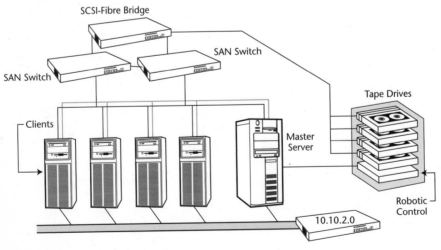

Figure 9.12   SAN attached master server.

There are many more possibilities with SANs in a NetBackup environment, which we discussed in the *Backing Up and Restoring in a SAN Environment* section of Chapter 7.

Summary

In this chapter we covered quite a bit of ground, from capacity planning techniques and dividing our backup domains, to exploring the different types of networks that may be used to increase the performance of our backup environment. Here are the highlights of what we covered:

- Advantages and disadvantages of multiple- and lone-master backup servers
- How to determine additional resource needs
- When to add more device hosts
  - Evaluating your network for bottlenecks
  - Adding more backup hardware
- When to add more tape drives
- Tape technologies
- Alternative network solutions

We could probably dedicate an entire book to the topics in this chapter, and if the demand is there, we just might do that. Until then, this should give you a good solid foundation on which to build your backup architecture decisions.

The Enterprise Impact
of Backup Systems

## CHAPTER 10

The Future of Backup

The future of backup sounds like an oxymoron: The future involves forward thinking, and backup involves an archive or history. However, it is critical to consider that sometime in the future, we will need to recover what was done in the past to protect the present. This consideration is as critical as architecting, planning, installing, configuring, and even updating the backup and recovery solution for your enterprise.

So far, everything we have talked about has been based on the current technologies and techniques available to perform backup storage management for the enterprise. Throughout this book, we have made every effort to ensure that our content is not speculative and that the solutions and methods mentioned are real and available solutions today. In this chapter, however, we take a peek into the crystal ball and see how possible changes in technology and business requirements will affect the way you do backup and recovery. While this chapter contains some ideas and methods that are underway, it also contains some speculation and conjecture, in hopes that the visionaries and innovators of this space might take note or at the very least become inspired to develop our thoughts further. Having said that, we make no claims to having a better crystal ball than anyone else as we have tried to gather information from some of these very same visionaries and innovators. We are not saying this is the way it will be—just that these are some of the things that could happen.

The trends in technology are responsible for some of the changes. We are seeing storage capacity doubling every year, resulting in our having more and more data to protect. Network bandwidth is doubling every nine months. Network backups will remain plausible in some environments, but the overall amount of data to be protected will necessitate changes. Networked storage is becoming more common, along with more intelligence being distributed throughout the SAN. These are seen as enablers to some of the new backup technologies. Will we begin to see these hardware solutions and software solutions integrate more closely from the backup perspective?

Still, the greatest visionaries and innovators have not been able to expand the day beyond 24 hours to provide us the ability to back up this ever-growing critical data in light of the most prevalent problem, the need for 24 × 7 backup operations. Backup servers cannot be taken down for maintenance, as they are expected to be running even during the production window. The backup windows are disappearing, or rather, merging with the traditional production window, but at the same time, the recovery requirements are increasing. There is a need for almost instant recovery options. In fact, backup and recovery is now being seen as an integral part of data availability, instead of just data insurance. Everyone wants to make the storage available on demand so that it can be logically moved around the enterprise and be used where it is most needed, but it still must be backed up. When you couple this with the requirement to cluster everything, including the applications, the data, and the data protection services, it makes backup and recovery even more challenging. This is leading to the idea of hot backup systems or even hot backup sites. Will we see more intelligent backup server software? Will backup become an appliance much like we have seen happen with Network File System (NFS) and electronic mail?

As the futurists look at these trends and requirements, one important hardware trend stands out. The cost of disk versus the cost of tape hardware, along with relative performance, is changing very quickly. Tape drives are getting faster and media has more capacity, but the costs of both are going up. Disks are getting cheaper per bit every day, and now we are seeing inexpensive high-density disks with good performance and reliability. This trend makes disk attractive as a backup device or at least suitable for use in the backup formula. The high-speed access makes it very attractive as a recovery device. Will disk be the new backup medium, as we have seen in some cases today? What will happen to tape? Will solid-state solutions prevail? What will the longevity of these solid-state devices mean, if anything, for off-site storage capabilities?

Another area being explored is the potential of merging or integrating different software products to provide an overall data protection strategy. The focus is not just on traditional backup anymore. This integration is already happening with the introduction of some of the frozen image backup products available today. It looks like this trend is going to continue and include several different technologies.

Some of the ideas and thoughts we explore in this chapter then are as follows:

- Virtual backup
- Real-time backup
- Synthetic backups
- Hardware/software integration (embedded agents)
- Intelligent backup server software
- Backup appliances
- Disk, solid-state disk as backup storage

As we found out when researching this chapter, many companies, unless they were ready to release the generally available (GA) version of their products, were reluctant to talk about their futures, and rightly so. Therefore, we have used our own industry experience and customer interactions to develop this chapter. This is our attempt at backup utopia. Even though it may never come to fruition, it's good to dream.

Virtual Backup

The future is now, or at least portions of it, for we are seeing some of the virtual backup technologies today with the integration of current technologies. However, it hasn't made the main stage yet. This virtual backup feature involves making persistent frozen images of the data being protected and managing these images. The frozen image can be either a mirror or a snapshot. This offers a way for you to use disk storage to provide high-performance data protection, and it allows you to encompass several technologies capable of providing versioned frozen images of filesystems or volumes. These local versions can then be accessed during restoration, instead of the data being accessed on tape or remote storage, allowing you to protect your data "instantaneously" via an automated and manual facility. In this way, the restoration of user data can be just as instantaneous as backups. The hope is to keep most differences in the underlying technologies away from you, the end user. If data was protected to tape or locally via a virtual backup, the user should be comfortable in locating and recovering either version of a file. This technology was actually introduced with VERITAS Software's NetBackup 4.5.

The implementation of this feature involves the integration of the frozen image technology with the backup technology. The real innovation is that the backup product controls the creation of the frozen images, catalogs the data in the frozen image, tracks the versions of the frozen images, and facilitates restores from the frozen image. You can configure the number of frozen images to be kept (versions) and how often they will be made. Since no data is actually transferred during the backup, this offers a very low impact backup option. The only real constraint is available disk space. The frozen images are disk images of the data, so the restore performance should also be almost instantaneous.

Figure 10.1 shows an example of doing virtual backups using VERITAS Software's VxVM mirrors. In this example, NetBackup is managing three mirrors plus the live volume. This gives the appearance of rotating mirrors. The concept is very similar with storage checkpoints. The biggest difference is that with the mirror model, you must allocate all the disk space for all the mirrors before initiating virtual backup. With storage checkpoints, the disk space is allocated as needed, and the disk space is deallocated as a checkpoint becomes obsolete. The mirrors potentially have less system overhead but will use more disk space.

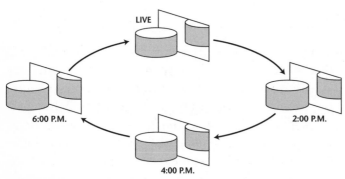

Figure 10.1   Virtual backups.

Other software solutions perform similarly by making periodic, scheduled point-in-time copies of the data. These solutions contain the changes only and not the entire file; therefore, they do not take up a significant amount of storage. The solutions typically will integrate with most backup solutions via some type of pre- and post-processing scripts. The future of virtual backups will be led by the backup software vendors and most certainly validated by the emerging technology companies that will provide this in a cross-backup-platform solution.

Real-Time Backup

Real-time backup is another feature that combines different technologies. Here the data is backed up (or replicated) as it changes, resulting in continuous backups. The data is replicated to a second host and then backed up from the second (target) host to tape. This moves the backup burden to the target system in exchange for a steady impact on the source system and the network. Real-time backup also offers you the opportunity to create versions based on more system-based events. Markers would be used in the log stream to synchronize the source and target checkpoints with application quiescence. Some solutions today actually sit at the application layer, above the cache, and will replicate changes incrementally, rather than the entire filesystem. These software solutions may provide a higher level of protection in the event of a failure, since the replication may be committed before the actual source information is committed.

Backup and Replication

Backup of a filesystem is typically accomplished by copying files from the source hard disk across the network to a network server hosting tape drives. The backup system would need to "walk" the filesystem in order to accomplish its task. The frequency of the backups is governed by practical considerations such as network impact, system impact, and available media. On the other hand, remote filesystem replication products monitor changes to file objects and copy these changes to a remote disk location for safekeeping. Some solutions choose to do a full file copy, block-level changes, or simply incremental or delta changes of a file when they sense a file change. The remote replica can be utilized for disaster recovery in the case of major physical damage to the primary filesystem. Data protection in this scenario occurs in real time as objects change. Its use is usually governed by network impact, available replica storage, and overhead on the server. Figure 10.2 is an example of a real-time backup configuration.

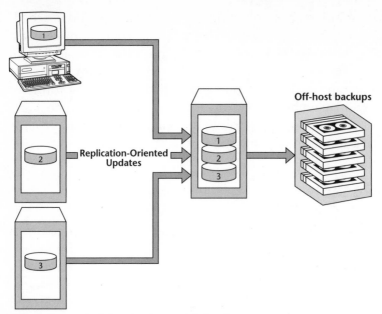

Figure 10.2 Real-time backup—High level.

What if we replicate only the block changes? Well, that's being done today, with VERITAS Volume Replicator, FalconStor's IPStor, EMC, Hitachi, and other solutions. What if we were able to back up only those changes for an infinite recovery level based on the retention of those blocks written to tape, as shown in Figure 10.3? Taking the block-level replication to the next level may include an option to integrate with the backup software that allows only those incremental changes to be written to tape, either continuously or scheduled. In the future, we may have the ability to recover a particular file from a particular point in time from blocks that are backed up or archived to tape after being migrated from the disk-based solution, providing an infinite level of recovery. The challenges that we will continue to face will be the backup of these very large databases and filesystems, and how to best protect this critical data while ensuring we have a more than reasonable recovery time in the event of online data loss. The trade-off with this type of solution is the dependence on the potentially proprietary nature of the data written to tape depending on the backup software with which this solution was integrated. However, in this solution, disk would be the primary backup medium and the tape backup would only be for the backup server's purposes.

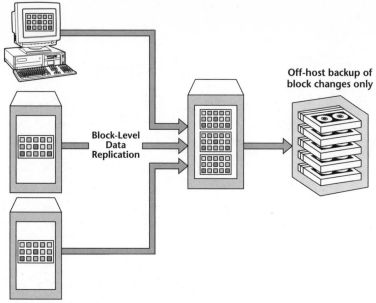

Figure 10.3   Future real-time backup—Block-level replication.

Replication will play a major role in the future of backup, especially as we continue to see the data growth scale higher and higher. Many of these replication solutions have been around for quite some time, but because of our general business requirements, we either didn't require that level of availability, found it to be cost-prohibitive, or simply didn't know it existed and worked as well as some of the proprietary hardware solutions. One of the products that has found success in the mid-tier level is NSI Software's Double-Take, shown in Figure 10.4. It will replicate a set of data at the application level, before it reaches the cache. It has been around for quite some time, but has not gotten proper attention because general business requirements have not been sufficiently compelling to evaluate this as a solution. Now we are facing new challenges and new requirements that ask us to stage data in two or three different locations: source, electronic vault, and perhaps a third location for sanity purposes. Solutions like Double-Take allow you to stage the data in such a manner, allowing for more granularity in the replicated data sets. For instance, the first set of data to the staging server might only replicate a subset of that data to the next stage, and so on.

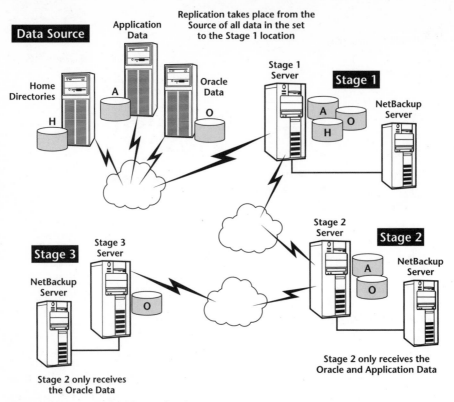

Figure 10.4   Double-Take replication.

It is assumed that clients will target a remote protection server that will host replicas of their data. These replicas will be backed up to tape via normal scheduled backups. In this scenario, the protection server acts as a disk consolidation server and then performs optimized backups from this consolidated storage. This type of backup does not require a SAN, but the protection server storage certainly could justify SAN connectivity. The replica data on the protection server can be backed up using traditional backup methods or any of the supported frozen image backups.

An anticipated way to further leverage technologies and get even more benefits from real-time backup is to use injected markers in the replication stream to notify the remote target or protection server that the application has been quiesced and that it is safe to take a snapshot. This allows the creation of consistent point-in-time snapshots that can potentially be used for rollback and can be written to tape. Figure 10.5 shows an example of this.

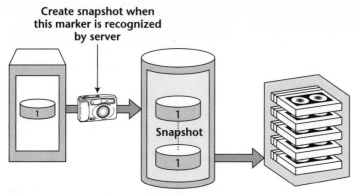

Figure 10.5 Consistent snapshots.

Many different scenarios based on the combination of these technologies are being investigated, and we are sure we will see many of them come to market in the not too distant future. The ability to create consistent versions of data to protect against corruption while allowing for disk-based rollback to a point in time is very attractive. Coupled with this is the ability to move data to tape for true data protection with minimal impact on production systems and applications—a very attractive feature.

Synthetic Backups

Synthetic backups will offer the technology to allow less frequent full and cumulative incremental backups while still allowing acceptable restore performance. Generally speaking, you establish the frequency for full backups based on recovery requirements and volatility of data. The less frequently you do full backups, the more images will be required to do a full filesystem or volume recovery. Synthetic backups will create new (synthetic) full backups from a series of incremental backups and new (synthetic) cumulative incremental backups from a series of differential incremental backups. The intent is that you will be able to schedule synthetic backups just like normal ones.

The basic idea behind synthetic backups is to manufacture a compact set of data from a disparate set of data spread among many pieces of removable media. It is essentially a restore operation used to manufacture a new full backup. The first task in creating a synthetic backup is to determine the data that needs to be collected to manufacture your new image. For a synthetic full backup, the last full backup is used as a reference point for collecting this data. For a synthetic cumulative backup, the backup sets or images are peers of each other and can span any time period between the last full backup and the current date.

The next task is to look into the catalog entries for the constituent backup sets or images and determine which files are necessary for the final new synthetic image. Basically, the most recent unique sets of objects are the ones desired for the synthetic backup. The time of the backup is used to order the objects correctly. Based on this information, the selected data is routed to a destination media that will constitute a synthetic backup. At the conclusion of the operation, the files now need to be appropriately cataloged as either a new full or cumulative incremental backup. You would now have a viable new compact set of media that represents a point in time of your data as recent as your latest offline copy.

Once again, disk-based backup solutions will add tremendous value when creating these synthetic full backups to tape; its random access serves quite well in this scenario.

Embedded Agents

There is a lot of discussion between hardware vendors and software vendors about actually embedding some level of the software application in the hardware. This could include backup software as well as storage management and SAN management software. It could also involve shipping the backup agent within an appliance or actually having some level of the software embedded in a storage library. One also must consider the implications this would have on the manufacturer of the hardware. This whole concept may birth an ever-needed standard for backup agent technology. Without this, the costs of this type of equipment may skyrocket because of the complexity found in the manufacturing of such a solution. The end user may have an option to install or upload an enhanced agent for the backup software you are using or decide to stay with the generic agent stub for cross-product backup support. With a generic agent stub embedded in the hardware, one of the benefits to the end user would be the ability to use the "best of breed" products to back up your devices. Your decision would no longer be tied to the proprietary agent structure, if you didn't want it to be.

Embedded technology opens up the door for true server-independent backups as well. The device will no longer need to be mediated by a server; embedded technology would allow it to go directly to the backup storage device, eliminating the middleman and increasing the effective backup speeds of the environment.

Or perhaps this agent stub wouldn't get updated at all by the reigning backup tool of choice. Perhaps it would simply be configurable enough to connect on a particular socket to communicate with the reigning backup tool of choice to receive all of its instructions for the particular process it is about to perform. It becomes limitless in what it would be able to accomplish.

It is much too early to know exactly where this will finally lead, but it will be interesting to watch—and it's even more interesting to speculate.

Intelligent Backup Software

How intelligent do we want the backup software to be? Well, let's speculate. First of all, let's all agree that backup administrator isn't the most appreciated position in the company. In fact, the only time we seem to hear any kind of comment is when there is a problem. In most cases, we find ourselves having to track down problems that may have been introduced by an undocumented system change thanks to a hasty system administrator who wanted to get his weekend started a little bit early on a Friday afternoon. We don't find out that the problem exists until backup starts at 10:00 P.M. or even later. Wouldn't it be great if the backup software could have some level of intelligence built in, to the point that it may be capable of re-installing backup client software, discovering additional filesystems, performing some self-tuning, and handling other tasks that we usually have to perform?

In today's production environments, we rarely seem to optimize the server performance for fear that we may stop something from working. The basic rule of thumb is, "if it ain't broke, don't fix it," and if we decide to optimize, we hire consultants to perform an audit, which isn't a bad idea. But wouldn't you like to have a self-tuning backup server, or at least one that would email you an update of its findings so you might proactively make adjustments and changes based on the recommendations of the intelligent backup server? What about one that would periodically query clients to ensure that the client software is installed and that the backup server can properly authenticate to the client? As administrators, we would rather find out about the problems at lunchtime than dinner or bedtime.

What about true load balancing? Perhaps the backup servers in the future will dynamically load balance their ever-increasing data loads to the backup storage devices. Optionally, they would make some logical choices before the backup window opens and further refine those choices during the backup process. Or even, as previously stated, this intelligent server could email us with recommendations for load balancing before we allow it to make those changes.

Backup Appliances

Why not? It has happened with NFS, mail servers, Web servers, Web caching, firewalls, and routers. You can get an appliance for just about anything today. So why wouldn't it work with backup? The model seems to be fitting for this type of solution; some companies are trying to present turnkey backup solutions with industry-leading products, but that is not a true appliance. That is a very nicely integrated package of a tape library, SCSI/fiber bridges, headless server, network connectivity with a software solution—all nicely installed in the 19-inch rack or even in the tape library itself. That looks like an appliance, but it isn't there just yet. Perhaps the intelligent backup server and the appliance server would come together at some point in the future, then tape libraries or large disk subsystems or server arrays would become the appliances of the future for backup.

By definition, an appliance would have to contain some of the intelligence we talked about previously, with much of the self-discovery built in for scalability as well. When you plug in an appliance at home, shouldn't you just have to turn the switch on to get the benefit? Perhaps the backup appliance model will follow this in the future—a self-discovering, self-configuring, self-tuning, highly available decentralized backup database with workload sharing. An additional backup appliance will first configure itself on the network, look for a previously installed appliance, and either place itself subject to this primary server or promote itself to the primary position.

Having highly available backup servers with no dependency on a particular server that holds the "keys" for recovery would be a future all of us would like to see. However, this is a very new concept. There aren't many people out there working backup into an appliance model, at least not yet.

Disk and Solid-State Devices

Well, this isn't a future per se, but it isn't something we would call an available commodity either. The proliferation of disk-based and solid-state devices will hinge upon the backup storage companies, both software and hardware, having the ability to adequately integrate hierarchical storage management (HSM) features into the use of these devices. Perhaps, the backup software will rely on a finely tuned hardware solution that manages the migration of the data to tape for you without having to worry about the backup application integrating with an HSM tool. This would help to untie the vendor-specific solutions and allow you to choose based on best of breed.

Time to recovery will continue to be the biggest hurdle for us in the future; therefore, disk or solid-state devices may be the answer. As we all know, these are not limitless devices; we must have the tools to manage them effectively and with limited administration intervention. This again speaks to the intelligent software we hope to see in the future—built-in management of the storage from a much higher level. When disk or solid-state devices are integrated with a backup solution that provides some of the HSM technology, it becomes that proverbial bottomless cup of coffee that we long to have available to us for backup and, more importantly, recovery. High-speed recovery won't come from tape. As much as we love tape devices, we do not foresee a tape device that will be able to match the speed of disk or solid-state disks. However, since we are in the chapter about the future, perhaps we will see a nice implementation of a "RAID" tape solution that would provide those kinds of speeds. Unfortunately, you will still be required to mount those tapes, and since it is a sequential media, you will be able to perform only one restore at a time. That's the beauty of the disk-based solutions for recovery: It is a random access device capable of serving many, many requests at once; the only limitations would be I/O and other factors.

Summary

Well, this was a fun chapter...all of the speculation and conjecture one can muster without having to apologize. Just as in any other industry, the future is uncertain; however, the forecast becomes a bit easier when we talk about the near future. We have tried to give you some of that in this chapter, and we have also taken creative license to speculate on technologies that would be nice to have in place to improve the climate for the backup administrator. While our crystal ball may have some flaws, we think the future should at least include some of what we discussed here. We will definitely see more integration of software technologies in the backup arena, and we will see disks being utilized more as their costs keep coming down.

It will make the future very interesting. Perhaps in the next edition of this book, "The Future of Backup" chapter will be titled "New Technologies."

In the next, and final, chapter, we look at several of the primary backup and recovery application providers.

CHAPTER 11

Major Players in the Backup Arena

Someone once said, "Backup is just a tool. It doesn't matter which one you have; it's just a matter of how you utilize it." I vehemently disagreed with that person back then: "Backup isn't *just* a tool; it is an integral part of your organization's business functions. Being a very critical tool, it does make a difference which tool you eventually decide to use. Your data and sometimes your job or reputation depend on it." It's interesting to read those words now and have discussions with colleagues throughout the years about backup storage management. We use the word "tool" quite a bit in reference to backup, something I didn't even realize until the first draft of this chapter had been written.

Backup *is* a tool, like a hammer—it serves a unique purpose with an anticipated outcome. When you hit a 16-penny nail on the head with a hammer, the force causes the nail to drive down into the wood until, eventually, the nail is firmly implanted into the piece of wood. Given the same scenario but with a slab of concrete instead of the wood, the outcome would be different. The anticipated outcome now is quite variable, because we are not using the right set of tools for the job.

Backup, as a tool, is exactly the same. Very simplistically, backup is designed to carry data from the clients to some end repository, in most cases tape, to provide protection from loss by having the ability to recover this data at some future point in time. If your environment's characteristics or requirements are unique, the very simplistic "hammer and nail" approach to backup may need to be reviewed to properly select the right tool for the job. A number of vendors in the market offer backup solutions; all store the data on some end repository and all provide a means to recover that data in the event of a loss. However, the methods by which they accomplish these things play a role in the selection process.

In this chapter, we present an overview of the major players, the features, and the functions of the various products to help you identify the best tool for your environment. The selection was quite scientific; we actually used what the technology research bodies listed as the market leaders, then selected the top four: Hewlett-Packard (HP), IBM, Legato, and VERITAS Software. We discuss them in alphabetical order by company name. When we did the research for this chapter, we asked the individual vendors to provide their responses to the chapter outline. The outline was very simple:

Company/Product Overview.   A brief history of the company and how the product was developed over the years into the current product available to the consumer market.

Backup Methodology.   The company's approach to backup, such as full plus incremental, progressive incremental, and synthetic full.

Principles of Recovery.   A philosophical view of recovery based on the specific vendor product, such as tape cloning, duplication, or copy, depending on terms used by the vendor for the purposes of recovery of an entire system, server, data center, or even critical files or directories.

Storage Support.   What if any unique devices or number of devices are supported? If there were none that fit this criteria, this heading was not included in the Vendors section. Suffice it to say that each of these four vendors supports a wide range of backup storage devices. None of them seem to be lacking support for any of the most popular media types.

High Availability.   HA-aware products are more and more important to the 7x24x365 data centers, so we want to know who integrates with what product.

Key Differentiators.   How the vendors would position themselves up against the major players if you had them in a room together. This is the chance you have been waiting for. Here we document what each company views as their key differentiators—what makes them better, faster, easier than the rest.

As far as agent support or backup options, such as database agents, Microsoft product support, and Network-Attached Storage (NAS) support, we found that for the most part all of the vendors had agent support for Oracle, Informix, Sybase, MS SQL Server, MS Exchange, SAP, Lotus Notes, and NDMP, just to name a few. And giving them the benefit of the doubt when there seemed to be some confusion, we added to the outline based on information publicly available on their Web sites.

Finally, in order to make this as even a playing field as possible, we took some editorial license with some of the vendor responses, such as removing blatant slams against the competition and self-promotional marketing speak. We believe the following accurately and equally represents all of these major players.

HP Data Protector (Formerly Omniback II)

Hewlett-Packard, founded in 1939 by Bill Hewlett and Dave Packard, has evolved over the last several decades into the new HP, one of the leading technology solution providers in the storage industry. HP recently launched a new data protection software product family, HP OpenView Storage Data Protector, or Data Protector for short, that builds upon and enhances their previous generation of data protection software, HP OpenView Omniback II. Data Protector adds new levels of disk-based recovery and additional features for service-level management as part of the newest release of the software.

The HP OpenView Storage Data Protector software builds on a foundation of backup and recovery software using distributed agent technology first acquired by HP with their purchase of Apollo Computers in the late 1980s. The second generation of this technology, HP OpenView Omniback II, was first launched by HP in September 1994, and had been continually enhanced and improved since then. The current incarnation of HP's data protection software, HP OpenView Storage Data Protector, was launched in June of 2002.

Methodology of Backup

Data Protector incorporates a flexible architecture that enables any combination of full and incremental backups that can span up to nine generations, Incremental-1 through Incremental-9. This is a variation on the traditional grandfather-father-son approach for backups. Typically, users will concentrate on combinations of full and a small number of incremental backups to accommodate their specific protection and recovery needs.

Even though the power of up to nine levels of incremental backup is available, recovering a lost directory from that deep a level would require copies of all nine levels of incremental backups and the most-recent full backup, potentially a large number of tapes, and it would take a bit of time to recover.

Principles of Recovery

Data Protector can support a variety of disaster recovery options. These options consist of the following:

Traditional manual disaster recovery.   Reinstallation of the operating system, reinstallation of the Data Protector agent, and then recovery of the applications and data from a previous backup.

Assisted manual disaster recovery.   After a staff person manually reinstalls the operating system on the downed server, the staff person uses the Data Protector's restore command from the management station to automatically restore the Data Protector agent to the downed server and automatically initiate the restoration of the applications and data to the server from tape.

Enhanced automatic disaster recovery.   This approach uses recovery diskettes, or a recovery CD, that are prepared ahead of time using Data Protector to facilitate the unattended reinstallation of the operating system and Data Protector agent. The recovery of the applications and data can then be initiated in the usual fashion using Data Protector.

One-button disaster recovery (OBDR).   For Windows NT or 2000 servers having directly connected tape drives compatible with OBDR, Data Protector enables the creation of disaster recovery tapes supporting this approach. With One-Button Disaster Recovery, a recovery staff person can simply reboot the downed server while holding the reset button on the tape drive, with the OBDR tape loaded in that drive, and the server automatically identifies the tape drive as a bootable device and begins to load from that drive. When the process completes, the server has reloaded the operating system, applications, and data from the tape and copied them to its disk, and it is running in a fully operational state.

Disk-image delivery.   In a SAN environment, recovery staff can connect a recovery server running Data Protector to the boot volume of the downed server over the SAN; restore the operating system, applications, and data of the downed server to that boot volume from tape; and then simply reboot the downed server, which comes up in a fully operational state. In a standalone disk environment, when a server's disk becomes corrupted and that server goes down, the recovery staff can use a recovery server that accommodates physical disk mechanisms compatible with the original downed server to restore the operating system, applications, and data of the downed server from tape to the disk. Then the recovery staff can physically remove the disk from the recovery server, replace the corrupted disk on the downed server with the new physical disk, and reboot the downed server to come up in a fully operational state.

Data Protector also supports copying backup tapes, for the purposes of providing added redundancy or sending a copy of backup tapes off-site for disaster recovery purposes.

High Availability

Data Protector is fully cluster-aware; the management station, disk agents, and media agents are all cluster-aware components, operating as virtual resources within a cluster, and they fully take advantage of the automatic failover capabilities within the clustering software. HP MC/ServiceGuard, Microsoft Cluster Server, and VERITAS Cluster Server (with only disk agent support) have been tested.

Data Protector supports additional capabilities within selected disk array architectures, including zero-downtime backup. This is the ability to eliminate backup windows by automatically invoking an application-server-less, split-mirror, or snapshot backup, enabling 24×7 continuous operation without performance impact on the application server. It also provides instant recovery, which is the restoration of selected information from a split-mirror or snapshot recovery image on disk, rather than from a recovery image on tape. This instant recovery capability occurs much more rapidly than restoring information from disk, and in some cases, it can occur with no bulk movement of data within the disk array at all. Both zero-downtime backup and instant recovery facilitate 24×7 continuous operations, and are available out –of –the box, integrated with Oracle, SAP, Exchange 2000, and MS-SQL, across Windows 2000, HP-UX, and Solaris environments.

Key Differentiators

Data Protector's key differentiators versus other data protection approaches are its tight integration with applications and storage arrays to enable capabilities such as instant recovery and zero-downtime backup. HP Data Protector provides a healthy breadth of capabilities, across the range of operating systems, applications, and storage arrays, as does HP itself. In particular, since Data Protector can work with a combination of both local and remote mirroring software (in the case of the HP XP array as well as EMC Symmetrix), Data Protector can very easily form a part of a disaster-tolerant high-availability configuration, where two separate sites, each with clustered servers and remotely-mirrored data on external disk arrays, can operate in a 24 × 7 disaster-tolerant configuration while still enabling routine protection operations utilizing split-mirror backups. Data Protector's tight integration with the applications in such environments, such as Oracle, SAP, and MS-SQL, enables automatic and dynamic selection of the data to be protected to ensure that each backup produces a fully recoverable image.

As part of HP's industry-leading OpenView management environment, Data Protector has built-in integrations with many of the other components within OpenView, enabling the data protection functions to be managed using sophisticated service-level management techniques, and reporting on service-level compliance without extensive scripting or any manual analysis. These integrations with HP OpenView Operations, OpenView Performance, OpenView Service Desk, OpenView Service Navigator, OpenView Service Reporter, and OpenView Service Information Portal enable tremendous flexibility in managing an organization's data protection environment as a protection service, not just as a combination of tasks and technologies. It also enables protection service to be managed in the same way other IT services, such as servers, networks, and applications, are using the industry's most popular enterprise management environment.

IBM Tivoli Storage Manager

IBM's Workstation DataSave product was developed in the late 1980s at the Almaden Research Center to meet customer requirements for distributed network backup. The product underwent significant redevelopment to become the ADSTAR distributed storage Manager (ADSM) in 1993 and was later renamed IBM Tivoli Storage Manager (TSM). The need for network backup emerged from distributed client/server computing driven by the proliferation of personal computers and workstations. The goal was to centralize the protection of distributed data in an environment where information assets were no longer restricted to controlled mainframe environments. Backing up individual computers to locally attached devices was, and still is, costly and error-prone, and often does not meet requirements for disaster recovery. With IBM TSM, clients can back up their data to central servers, which store the data on a variety of media and track its location for later retrieval. TSM protects data from hardware failures and other errors by storing backup and archive copies of data on offline storage.

Scaling to protect hundreds of computers running a dozen operating systems ranging from laptops to mainframes and connected together via the Internet, WANs, or LANs, TSM's centralized Web-based management, smart-data move and store techniques, and comprehensive policy-based automation all work together to minimize data protection administration costs and the impact to both computers and networks. Optional modules allow business-critical applications that must run 24×365 to utilize TSM's centralized data protection with no interruption to their service.

Methodology of Backup

IBM TSM uses progressive incremental backup rather than the full-plus-incremental/differential methodology of some of the other backup solutions. Its sophisticated architecture allows it to just back up new or changed files. Likewise, when you are doing a restore, only the version of the files requested is restored, so there is no need to restore a full and then incremental or differential backups on top of that.

Principles of Recovery

TSM has the ability to automatically create as many copies of the backed-up data onto whatever type of media you specify. This capability can be scheduled for administrator ease. TSM only creates copies of the files that were not previously backed up. TSM can also reclaim space on off-site copies. TSM also can simultaneously create copies of data at the time of initial backup. This is done with a simultaneous write to primary and copy storage pools. TSM has an open API that allows for integration by any interested third party or any company who wants to further integrate with TSM. The Kernel Group (acquired by VERITAS Software) has integrated their Bare Metal Restore product with TSM, providing true bare metal recovery of a failed system.

High Availability

IBM TSM supports integration with Windows clustering and AIX HACMP from a hardware integration perspective, and works well with IBM ESS (Shark) FlashCopy and EMC Symmetrix TimeFinder.

Key Differentiators

One of the things that differentiates IBM TSM's product from the field is its relational database architecture and transaction logging. This enables a host of unique capabilities including:

- Backing up just files that have changed or are new
- Migrating data from one type of media to another
- Performing advanced tape management capabilities that allow for the reclamation of dead space on tapes caused by expiring files
- Managing archives of data for a specified amount of time
- Performing accurate restores of files so that only the requested version of the files is restored
- Allowing highly flexible policies that can be easily changed and made retroactive

Legato NetWorker

Legato Systems was founded in 1988 by four engineers from Sun Microsystems (Jon Kepecs, Bob Lyon, Joe Moran, and Russell Sandberg) to provide an integrated set of storage management solutions and services that simplify the administration of client/server computing. Legato has a long tradition of adopting and driving storage-specific standards. Legato was the first in the market to introduce a common tape format (OpenTape) and a common media management interface (SmartMedia), and it codeveloped the NetWork Data Management Protocol (NDMP). In the increasingly important SAN market, Legato is both a founding member and a member of the Board of Directors of the Storage Network Industry Association (SNIA) in the United States and Europe.

Legato NetWorker protects the critical business data by simplifying, centralizing, and automating backup and recovery operations across UNIX, Windows, Linux, and NetWare platforms in DAS, NAS, and SAN storage environments. Built upon open, highly scalable client/server architecture, the NetWorker product family reduces management overhead by providing "lights out" protection of storage assets in the largest corporate data centers and the smallest satellite branch offices. Advanced indexing and media management, cluster support, high-speed parallelism, cross-platform tape interoperability, comprehensive NDMP support, backup to disk, tape cloning, archive, serverless backup, and dynamic drive sharing are among the key components that enable IT organizations to protect storage assets and minimize downtime. Database, messaging, and ERP modules deliver online protection and granular recovery. Autochanger/silo modules enable hands-free protection using a wide variety of robotic devices. Storage nodes enable load sharing and distribution of backup traffic, and LAN-free protection of servers with large data volumes. NetWorker is also tightly integrated with complementary Legato applications, such as hierarchical storage management (HSM), systems management frameworks, simplified operator administration, and Web-enabled management of multiple NetWorker servers.

Methodology of Backup

A NetWorker's scheduled backup may perform a full, incremental, consolidated, and/or level backup. A full backup (considered a level 0) consists of all files whether or not they have changed. An incremental backup backs up files that have changed since the last backup regardless of the level. However, the incremental level backups, of which there are nine, allow you to creatively architect the manner in which you wish to protect your data. The incremental levels back up files that have changed since the last lowered numbered backup. For example, a level 1 backup backs up all the files that have changed since the last full backup (considered a level 0). A level 3 backup backs up all the files that have changed since the last level 2 backup, level 1 backup, or full backup. A level 9 backs up all the files that have changed since the last level 8,7,6,5,4,3,2,1,or full (0) backup. A consolidated backup backs up all data that has changed since the last full backup and subsequently merges these changes with the last full backup, effectively building a synthetic full backup. NetWorker also has what is called "skip" backup type, which skips a scheduled backup that may, for example, fall on a holiday or may be skipped if no one will be available to perform tasks such as change or add media volumes.

Principles of Recovery

NetWorker Data Recovery takes full advantage of the information stored in its client file index and media database to quickly locate files and recover them to their original location or an alternate location if desired. The two methods employed by NetWorker for recovery are as follows:

Client File Index-Based Recovery. An end user or administrator browses the client file index using graphical tools or command-line interface (CLI) and selects individual files or directories to recover.

Save Set Recovery.   An administrator or end user recovers an entire save set to the originating client from the NetWorker GUI or CLI.

In addition to these methods, NetWorker maintains the ability to recover data that has been expired by using a utility called scanner. Scanner reads a NetWorker volume independent of the NetWorker server, making it possible to rebuild the media database and client indices in the unusual event that the NetWorker database was inaccessible.

NetWorker is designed with disaster recovery as a primary focus. If a disaster occurs—whether it is isolated to a single system, strikes the NetWorker server itself, or affects an entire site—NetWorker is able to respond quickly so that data can be restored and operations can resume in minimal time. NetWorker protects its databases by the creation of *bootstraps*. A bootstrap contains the site-specific information that a NetWorker server requires to recover in the case of a disaster.

Legato's AlphaStor product provides drive sharing and advanced media management for the NetWorker servers. As with other products, Legato customers often implement multiple NetWorker servers to maximize backup performance, which naturally equates to increased complexity with multiple media databases and client file indexes having multiple points of administration. AlphaStor helps to reduce this complexity by providing a single and consolidated view of all NetWorker media, as well as other storage media.

AlphaStor's advanced media management includes the following:

- A simple-to-use, browser-based interface for data center operation personnel
- On-site and off-site tape rotation management and tracking
- The ability to schedule, track, and automate movement of all media, regardless of location, based on defined policies and utilizing tape retention policies defined within NetWorker
- Ability to share tape devices and libraries across multiple NetWorker servers and storage nodes
- A consolidated view of all media and drive usage
- Consolidated reporting of tape pools and media by location
- Support for SAN environments

Much of the disaster recovery principles are contained within the functionality of AlphaStor. This is an add-on product and not included in the base product.

High Availability

There is extensive support for clustered environments, including Sun Cluster, Hewlett-Packard MCSG, IBM HACMP, Compaq TruCluster, Microsoft Cluster Services, and Legato Availability Manager. It also has the ability to cluster NetWorker Servers.

Key Differentiators

The following are the key differentiators for NetWorker:

- The core product is engineered for performance, resiliency, and scalability.
- 13,000 enterprise customers utilize NetWorker worldwide; SAP standardizes on NetWorker (12+ TB daily), Sun protects six global data centers with NetWorker, 28 separate NetWorker OEM agreements (most in industry; example: Sun Solstice Backup is NetWorker OEM).
- It is the only data protection software shipping with every IBM LTO library, and the only data protection software shipping with every Oracle 8i and 9i database.
- It enables standardization on one application to protect information in the largest data centers, the smallest branch offices, and throughout a heterogeneous global enterprise.
- Open Tape Format provides tape interoperability between UNIX, Windows, Linux, and NetWare backup platforms, increasing disaster recovery and platform migration capabilities.
- Advanced indexing architecture eliminates risk of corruption and speeds file recovery.
- Single location for index data simplifies management and increases resiliency in the event of a storage node failure.
- It provides support for over 200 tape drives, 450 library models, and a variety of tape silos.
- It provides comprehensive protection for NDMP-based Network-Attached Storage devices using UNIX, Windows, or Linux backup platforms.
- It features the ability to back up locally, via third-party copy, or , remote to UNIX-attached library, to ATL network attached library, or over SAN.

- Through Direct Access Restore (DAR), it pinpoints file location for faster file recovery of NDMP-based backups. Also featured are separate browse and retention policies and the ability to recover data without administrator assistance.

- It features native library sharing plus an option to dynamically share drives between storage nodes and NDMP NAS in SAN.

- It allows backup server, storage node, client, and application support for Linux.

- The live, serverless backup option frees applications and network from the impact of backup operations.

- You can automatically back up to disk (JBOD and RAID), clone backups on disk to tape, or stage backups to disk before moving to tape—all with one-step recovery.

- New hardware snapshot modules enable instant "backup" and near line recovery.

VERITAS NetBackup

VERITAS Software Corporation is the acknowledged leading provider of storage management software solutions that allow enterprises to protect, access, and manage data. No other company can claim the depth and breadth of heterogeneous solutions, from high availability to backup and recovery to data management. By choosing VERITAS, enterprises are not tied to any proprietary platform—hardware or software. Rather, VERITAS solutions facilitate choice—the implementation of best-of-breed technologies for data protection, access, and management. Of Fortune 500 companies, 86 percent rely on VERITAS solutions.

In 1997, VERITAS acquired OpenVision Technologies and in doing so added VERITAS NetBackup to its product arsenal. Originally developed over 10 years ago to provide scalable backup and recovery services at Chrysler Motor Corporation, NetBackup today remains VERITAS' flagship backup and recovery solution. NetBackup commands the coveted number 1 market share position, based on new license revenue, and a reputation for delivering innovative, visionary functionality that provide real business value today. NetBackup's list of industry firsts and accomplishments includes the following:

- First backup and recovery software solution based on a core three-tier architecture designed for performance and scalability

- First backup and recovery software solution to support multihost tape library sharing between heterogeneous systems

- First backup and recovery software solution to break the 1 TB/hour backup barrier (July 1997)

- First backup and recovery software solution to offer dynamic tape drive sharing between UNIX and Windows systems (June 1999)

- One of only three solutions to back up 1 TB of data in under an hour and restore the same 1 TB of data in under an hour at a Storage Networking Industry Association (SNIA) benchmarking event (March 2002)

- First backup and recovery software solution to break the 2 TB/hour backup barrier (April 2002)

VERITAS offers two versions of NetBackup to address the needs of the varied customer data centers:

- VERITAS NetBackup DataCenter

- VERITAS NetBackup BusinesServer

NetBackup DataCenter's core three-tier architecture—master server, media server, and client—offers truly flexible deployment options. Companies can create consistent policies across the business, whether data is local, distributed, or remote. Leveraging the intuitive graphical user interfaces to perform all backup and recovery operations centrally, customers can manage more data per administrator.

Based entirely on the code for NetBackup DataCenter, VERITAS Net-Backup BusinesServer offers an alternative for companies who require the same enterprise-class backup and restore performance but for smaller, less complex environments. Targeted at heterogeneous (UNIX and Windows) workgroups, departments, and remote offices, NetBackup BusinesServer combines the concept of a master server and media server into a single BusinesServer Server.

Mixed NetBackup BusinesServer and NetBackup DataCenter environments can be administered centrally via VERITAS Global Data Manager. In addition to managing all facets of backup and recovery through the launch of the NetBackup Administration Console, Global Data Manager also provides enhanced monitoring capabilities. Thresholds may be set to alert the administrator to abnormal situations, such as an unusual amount of down tape drives for a given server.

Methodology of Backup

VERITAS NetBackup utilizes the very traditional, tried-and-true method of backup, full and incremental. Incremental backups copy files that have changed since the last backup; this type of NetBackup backup is called a differential incremental. However, in Version 2.0 of NetBackup, engineering introduced True Image Recovery (TIR) that allowed the backup storage administrator to recover a failed disk or a deleted directory or directories to a specific point in time. One of the dilemmas of the old method was the fact that you may recover *more* data than you have disk space and potentially more files than the user remembered being there when the loss occurred. TIR addresses that problem by maintaining a "rest-in-peace" database of all the deleted files. This requires very little disk space, typically no more than 2 percent of your total image database. When a TIR restore is invoked, the software determines which tapes are required and which files need to be recovered based on the restore criteria. The ending result is a disk or directory or directories with exactly what the user had anticipated from the last backup, a true image restore.

While this is a significant improvement over the traditional method, it still requires all of those differential incremental backup tapes, which may delay your restore slightly. This is why VERITAS introduced another type of incremental backup, cumulative incremental, a backup that copies all files changed since the last full backup. The benefit of implementing cumulative incremental backup jobs is reducing the number of tapes required for a full recovery. Many customers have blended both differential and cumulative incremental backups to aid in shortening their recovery times from tape.

Principles of Recovery

VERITAS views recovery in terms of information availability. How much do down systems cost your business? VERITAS offers integrated solutions that can deliver as much as 95 percent uptime to 99.9999 percent uptime or more. Via backup, Replication, Clustering, and global clustering, the VERITAS product suite supports the creation of comprehensive disaster recovery plans based on the required level of information availability.

Through VERITAS Software's recent acquisition of The Kernel Group, it now has added Bare Metal Restore (BMR) to their product offerings. BMR utilizes the TIR function of NetBackup to completely recover systems to full operation without administrator intervention beyond a few clicks of the mouse via the browser-based interface. During a BMR installation, OS images are installed to the BMR server for the clients that are being protected by the NetBackup servers. Next, disk partition information is saved to the BMR server for the clients that will have BMR protection to facilitate the complete and total recovery.

Bare Metal Restore protects systems running HP-UX, IBM AIX, Sun Solaris, and Microsoft Windows NT 4.0/2000, with additional platform support planned for future releases.

At the base level of any disaster recovery plan, however, is backup and recovery with off-site tape vaulting. The essence of vaulting is the process of creating duplicate backup tapes, which are brought from the primary site to an off-site location (vault). If the primary site is rendered inaccessible and data and applications are no longer available, the duplicate tapes at the remote location may be used with backup hardware to recover data and restore information availability.

NetBackup Vault is now tightly integrated within NetBackup 4.5. Vault automates the duplication, tracking, and reporting for the purposes of off-site storage as a disaster recovery component. In the event of a complete facility loss or on-site media failure, a Vault-protected environment has the option of retrieving duplicated media for recovery. NetBackup 4.5 now supports up to 10 copies of a backup image versus the previous version two-copy limitation.

High Availability

Keeping with VERITAS' end-to-end solutions of data and storage management, VERITAS Cluster Server provides you proactive management of service groups (application services) and protection against hardware failures, power outages, and other disasters. A Java-based management GUI provides a single point of administration for multiple VERITAS Cluster Server clusters. VERITAS Cluster Server provides a comprehensive availability management solution designed to minimize both planned and unplanned downtime.

VERITAS NetBackup has also been tested with Microsoft Cluster Server, and support for additional clustering technologies is planned for future releases.

Key Differentiators

VERITAS' key differentiators obviously rest in their ability to say they are an end-to-end solution provider, from the operating system to the application. It can also be integrated with other VERITAS products such as the

VERITAS File System, VERITAS Volume Manager, VERITAS Cluster Server, and VERITAS Bare Metal Restore. The key differentiators are as follows:

- Is the number 1 backup and recovery software solution worldwide.

- Offers unparalleled performance and scalability.

- Offers a core three-tier architecture that provides the foundation for unparalleled backup and restore performance.

- Supports heterogeneous environments.

- Offers comprehensive data protection across operating systems, databases and applications, storage devices, and network topologies.

- Offers application-specific backup and recovery.

- Supports the broadest range of database/application/platform combinations and leverages native (nonproprietary) utilities and APIs on all accounts.

- Features tools that allow for ease-of-use and ease-of-administration.

- For an enterprise-class solution, provides an unmatched suite of wizard-driven interfaces that simplify installation, configuration, and administration. A plethora of standard reports deliver critical information, such as the status of backup jobs, without the administrator having to parse transaction logs, and an integrated troubleshooting wizard offers online access to remedies for various errors.

- Features industry-known, "bulletproof" catalog scales to address the largest environments while commanding comparatively the smallest amount of reserved space among leading competing solutions.

- Relies on the establishment of key partnerships to help drive integration and success among hardware and software solutions. Where applicable, VERITAS NetBackup is a recognized solution in partner programs, such as Sun Microsystems SunTone Certification program, IBM ServerProven, and more.

Through acquisition, innovation, and partnerships, VERITAS has been able to set themselves clearly apart from the list of industry leaders.

Summary

As you can see, there are different ways to accomplish the same task. This chapter provided you a good introduction into the major players in the marketplace. This is by no means the "short list"; there are others out there who are innovating and have a distinct vision for the future of backup and recovery. Perhaps by the next edition of this book, the list will grow and even change. So when you are considering either a new tool or a change to your existing tool to protect your data, this chapter should help you determine what methods, principles, and philosophical approaches best fit your organization's specific requirements.

Command-Line Interface Guide

Just about any backup and recovery application you use will offer a graphical user interface (GUI). These are very helpful in the normal day-to-day operations, but there are times when they just aren't what you are looking for. If you want to access, control, or configure your backup application using a slow-speed dial-up line, for example, a GUI can be painful to try to use—if it will work at all. There are also situations where you might want to schedule your backups with a third-party scheduler. In these cases, what you need is access to a good command-line interface (CLI). A good understanding of the CLI for your backup and recovery application gives you the ability to access, configure, control, and monitor both backups and restores from a nongraphic terminal or over a slow line. It also offers a method to interface the backup application with a third-party scheduler.

In this appendix, we list the most commonly used commands for VERITAS NetBackup. We also define the command. A complete listing of the supported commands, along with their options and switches, can be found in the man pages for NetBackup and in the System Administrator's Guide. There is a UNIX and Windows NetBackup System Administrator's Guide and a UNIX and Windows Media Manager System Administrator's Guide. Maybe at some point, if demand is high enough, we will write a companion book on the CLI and greatly expand on their uses. For sample UNIX and Windows NT and 2000 scripts, check out www.NetBackupCentral.com.

NetBackup Commands for UNIX

bp   Starts the NetBackup menu interface that lets users archive, back up, and restore files, directories, or raw partitions from their client workstations.

bpadm   Starts the NetBackup menu interface for administrators, which an administrator can use to configure NetBackup and monitor its operations. bpadm requires root privileges.

bparchive   Archives files to the NetBackup server by processing files that you list on the command line or in the file you specify with the -f *listfile* option. Any file path entered can be a file or directory name. If the list of files includes a directory, bparchive archives all files and subdirectories of that directory starting at the directory itself.

bpauthorize   Manages the authorize.txt file on remote servers. This command is available only on NetBackup master servers and sets up authentication files on NetBackup servers and clients according to the options that are specified with the command.

bpauthsync   Synchronizes authentication files on NetBackup servers and clients. This command is available only on NetBackup master servers and sets up authentication files on NetBackup servers and clients according to the options that are specified with the command.

bpbackup   Backs up files to the NetBackup server. If issued on a client, bpbackup starts a user backup that is the equivalent to what is performed by using the interface on the client. This type of backup can be started from any NetBackup client in order to back up files from that client. The bpbackup command processes the files that you list on the command line or in the file that you specify with the -f listfile option. A file path can be a file or directory name. If the named files include a directory, bpbackup backs up all files and subdirectories of that directory starting at the directory itself.

If issued on the master server, bpbackup starts an immediate-manual backup of a client. This variation requires the -i option on the bpbackup command and is available only to the administrator on the master server. It is the equivalent of starting a manual backup from the Net-Backup administrator's interface. Use the -h option to specify the host.

bpbackupdb   Initiates a backup of one or more NetBackup image catalogs specified on the command line. It also backs up the default set of NetBackup catalogs, unless the command line contains -nodbpaths. If the command line specifies a destination, the backup is stored there. Otherwise, the backup is stored at the default location for backups of the NetBackup internal databases, which are called catalogs.

bpchangeprimary   Promotes a copy of a backup to be the primary copy.

bpclient   Manages client entries on a master server.

bpconfig   Modifies or displays the global configuration attributes for NetBackup. These attributes affect operations for all policies and clients.

bpdbjobs   Interacts with the NetBackup jobs database and is useful in scripts or as a command-line administration tool. Use bpdbjobs to print the entire jobs database, print a summary, delete done jobs, cancel uncompleted jobs, and clean old jobs.

bpdbm   NetBackup database manager daemon that responds to queries related to the NetBackup internal databases, which are called catalogs. bpdbm must be running in order for NetBackup commands and utilities to work properly. This daemon runs only on the master server and can be started only by the administrator.

bpduplicate   Creates a copy of backups created by NetBackup; can also change the primary copy in order to enable restoring from a duplicated backup. The primary copy is used to satisfy restore requests and is initially the original copy.

bperror   Displays NetBackup status and troubleshooting information or entries from the NetBackup error catalog. It displays information from either the same source as the online troubleshooter (in the Activity Monitor or Reports applications) or from the NetBackup error catalog.

bpexpdate   Changes the expiration date of backups in the image catalog and media in the media catalog. It is also used to change the expiration of removable media in the NetBackup media catalog.

bpimagelist   Queries the NetBackup catalog and produces a report on the status of the NetBackup images. It will produce one of two types of reports:

- Report images satisfying a set of criteria (if -media is absent)
- Report on removable media satisfying a set of criteria (if -media is present)

bpimmedia   Queries the NetBackup image catalog and reports on the NetBackup images. It can produce two reports:

- An Images-on-Media report
- A Spangroups report

bpimport   Imports NetBackup and Backup Exec backups that are expired or are from another NetBackup or Backup Exec server.

bplabel   Writes a NetBackup label on tape media. Labeling is required only for media that was last used for NetBackup catalog backups or by a non-NetBackup application. You can also use it to assign specific media IDs.

bplist   Lists backed-up and archived files on the NetBackup server according to the options that you specify.

bppldelete   Deletes policies from the NetBackup database.

bppllist   Lists policies and policy information within the NetBackup database.

bpmedia   Freezes, unfreezes, suspends, or unsuspends an individual NetBackup media ID, allowing or disallowing future backups or archives to be directed to the media. Note that this command applies only to media managed by Media Manager.

bpmedialist   Displays NetBackup media status by making queries of one or more NetBackup media catalogs and produces a report on the status of the NetBackup media.

bpminlicense   Manages NetBackup license file.

bpplclients, bpclclients   Administers the clients within NetBackup policies.

bpplinfo, bpclinfo   Initializes, modifies, or displays policy attributes for a NetBackup policy.

bpplinclude, bpclinclude   Maintains the policy file list for a Net-Backup policy. This is the list of files backed up when NetBackup runs an automatic backup for the policy.

bpplsched, bpclsched   Adds, deletes, or lists NetBackup schedules to/from a policy.

bpplschedrep, bpclschedrep   Modifies the attributes of a NetBackup schedule. The schedule and policy named by the command should already exist when it is run.

bppolicynew, bpclassnew   Creates, copies, or renames a NetBackup policy.

bprd   Initiates the NetBackup request daemon, which is responsible for starting automatic client backups and responding to client requests for file restores and user backups and archives.

bprecover   Initiates the NetBackup utility for restoring the NetBackup internal databases called catalogs and recovers catalogs that were backed up by using the procedures described in the NetBackup system administrator's guide. The command has two main modes: list and recover.

bprestore   Restores files or directories from the NetBackup server.

bpstuadd   Creates a NetBackup storage unit group or a storage unit.

bpstudel   Deletes a NetBackup storage unit or storage unit group.

bpstulist   Displays the attributes for one or all of the NetBackup storage units or storage unit groups.

bpsturep   Modifies an existing NetBackup storage unit by replacing selected storage-unit or storage-unit-group attributes in the Net-Backup catalog.

bpverify   Verifies the backups created by NetBackup.

cat_convert   Converts NetBackup catalog .f files between Versions 3.4 and 4.0, or between 4.5 ASCII format and 4.5 binary format.

jbpSA   Starts the Backup, Archive, and Restore client interface on Java-capable UNIX machines.

jnbSA   Starts the NetBackup Administration Console on Java-capable UNIX machines.

nbdbsetport   Sets TCP/IP port used by the nbdbd database service.

nbdbsetpw   Modifies passwords used by the nbdbd database service.

vopied   Daemon to provide VERITAS one-time password user authentication.

vopie_util   Manages local vopie authentication files.

xbp   Starts the X Windows-based interface for NetBackup users.

NetBackup Commands for Windows

beconv   Converts Backup Exec on-disk catalogs to NetBackup on-disk catalogs.

bephyinv   Updates the Media Manager database, NetBackup media database, and Backup Exec database for a set of Backup Exec media.

bparchive   Archives files to the NetBackup server by processing files that you list on the command line or in the file you specify with the -f *listfile* option. Any file path entered can be a file or directory name. If the list of files includes a directory, bparchive archives all files and subdirectories of that directory starting at the directory itself.

bpauthorize   Manages the authorize.txt file on remote servers. This command is available only on NetBackup master servers and sets up authentication files on NetBackup servers and clients according to the options that are specified with the command.

bpauthsync   Synchronizes authentication files on NetBackup servers and clients. This command is available only on NetBackup master servers and sets up authentication files on NetBackup servers and clients according to the options that are specified with the command.

bpbackup   Backs up files to the NetBackup server. If issued on a client, bpbackup starts a user backup that is the equivalent to what is performed by using the interface on the client. This type of backup can be started from any NetBackup client in order to back up files from that client. The bpbackup command processes the files that you list on the command line or in the file that you specify with the -f *list-file* option. A file path can be a file or directory name. If the named files include a directory, bpbackup backs up all files and subdirectories of that directory starting at the directory itself.

If issued on the master server, bpbackup starts an immediate-manual backup of a client. This variation requires the -i option on the bpbackup command and is available only to the administrator on the master server. It is the equivalent of starting a manual backup from the NetBackup administrator's interface. Use the -h option to specify the host.

bpbackupdb   Initiates a backup of one or more NetBackup image catalogs specified on the command line. It also backs up the default set of NetBackup catalogs, unless the command line contains -nodbpaths. If the command line specifies a destination, the backup is stored there. Otherwise, the backup is stored at the default location for backups of the NetBackup internal databases, which are called catalogs.

bpchangeprimary   Promotes a copy of a backup to be the primary copy. The bpchangeprimary command lets you change which copy is the primary copy for a set of backup images.

bpclient   Manages client entries on a master server.

bpconfig   Modifies or displays the global configuration attributes for NetBackup. These attributes affect operations for all policies and clients.

bpdbjobs   Interacts with the NetBackup jobs database and is useful in scripts or as a command-line administration tool. Use bpdbjobs to print the entire jobs database, print a summary, delete done jobs, cancel uncompleted jobs, and clean old jobs.

bpduplicate   Creates a copy of backups created by NetBackup and can also change the primary copy in order to enable restoring from a duplicated backup. The primary copy is used to satisfy restore requests and is initially the original copy.

bperror   Displays NetBackup status and troubleshooting information or entries from the NetBackup error catalog. It displays information from either the same source as the online troubleshooter (in the Activity Monitor or Reports applications) or from the NetBackup error catalog.

bpexpdate   Changes the expiration date of backups in the image catalog and media in the media catalog. It is also used to change the expiration of removable media in the NetBackup media catalog.

bpimagelist   Queries the NetBackup catalog and produces a report on the status of the NetBackup images. It will produce one of two types of reports:

- Report images satisfying a set of criteria (if -media is absent)
- Report on removable media satisfying a set of criteria (if -media is present)

bpimmedia   Queries the NetBackup image catalog and reports on the NetBackup images. It can produce two reports:

- An Images-on-Media report
- A Spangroups report

bpimport   Imports NetBackup and Backup Exec backups that are expired or are from another NetBackup or Backup Exec server.

bplabel   Writes a NetBackup label on tape media. Labeling is required only for media that were last used for NetBackup catalog backups or by a non-NetBackup application. You can also use it to assign specific media IDs.

bplist   Lists backed up and archived files on the NetBackup server according to the options that you specify.

bppldelete   Deletes policies from the NetBackup database.

bppllist   Lists policies and policy information within the NetBackup database.

bpmedia   Freezes, unfreezes, suspends, or unsuspends an individual NetBackup media ID, allowing or disallowing future backups or archives to be directed to the media. Note that this command applies only to media managed by Media Manager.

bpmedialist   Displays NetBackup media status by making queries of one or more NetBackup media catalogs and produces a report on the status of the NetBackup media.

bpminlicense   Manages NetBackup license file.

bpplclients, bpclclients   Administers the clients within NetBackup policies.

bpplinfo, bpclinfo   Initializes, modifies, or displays policy attributes for a NetBackup policy.

bpplinclude, bpclinclude   Maintains the policy file list for a Net-Backup policy. This is the list of files backed up when NetBackup runs an automatic backup for the policy.

bpplsched, bpclsched   Adds, deletes, or lists NetBackup schedules to/from a policy.

bpplschedrep, bpclschedrep   Modifies the attributes of a NetBackup schedule. The schedule and policy named by bpplschedrep should already exist when this command is run.

bppolicynew, bpclassnew   Creates copies, or renames a NetBackup policy.

bprecover   Initiates the NetBackup utility for restoring the NetBackup internal databases called catalogs and recovers catalogs that were backed up by using the procedures described in the NetBackup System Administrator's Guide. The command has two main modes: list and recover.

bprestore   Restores files or directories from the NetBackup server.

bpstuadd   Creates a NetBackup storage unit group or a storage unit.

bpstudel   Deletes a NetBackup storage unit or storage unit group.

bpstulist   Displays the attributes for one or all of the NetBackup storage units or storage unit groups.

bpsturep   Modifies an existing NetBackup storage unit by replacing selected storage-unit or storage-unit-group attributes in the NetBackup catalog.

bpverify   Verifies the backups created by NetBackup.

cat_convert   Converts NetBackup catalog .f files between Versions 3.4 and 4.0 or between 4.5 ASCII format and 4.5 binary format.

nbdbsetport   Sets TCP/IP port used by the nbdbd database service.

nbdbsetpw   Modifies passwords used by the nbdbd database service.

vopied   Daemon to provide VERITAS one-time password user authentication.

vopie_util   Manages local vopie authentication files.

Media Manager Commands for UNIX and Windows

Most of these commands are common between UNIX and Windows. The exceptions are noted.

acsd   Automated Cartridge System (ACS) daemon that interfaces with Media Manager to automatically mount and unmount tapes that are under Automated Cartridge System (ACS) control.

lmfd, lmfcd   Library Management Facility (LMF) daemon and control daemon to interface with Media Manager to mount and unmount tape volumes in an LMF robot.

ltid   Starts the Media Manager device daemon. The ltid command starts the Media Manager device daemon (ltid) and Automatic Volume Recognition daemon (avrd). These daemons manage Media Manager devices. The ltid command also starts the appropriate robotic daemons, if robotic devices were defined in Media Manager, as well as the Media Manager volume daemon, vmd.

odld   Optical Disk Library (ODL) daemon interfaces with Media Manager to mount and unmount optical platters in an optical disk library.

rsmd   Removable Storage Manager (RSM) process interfaces with Media Manager to automatically mount and unmount tapes that are under Microsoft Windows 2000 Removable Storage Manager (RSM) control.

stopltid   Stops the Media Manager device daemon, avrd, and the robotic daemons.

tl4d   Tape Library 4MM (TL4) daemon interfaces with Media Manager to mount and unmount tapes in a Tape Library 4MM (TL4) robot.

tl8d, tl8cd   Tape Library 8MM (TL8) daemon and control daemon interface with Media Manager to mount and unmount volumes in a Tape Library 8MM robot.

tldd, tldcd   Tape Library DLT (TLD) daemon and control daemon interface with Media Manager to mount and unmount volumes in a Tape Library DLT (TLD) robot.

tlhd, tlhcd   Tape Library Half-inch (TLH) daemon and control daemon interface with Media Manager to mount and unmount tape volumes in a Tape Library Half-inch (TLH) robot.

tlmd   Tape Library Multimedia (TLM) daemon interfaces with Media Manager to mount and unmount tapes in a Tape Library Multimedia (TLM) robot.

tpautoconf   Manages the global device database host and is normally used by the Device Configuration Wizard to automatically discover and configure devices.

tpclean   Manages tape drive cleaning by allowing you to monitor Media Manager tape drive usage and optionally configure tape drives to be automatically cleaned (except drives in ACS, LMF, ODL, RSM, or TLH robots; or shared (SSO) drives).

tpconfig   Tape configuration utility. tpconfig can be used as a command-line interface or menu interface (only on UNIX) to configure robots and drives for use with NetBackup or to display the current configuration.

tpformat   Formats optical disks for use by Media Manager.

tpreq   Requests a tape volume for mounting and associates a filename with the assigned drive.

tpunmount   Removes a tape volume from a drive and the associated tape file name from the directory.

ts8d   Tape Stacker 8MM (TS8) daemon interfaces with Media Manager to mount and unmount tapes in Tape Stacker 8MM robots.

tsdd   Tape Stacker DLT (TSD) daemon interfaces with Media Manager to mount and unmount tapes in Tape Stacker DLT (TSD) robots.

tshd   Tape Stacker Half-inch (TSH) daemon interfaces with Media Manager to mount and unmount tapes in Tape Stacker Half-inch (TSH) robots.

vmadd   Adds volumes to the volume database.

vmadm   Character-based media management utility used to manage volumes and volume pools, manage barcode rules, and inventory robots controlled by the Media Manager volume daemon (vmd).

vmchange   Changes media information in the Media Manager volume database.

vmcheckxxx   Reports the media contents of a robotic library and optionally compares its contents with the volume configuration.

vmd   Media Manager volume daemon that manages the volume database, responding to requests to add, change, list, or delete volumes.

vmdelete   Deletes volumes from the volume database.

vmoprcmd   Performs operator functions on drives.

vmpool   Manages volume pools, allowing you to add, change, delete, or list volume pools.

vmquery   Queries the volume database, or assigns and unassigns volumes.

vmrule   Manages barcode rules.

vmupdate   Inventories the media contents of a robotic library and updates the volume database.

Glossary

active job   A job for which NetBackup is currently processing backup or restore data.

activity logs   Logs that may be optionally enabled for specific NetBackup programs and processes and then used to further investigate problems.

Activity Monitor   A NetBackup administration utility that displays information about NetBackup jobs, services, and processes, and provides limited control over them.

backup identifier (backupid)   The unique identifier assigned to each backup image. This is the identifier that is stored with the backup information in the NetBackup image catalog and used to track all backup images.

backup window   The time or window of opportunity given to the backup process in which to execute either scheduled or user-directed backups.

barcode   A label that is affixed to a cartridge and read by a barcode reader to allow the storage library to identify the media.

bpduplicate   Command-line interface used to duplicate NetBackup backup images. Also used by bpVault if configured to automate the duplication processes.

bpVault   A utility used to automate the off-site vaulting process of tape media, whether duplicated media or original media. Replaced by NetBackup 4.5 Vault.

bpVault Reports   bpVault generates several reports; the most common ones are the Picking List for Library, Distribution List for Vault, Picking List for Vault, and Distribution List for Library and Volume Inventory.

catalogs   The internal NetBackup and Media Manager databases; these catalogs contain information about configuration, media, devices, status, errors, and the files and directories in the stored backup images.

class   *See* policy. This was the NetBackup term before the current 4.5 release.

command-line interface (CLI)   Commands that users can execute either from the system prompt or in scripts.

cron   The cron command starts a process that executes commands at specified dates and times. Regularly scheduled commands can be specified according to instructions found in crontab files in the directory /var/spool/cron/crontabs. Users can submit their own crontab file using the crontab(1) command. Commands that are to be executed only once may be submitted using the at command.

cumulative-incremental backup   An attribute of a class schedule, this type of backup collects all files that have changed since the last successful full backup. All files are backed up if no prior backup has been done. *See also* differential-incremental backup.

database-agent clients   NetBackup clients with additional software designed to allow backup of certain relational databases.

database-extension clients   *See* database-agent clients.

device host A Media Manager host with either a physical attachment or a definition of a drive or robotic control.

Device Monitor A Media Manager administration utility that allows monitoring and manual control of Media Manager storage devices. For example, an administrator or computer room operator can use this utility to manually reset devices or set them to the UP or DOWN state.

DHCP Dynamic Host Configuration Protocol. This TCP/IP protocol automatically assigns temporary IP addresses to hosts when they connect to the network.

differential-incremental backup Scheduled by the administrator on the master server, this backup type backs up files that have changed since the last successful incremental or full backup. All files are backed up if no prior backup has been done. *See also* cumulative-incremental backup.

directory depth The number of levels below the current directory level that the NetBackup interfaces show in their directory and file list displays.

directory tree The hierarchy of how the files are organized on a disk. Each directory lists the files and directories that are directly below it in the tree. On UNIX, the topmost directory is called the root directory.

disaster recovery (DR) The act or process of recovering data from backups after a disk crash or other catastrophe.

disk-image backup A bit-by-bit rather than a filesystem backup of a disk drive on Windows NT/2000.

Distribution List for Library Part of bpVault. Lists all of the VOLSERs or media IDs that are due to be returned from the Offsite Vendor. This report may be blank if none of the VOLSERs have met their expiration date. The report contents are the same as the Picking List for Vault report with the VOLSERs listed by slot number instead of VOLSER number.

Distribution List for Vault   Part of bpVault. Lists all of the VOLSERs or media IDs that have been sent off-site to the Vaulting Vendor. This report is listed in numerical order by slot number and should be used by the Offsite Vendor to ensure all of the tapes sent are accounted for based on the report. The report contents are the same as the Picking List for Library.

duplicate image   A duplicate copy of a particular backup image.

EVSN   External volume serial number. An identifier written on a media cartridge or canister so the operator can identify the volume before inserting it into a drive or robot. For labeled media, the EVSN must be the same as the RVSN (identifier recorded on the media). For all media, the EVSN is the same as the media ID.

exclude list   Files or directories to exclude from automatic backups are contained within this list.

expiration (image)   The date and time when NetBackup stops tracking a backup image.

expiration (volume)   The expiration date of a volume is the date and time when the physical media (tape) is considered to be no longer usable.

Fibre Channel   The collection of physical interconnect hardware and the Fibre Channel protocol.

frequency (backup)   This determines how often NetBackup performs automatic scheduled backups within a particular policy (class). For example, if the frequency is seven days, then backups occur once a week.

FROZEN media state   If a volume is FROZEN, NetBackup keeps it indefinitely and can restore from it but not use it for further backups or archives.

full backup   A backup that copies to a storage unit all files and directories that are beneath a specified directory.

FULL media state   If this appears in a report or listing, it indicates the volume is full and cannot hold more data or be used for further backups.

global attributes   These are configuration attributes that affect the entire NetBackup master domain.

Global Data Manager (GDM)   An optionally purchased utility that provides a tree view and administration of multiple master servers within the enterprise. The server where the option is installed is called a master of masters.

GNU TAR   A public domain version of the UNIX TAR program.

image   The collection of data that NetBackup saves for an individual client during each backup or archive. The image contains all the files, directories, and catalog information associated with the backup or archive.

import   The process of re-creating NetBackup records of images that have previously expired or are not included in an active environment so the images can be restored.

include list   This list designates files or directories to add back in from the exclude list.

incremental backup   *See* cumulative-incremental backup, differential-incremental backup.

library   Refers to a robot and its accompanying software. A library includes a collection of tapes or optical platters used for data storage and retrieval. For example, a Tape Library DLT (TLD) refers to a robot that has TLD robotic control.

Mail CAP   A tape library term. A place where tapes may be transferred in and out of the tape library without compromising the integrity of the tape library's inventory. CAP stands for Cartridge Access Port.

master and media server cluster   This is defined as the NetBackup master server and the remote media servers in an enterprise configuration. It is possible to configure clusters only with NetBackup Data-Center servers.

master of masters   The master of masters is a NetBackup host where Global Data Manager software is installed. When logging into this host, the interface has a tree view where the administrator can view and administer multiple master servers.

master server   The NetBackup server that provides administration and control for backups and restores for all clients and servers in a master and media server cluster.

media   The physical magnetic tapes, optical disks, or magnetic disks where data is stored.

media host   The NetBackup host writing the data to the attached storage device that is received from the client.

media ID   An identifier that is written on a volume as part of the recorded label.

Media Manager   Software that is part of NetBackup and manages the storage devices and removable media.

Media Manager host   Simply put, a host where Media Manager software is installed.

media server   A NetBackup server that provides storage within a master and media server cluster. The master can also be a media server. A media server that is not the master is called a remote media server (or slave server).

Multi-Hosted Drives   Also known as SSO (Shared Storage Option), an additional piece of software that allows tape drives (standalone or in a robotic library) to be dynamically shared between multiple Net-Backup and Storage Migrator servers. This option is supported only on NetBackup DataCenter servers. *See also* SSO.

Multiple Data Streams (MDS)   Policy (class) attribute that allows more than one data stream from a client to be simultaneously backed up. *Note:* This implies that the global attribute Max Jobs Per Client has been modified to greater than one or a client database has been created using the bpclient command.

multiplexing   The process of sending data from multiple sources (clients) to a single destination (single storage device), interleaving those streams onto one piece of media.

NetBackup Client Service   NetBackup Windows NT/2000 service that runs on clients and servers and listens for connections from NetBackup servers and clients in the network. When a connection is made, this service starts the necessary programs.

NetBackup configuration options   On UNIX servers and on UNIX and Macintosh, clients, these settings are made in the bp.conf file. On NetWare target and OS/2 clients, they are in the bp.ini file. On Windows NT/2000 servers and Microsoft Windows clients, these settings are called properties and are made through the Backup, Archive, and Restore interface or the Configure-NetBackup window in the administration interface. With NetBackup 4.5 these can be set from the Java GUI through properties settings.

NetBackup Database Manager Service   NetBackup Windows NT/2000 service that runs on the master server and manages the NetBackup internal databases (called catalogs). This service must be running on the master server during all NetBackup administrative operations.

NetBackup databases   *See* catalogs.

NetBackup Device Manager Service   The NetBackup Windows NT/2000 service that runs on a NetBackup server and starts the robotic control processes and controls the reservation and assignment of volumes. This service runs only if the server has devices under Media Manager control. The process is ltid, logical tape interface daemon.

NetBackup properties   Same as NetBackup configuration options. Called NetBackup properties on Microsoft Windows platforms and UNIX platforms with NetBackup 4.5.

NetBackup Request Manager Service   The NetBackup Windows NT/ 2000 service that runs on the master server and starts the scheduler and receives requests from clients.

NetBackup Volume Manager Service   A NetBackup Windows NT/ 2000 service that runs on a NetBackup server, allows remote administration of Media Manager, and manages volume information. The process is vmd.

nonrobotic   *See* standalone.

parameter file   This is a bpVault term. The basic bpVault configuration requires setting up a parameter file to show which servers to use, how many drive pairs per server, which classes to duplicate (or eject), the name of the duplicate pool, the name of the vault, and the location for vault's working subdirectories. Bpvault can have several vaults running on the same server simultaneously as long as they have different vault names and different pools. If you have multiple vaults, you may wish to append the vault name to the end of the parameter file , for instance, dup_param_V1, dup_param_V2, and so on.

patch   A program that corrects a problem or adds a feature to an existing release of software.

pending request   When a request is made for a volume that is not either in the robot or a standalone drive, Media Manager displays a pending request in the Device Monitor interface.

Picking List for Library   Part of bpVault. Lists all of the VOLSERs or media IDs to be sent off-site to the Vaulting Vendor. This report is listed in numerical order by VOLSER number and should be used by operations to ensure all of the tapes retrieved from the Mail CAP are accounted for based on the report. The report contents are the same as the Distribution List for Vault.

Picking List for Vault   Part of bpVault. Lists all of the VOLSERs or media IDs that are due to be returned from the Offsite Vendor, sorted numerically by slot number. This report is to be used by the Offsite Vendor to facilitate the retrieval of the tapes. This report may be blank if none of the VOLSERs have met their expiration date. The report contents are the same as the Distribution List for Library report with the VOLSERs listed numerically.

policy   In NetBackup 4.5, defines the backup characteristics for a group of one or more clients that have similar backup requirements.

primary copy   The copy of an image that NetBackup uses to satisfy restores. When NetBackup duplicates an image, the original is designated as the primary copy.

queued job   A job that has been added to the list of jobs to be performed.

Registry   The Microsoft Windows 2000, NT, 98, or 95 databases that has configuration information about hardware and user accounts.

remote media server   A media server that is *not* the master. Note that only NetBackup DataCenter supports remote media servers.

residence   In Media Manager, information about the location of each volume is stored in a volume database. This residence entry contains information such as robot number, robot host, robot type, and media type.

retention level   An index number that corresponds to a user-defined retention period; there are 10 levels from which to choose (0 through 9) prior to NetBackup 4.5 and 25 levels at 4.5. The retention period associated with each level is configurable. *See also* retention period.

retention period   The length of time that NetBackup keeps backup and archive images. The retention period is specified on the schedule.

RVSN (Recorded Volume Serial Number)   This is an identifier recorded as part of the label on a volume and used by Media Manager to ensure that the correct volume is mounted. The RVSN is the same as the media ID.

schedules   Controls when backups can occur in addition to other aspects of the backup, such as the type of backup (full, incremental) and how long NetBackup retains the image.

Server-directed restores   Using the client interface on the master server to restore files to any client. Only the administrator can perform this operation.

Server-independent restore   Restoring files by using a NetBackup server other than the one that was used to write the backup; this feature is available only with NetBackup DataCenter.

server list   The list of servers that a NetBackup client or server refers to when establishing or verifying connections to NetBackup servers. On a Windows NT/2000 server and Microsoft Windows clients, you update the list through a dialog box in the interface. On a UNIX server and UNIX and Macintosh clients, the list is in the bp.conf file. In Net-Backup 4.5, this list can be configured and maintained from the Java GUI. On NetWare target and OS/2 clients, the list is in the bp.ini file.

service   Programs on a Windows NT/2000 system that runs in the background and performs some task (for example, starting other programs when they are needed). Services are generally referred to as daemons on UNIX systems.

session   An instance of NetBackup checking its schedules for backups that are due, adding them to its work list, and attempting to complete all jobs in the work list. For user backups and archives, a session usually consists of a single backup or archive.

SSO (Shared Storage Option)   SSO allows for individual tape drives to be shared dynamically among multiple NetBackup media servers. *See also* Multi-Hosted Drives.

standalone   A qualifier used with drives and media to indicate they are not associated with a robot. For example, a standalone tape drive is one where you must manually find and insert tapes before using them. A standalone volume is one that is located in a standalone drive or is stored outside of a drive and designated as standalone in the volume configuration.

status code   IA numerical code usually accompanied by a message that indicates the outcome of a particular operation.

storage area network (SAN)   A network used to connect hosts and storage devices. Typically these networks are built using Fibre Channel equipment.

storage unit   Logical representation of the physical storage devices that is used by NetBackup to identify storage resources and manage backups. It can be a set of drives in a robot or consist of one or more single tape drives that connect to the same host.

SUSPENDED media state   If a volume is suspended, NetBackup can restore from it but cannot use it for backups. NetBackup retains a record of the media ID until the last backup image on the volume expires. After the last image expires, the media is made available for backups.

TLD (Tape Library DLT)   Designates the type of tape library being controlled by the media server.

true image restore   Restores the contents of a directory to what it was at the time of any scheduled full or incremental backup. Previously deleted files are not restored.

user operation   A backup, archive, or restore that is started by a person on a client system.

Vault   NetBackup 4.5 feature that replaces bpVault, is integrated with NetBackup, and is configured with GUIs.

VOLSER   Volume serial number, otherwise known as the media ID, barcode label, or tape ID.

volume   Media Manager volumes are logical units of data storage or cleaning capability on media that have been assigned media IDs and other attributes, which are recorded in the Media Manager volume database.

volume configuration   Refers to configuration information that is stored in the Media Manager volume database.

volume database   An internal database where Media Manager keeps information about volumes, such as number of mounts and density.

All Media Manager hosts have a volume database. However, the database is empty unless the host is designated as a volume database host.

volume database host   The Media Manager (usually the NetBackup master) host that contains information about the volumes that Media Manager uses in a device.

volume database host (device allocation host)   The host that is defined as the volume database who is also the device allocation host in an SSO environment.

volume group   A logical representation of physical pieces of media that share a common residence (standalone or robotic).

volume pool   A set of volumes that are configured within Media Manager to be used by a single application and are protected from access by other applications and users.

Tuning Your Backup and Recovery Application

Tuning is a topic that just about everyone wants to talk about, and tuning your backup and recovery application is no exception. Because backup and recovery touch so many areas of the system, and in fact, the enterprise, tuning becomes more difficult to define clearly. The backup servers need to be tuned for optimum I/O performance, as well as shared memory, message queues, and network performance. The clients need to be tuned to their network performance, plus they need to have good disk performance. With all the variables that must be considered, tuning becomes a large task that sometimes appears to be more an art than a science.

Generally, we leave the majority of the operating system tuning to the appropriate system administrators and the different operating system specialists. In this appendix, we discuss some of the tuning that can be done specifically for the application, using NetBackup, and some OS tuning that directly affects the application. We also list some tuning references that you can use. If you go to the VERITAS Software's support Web site, http://support.veritas.com, and select Knowledge Base Search, you can search for a specific phrase and limit it to a specific product. We searched for "tuning" and the specific product "NetBackup DataCenter." We found several documents, but the two you really should concentrate on are "NetBackup Performance Tuning Guide for UNIX Platforms" (http://seer.support.veritas.com/docs/240733.htm) and "Tuning NetBackup on NT Systems for Optimal Performance" (http://seer.support.veritas.com/docs/248373. htm). These two documents contain a lot of the specific tuning steps for UNIX and Windows servers.

The key to tuning any of your backup servers is to understand what resources are being used and how they are being used. With a NetBackup media server, the primary function is to receive data from a client and move that data to tape. One of the first areas to tune is the size of the data buffers the application will be using as it moves the data to tape. You will generally get better performance if the application's write buffers more closely match the drive cache or are a function of the cache. After many tests, we have found that in most cases the best buffer size to use with Net-Backup is 256 KB, or 262144. This value usually gives the best tape write performance.

There is another buffering parameter that controls how many of these write buffers the application is allowed to use. This is a little harder to quantify, but 8 or 16 seems to be a good starting number. If you do not manually set up these configuration files, the application uses default values. These values can change with the version of the application and also depend on the platform type (UNIX or Windows) and whether you are using multiplexing.

As mentioned, tuning is more art than science. The art portion of the equation comes when you want to establish the exact values for each of these configuration files. The values we mentioned are generally good, but depending on the configuration and type of data, you might want slightly different ones. The only way to determine the best settings is to test and measure, and then test and measure again. Tables C.1 and C.2 list the default values for the common tuning parameters at NetBackup 4.5.

Table C.1   Default Values —SIZE_DATA_BUFFERS

	MULTIPLEXED	NONMULTIPLEXED
UNIX	64K	32K
Windows	64K	64K

Table C.2   Default Values—NUMBER_DATA_BUFFERS

	MULTIPLEXED	NON-MULTIPLEXED
UNIX	4	8
Windows	8	16

The NetBackup master server is mostly dependent on system resources, so tuning is not as much an issue as just making sure enough resources are configured. The resources that can give a master server problems are message queues, semaphores, and shared memory. The NetBackup Release Notes give minimum values for these resources. In addition, documents on the support Web site are available that discuss minimum settings for all the most commonly configured operating system resource parameters. Table C.3 shows an example of the minimum values for Solaris.

Table C.3   Minimum Kernel Settings on Solaris System

*
set maxusers=32
*
set shmsys:shminfo_shmmin=1
set shmsys:shminfo_shmmni=220
set shmsys:shminfo_shmseg=100
set shmsys:shminfo_shmmax=8388608
*
set semsys:seminfo_semume=64
set semsys:seminfo_semmap=64
set semsys:seminfo_semopm=32
set semsys:seminfo_semmni=1024
set semsys:seminfo_semmns=1024
set semsys:seminfo_semmnu=1024
set semsys:seminfo_semmsl=60
*
set msgsys:msginfo_msgmap=512
set msgsys:msginfo_msgmax=8192
set msgsys:msginfo_msgmnb=65536
set msgsys:msginfo_msgmni=256
set msgsys:msginfo_msgssz=8
set msgsys:msginfo_msgtql=512
set msgsys:msginfo_msgseg=8192

The tuning that we do for a client usually involves dealing with the way the client uses the network. There are settings on the client that will affect the buffer size used for network communications during backup. These are different for UNIX and Windows clients but are mentioned in the tuning documents cited earlier.

In addition, some operating system network parameters then sometimes are tuned. These are also mentioned in detail in the tuning documents. One of the most common things that can cause performance issues with network client backups is the duplex setting. To get the best performance, all networks should be set to FULL DUPLEX. Sometimes we see a mismatch where some settings are FULL DUPLEX and some are HALF DUPLEX, but the most common mistake is to set the duplex to AUTOMATIC. This very often results in a mismatch. Each OS has its own way to check the duplex setting. For example, on HP UNIX systems, you check this with the lanadmin command, whereas on Solaris, you use ndd.

Disaster Recovery Planning Kit: From End to Beginning

Recovery and backup—it's an interesting twist on a common term we have heard for years, backup and recovery. When was the last time you heard someone lead with *recovery*? So much emphasis is placed on backup—high speed, highly compressed data, and backing up very large amounts of data. Backup is important; however, restorability defines our success. We want very fast backups of very large amounts of data with a minimum impact on our networks—at least that's what our management team has been telling us (and they want it done by 4:00 P.M. Friday afternoon). Unless we have done our due diligence, we will be poorly prepared to rebut their expectations. Simple responses such as "that's just not possible" without the facts to back it up will fall on deaf ears.

Well, now that you are here, hopefully this appendix will help you better prepare your answers to management when certain expectations are placed on you for backup and recovery—or recovery and backup. Often, when we plan, we should consider starting with the end result and work backward. Just like the mazes that we used to do as children, it always seems to be easier when we start from the end and work our way back. Why? Well, we don't know of any specific scientific proof, but it probably has to do with the change in our perspective. Our perspective changes when we start to plan our data management policies backward: disaster recovery, recovery, and backup. When we plan backward, we can define

BACKUP IS IMPORTANT; HOWEVER, RESTORABILITY DEFINES OUR SUCCESS

Before we discuss the disaster recovery plan, let's talk about recovery plans in general. A recovery plan can be divided up into four parts. The first part of the document contains every step system administrators, database administrators, or applications developers take for granted when, during the normal course of the day, they are called upon to "fix" or maintain the server or application for which they are responsible. The second part contains the information documented as though these administrator and developers are not readily available. This is much more detailed and written to the level of the personnel most likely to be executing the plan. This means if the likelihood of a junior system administrator executing the plan is high, the person should be able to read and understand the recovery steps without question. The third part now includes a call tree to be used in the event any of the critical components (administrators) need to be contacted in their absence. Finally, the fourth part contains information as it pertains to differing levels of interruptions. These can range from severe weather to complete facility access having been cut off.

What rounds out the recovery plan and makes it a disaster recovery plan are the business impact analyses that tell you how much money it will cost the company if a particular application or server is unavailable for a period of time. A very strong element of your disaster recovery plan is the business impact analyses and assessments. These are prerequisites to beginning your DR plan. So if you haven't already done so, please begin with the business impact analysis planning kit that we prepared for this appendix or one that your organization has standardized on before you launch out into creating your DR plan. Without the valuable information that will be generated from these reports, your DR plan will be very weak.

our goals more clearly, identify management expectations, and present a concise message of the financial impact the expectations have on our overall plan.

How to Use This Kit

We used several Internet resources and past experiences for our research in developing this planning kit. We have been privileged to work with several DR professionals from various companies who had created excellent DR plans, and we have used their expertise to aid in putting this small planning kit together. It is not an exhaustive planning kit, but we believe it does touch on most of the high points of DR.

The purpose of this document is to assist in the planning and creation of a DR plan for your organization. While we have not included absolutely everything an administrator would want to cover in his or her DR plan, this is rather extensive and should provide you a good base on which to build your plan. One of the primary reasons for having a DR plan is to limit the decisions that must be made following a disaster. When disaster strikes, the decision-making process is tainted because of the events surrounding the disaster, as well as the physical demands a disaster has on the team without the aid of a plan such as this. It also removes any dependencies the company may have upon certain people or groups that would be required for the recovery process, such as consulting partners, hardware or software vendors, and so on.

NOTE When responding to a disaster, it is imperative that you follow your company's policies with regard to media communication, especially if your organization is a well-known target for media coverage.

You should decide what steps to take during the development of your DR plan. Many companies have been very successful using the model illustrated in Figure D.1, but it may be modified to suit your needs. It is a seven-layer model that covers most bases.

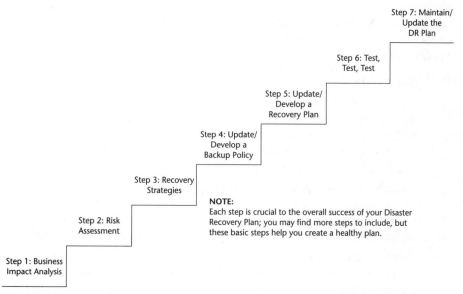

Figure D.1   Disaster recovery plan model.

Getting Started

Always include an objective, site-specific details, and a list of terms to be used throughout your document. This is all of your up-front information that you want to reader to understand; it should also give those who are not necessarily the ones executing the plan the ability to comprehend just what the plan will accomplish if done successfully. Doing it in this manner accomplishes a couple of things:

- Eliminates confusion
- Sets expectations for the use of this plan at the outset

Let's look at the following example of a DR plan.

SAMPLE DR PLAN

OBJECTIVE

Maintain the <Company Name>'s ability to continue to service customers, complete sales, and deliver their online services in a global market place. This ability hinges on four primary data centers located across the United States and Canada.

These data centers consist of mainly decentralized servers that once were singularly located on legacy mainframe hardware. Therefore, the protection of the data of these systems with regular duplications and off-site storage with enough detail to facilitate recovery is critical to the success of this plan. As part of this plan, regular testing will be scheduled to ensure the company's ability to survive a disaster.

DEFINITION OF TERMS

Assessment team. This person or group of persons will be responsible for assessing the level of damage the disaster caused to the organization's facilities, IT infrastructure, intellectual property (data), and so on. This team may consist of a number of different business units depending on the depth and breadth of the DR plan.

Business-critical. Defined as any resource, be it data, applications, personnel, and so on, that would be second (to mission-critical; see below) in priority in the plan of recovery in the event of disaster, loss, or interruption. An example of a business-critical application may be payroll and accounting.

Business interruption. Any event whether planned or unplanned that disrupts the normal course of business operations at one of your locations, which if not addressed within a predetermined amount of time may turn into a disaster.

Disaster.   A disaster is declared when an event or chain of events results in the inability of an organization to provide critical business functions for a period of time and/or causes the company to move from using standard operating procedures to employing its disaster recovery plan after a predetermined period of time, potentially at another facility.

Emergency on-call.   This is the front line in the event of a disaster. This person or group of persons will be contacted in the event of a disaster, and they, as part of the response team, will execute this plan and begin the process of recovery.

Functional critical.   Noncritical back-office functions such as file and print.

Management team.   The person or group of persons managing the entire execution of the DR plan. This team will ultimately have full responsibility for the success or failure of the DR plan.

Mission-critical.   Defined as any resource, be it data, applications, personnel, and so on, that would be of the highest priority in the plan of recovery in the event of disaster, loss, or interruption. An example might be online ordering or reservations systems.

Recovery team.   The person or group of persons that will take on the responsibility of the actual recovery process. This may involve restoration of the data from backup media or, in fact, the management of the restoration of physical infrastructure, facilities, and so on. This team may include a number of different people representing a number of different business units.

Response team.   The person or group of persons responsible for carrying out the declaration of and recovery from a disaster.

Scope

The scope defines the boundaries of this DR plan, such as when this plan will be invoked and how this plan will be most effective. It also gives the response teams and management teams a clear, concise image of the expectations for the execution of this DR plan. An example wording of a scope follows:

The DR plan has been developed for use in the event that access to the mission-critical data has been rendered unavailable. Recovery may be achieved from total disaster to component disaster by using all or part of this plan.

Component disaster describes anything that is not considered total destruction, such as server failure, hard drive failure, and so on. This plan will not cover recovery of client workstation data, which was considered nonessential at the point this DR plan was developed.

Assumptions

It is important to disclose the assumptions made during the development of this plan. This has gotten more attention since September 11, 2001. When the DR plans were developed, companies assumed that they would be able to get across town to their data; they never assumed that the roads would be completely shut down as they were in New York for a period of time. Disclosing these assumptions at the beginning of the plan will give the response teams the ability to make decisions that fall outside this plan should they find themselves in one of those situations. Here are some sample assumptions you might make at your company:

Certain assumptions have been made during the development of this plan. The following lists the assumptions:

- ◆ **Recovery site of choice is ready and available at the time of the declaration.**
- ◆ **Paging and telecommunication systems for public access are available.**
- ◆ **IT staff responsible for backup and recovery are on call and available.**
- ◆ **Access to public/private transportation will be available.**
- ◆ **Hardware will be available for use at the hot site.**
- ◆ **Software will be available from the off-site media storage facility.**
- ◆ **Air travel will not be interrupted.**

Off-Site Location

List the off-site location here, as well as a list of all authorized parties and their various capacities, such as retrieval of media and changing of permissions. The following procedure is used by the authorized personnel to contact the off-site data storage vendor and arrange for the media to be transported to the appropriate recovery location(s).

Define "off-site" for your organization.   Off-site can mean several things to different organizations. Some are completely secure with the data being 6 miles away in another data center that sits on a completely separate power grid, while others consider off-site to be more than 50 miles away from the primary location. Still others will not consider media to be off-site unless it is in a completely secured location sufficiently distanced from railways, large cities, or power facilities. Once again, "sufficiently distanced" should be defined here. An off-site vendor must restrict access to their facilities to only authorized personnel, yet make the data available anytime, day or night. The following is an example of a definition for an off-site location:

An off-site location is any location sufficiently distanced from any railways, large cities, or power facilities that offers a secure building and storage area that is restricted to authorized personnel only, but will allow immediate access to data anytime day or night in the event of a disaster. The off-site vendor will provide a contact list of individuals to be contacted in the event we declare a disaster. This off-site facility must be, at minimum, 45 miles from the primary data location(s). There are four data locations: Redmond, Washington; Chicago, Illinois; Minneapolis, Minnesota; and Rochester, New York. The locations of the off-site vendor's data vaults should be nondescript, low-key buildings, as should the transportation vehicles, in order to maintain security of the data during transport and storage.

A documented procedure must be in place that outlines the off-site rotation process.   At a minimum, this must include a list of who is authorized to send data off-site, who is authorized to recall data, and who is authorized to make changes in access levels of the company employees.

A process must be in place for reviewing who has access to off-site processes.   This review must be done at a minimum annually, or whenever there is a change in responsibilities that warrants it.

Business Impact Analysis

A business impact analysis (BIA) is an assessment of your company's strengths and weaknesses as they pertain to the company's ability to recover from a severe business interruption or a complete disaster. You should also be able to define what areas of your business are mission-critical, business-critical, or functional-critical. The level of criticality will determine your actions in the face of disaster. Typically, companies conduct BIAs for all areas of business, not just for IT. If your company is currently not conducting formal studies such as this, now is a great time to start as you begin the creation of your disaster recovery plan. No company is too small to conduct a BIA, because every company has something to lose in a disaster.

After the assessment has been done, a summary of the report should be included at the very least to inform the DR team of the expectations of the business units. The report should include items such as application/server, recovery location, recovery time, date BIA was done, and the parties that approved this BIA. Table D.1 shows an example of a BIA report template. If you do not have a template for a business impact analysis, you may use the business impact analysis planning kit to develop one.

You may also want to include where these BIAs are being stored, including both electronic storage and physical storage, such as is discussed in the next section.

Declaration of a Disaster

What does your company call a disaster? Clearly define the levels of disasters and what warrants the declaration of a disaster. Also take into consideration a definition of business interruptions and steps to take in the event the business interruption changes into a disaster. We consider a business interruption as any event, whether planned or unplanned, that disrupts the normal course of business operations at one of your locations, which if not addressed within a predetermined amount of time may turn into a disaster.

Table D.1 Sample BIA Summary Report Template

APPLICATION	RECOVERY LOCATION	RECOVERY TIME	BIA COMPLETION DATE	APPROVED BY

WHAT TO ASK BEFORE DECLARING A DISASTER

Operations, IT management, or facilities may declare a disaster and invoke the recovery process, depending on the answers to the following questions:

- ◆ Are you experiencing flash floods in your area?
- ◆ Has this affected any of the critical data centers?
- ◆ Are your facilities experiencing water problems, such as flood, broken pipe, and so on?
- ◆ As a result, are any of the critical data centers at risk? Facility at risk?
- ◆ Has a fire broken out in the building?
- ◆ Have you experienced a power failure?
- ◆ Do you see or smell smoke in the server room?
- ◆ Has natural disaster damage to the building limited normal access?

If you answered yes to any of these questions, immediately contact the primary on the call tree. If contact fails, contact the secondary and page the primary. Continue this process with the tertiary contact until you have reached someone on the declaration call tree.

Disaster Declaration Process

Define your organization's process for declaring a disaster, such as responsible parties, levels of criticality, and so forth. What would warrant a disaster? What would you consider a business interruption? When does a business interruption shift into a disaster? Following are some sample questions you might want to consider as a guide to help you determine if a declaration is necessary and what level of severity it would be.

Response Teams

DR plans are executed by a group of persons we call the response team. The team consists of all subgroups of teams responsible for executing this DR plan in a successful manner, including the emergency on-call, assessment, and recovery teams. Certain members of the response team should manage the overall execution of the DR plan; preferably, in order to remain focused, they should have no other subgroup responsibilities.

Emergency On-Call

The emergency on-call team is the first line of support when the declaration is made. The primary team lead will initiate the plan once they have confirmed the declaration. An example of some key positions and their responsibilities are listed in Table D.2.

Fill out completely the call tree shown in Table D.3, including as many alternates as possible.

Table D.2 Key Positions on the Emergency On-Call Team

KEY POSITION	RESPONSIBILITY
Primary contact	Leader of the recovery teams, assignment of tasks, and management of the DR plan.
Secondary contact	Second in command to the Primary and would assume all responsibilities of the primary in the event the primary is not available.
Tertiary contact	Assumes primary role in the event both primary and secondary leaders are not available.
Management representative	Business unit representative who's responsible to act as a liaison between the recovery team and corporate management. This individual should be instrumental in acquiring any additional resources necessary to make the recovery successful.
Networking	Primary contact with group managing wide-area and local-area network infrastructure.
Finance	This individual has appropriate authority to authorize purchases of assets or services in order to successfully recover from the declared disaster. This person should have limits on his or her authority, and beyond that, a senior finance representative should be available for additional authorization.
Facilities	Physical building, environmental controls, and so on.
P.R.	This group will be responsible for all media communication when necessary.

Table D.3   Emergency On-Call Team

KEY POSITION	NAME	PHONE #	CELL PHONE/ PAGER NUMBER	HOME PHONE #/ ALT. PHONE#	ADDRESS
Primary contact					
Secondary contact					
Tertiary contact					
Management representative					
Networking					
Finance					
Facilities					
P.R.					

Assessment Team

This team evaluates the situation, identifies the severity of the damage, and reports back to the emergency on-call team leader. The report should include estimates and rough time lines for recovery. Once again, there should be a list of people involved in this team. A sample of this team is listed in Table D.4.

Table D.4   Key Positions on the Assessment Team

KEY POSITION	DESCRIPTION
Primary contact	Organizes and mobilizes the team.
Secondary leader	Assists primary, assumes role in the event the primary leader is not available.
Tertiary leader	Assumes primary role in the event both primary and secondary leaders are unavailable.
Networking	Assesses damage to wide-area and local-area network infrastructure.
Sys administrators	Assesses their appropriate areas.

(continued)

Table D.4 *(continued)*

KEY POSITION	DESCRIPTION
Application developers	Assesses their appropriate areas.
Database administrators	Assesses their appropriate areas.
Vendors	Provides information regarding repair, replacement, pricing, and resource availability.

You should list the members of the damage assessment team using the example shown in Table D.5.

NOTE Please list alternate members wherever possible.

Recovery Team

The recovery team manages the overall recovery of the data, systems, and hardware. There may be some crossover from the other teams, but primarily this team will be composed of system administrators, DBAs, and application support. Table D.6 shows the key positions on the recovery team.

Table D.5 Assessment Team

KEY POSITION	NAME	PHONE #	CELL PHONE/ PAGER NUMBER	HOME PHONE #/ ALT. PHONE#	ADDRESS
Primary					
Secondary					
Tertiary					
Networking					
System administrators					
Application administrators/ developers					
Database administrators					
Facilities manager					
Vendors					

Table D.6   Key Positions on the Recovery Team

POSITION	DESCRIPTION
Primary	Responsible for management of the team, assignments, and reports.
Secondary leader	Assists primary leader, assumes role in the event the primary leader is not available.
Tertiary leader	Assumes primary leader role in the event both primary and secondary leaders are unavailable.
System administrators	Coordinates restoration of hardware, OS, and data from backup media
Network	Coordinates restoration of network services to the local and/or wide-area network(s).
Application administrators/developers	Coordinates the recovery of key applications. Works very closely with the system administration members.
Database administrators	Recovers, restores, and tests the database applications and data to the servers.

Table D.7 is a contact list or call tree for the recovery team.

Table D.7   Recovery Team

KEY POSITION	NAME	PHONE #	CELL PHONE/ PAGER NUMBER	HOME PHONE #/ ALT. PHONE#	ADDRESS
Primary					
Secondary					
Tertiary					
System administrator					
Network					
Hardware systems specialist					
Application administrator/ developers					
Database administrators					

Infrastructure Inventory

Hardware and software inventories are very important to any DR plan. Without this information, you expose yourself and your company to potential failure during the execution of the plan. While this may seem like a great deal of work, the outcome far outweighs the grief you are putting yourself through today. The success of the plan will be measured by the thoroughness of your work during the development of your plan.

Hardware Inventory

Include as much detail as possible about the hardware that will be protected by this DR plan. The more detail the better. Also include as much information about the maintenance contract as possible for the hardware as well. Here's a brief sample list of what you may want to include in your hardware inventory:

- Server name
- Make/model
- Serial number
- OS
  - Patch level
- Memory
  - Amount
  - Type
- Disk controllers
- Disk drives
- Partitions
- Network interface card
- IP address

For your UNIX servers, try to script as much of this as possible; if you are using VERITAS NetBackup, use the NetBackup Configuration Verification Utility (NCVU) found on VERITAS' support Web site. It will make running this inventory much easier. For Windows NT and 2000 servers, formal software packages are available that will help you create this type of information. How it is gathered is not the issue; the fact that you gather it for all machines deemed critical is what is important.

Architecture Inventory

The reason we included this heading under Hardware Inventory is that we feel the two go hand in hand. We want to stress the importance of diagrams that illustrate your network configuration, server configuration, drive partitioning, and so on. Include any and all diagrams necessary for this DR plan here. We're sure many of you have spent hours creating your Visio diagrams; now is the time to display them. Any paper or electronic diagrams should be recorded in your DR plan. If your company has an information librarian, then have him or her mark and track these documents; if not, include a table similar to the one in Table D.8.

Software Inventory

Equally as important as the hardware inventory, the software inventory will play a critical role in a successful recovery. Following is another sample list of the information you may want to include in your software inventory list:

- Application name
- Functional name (Finance, for example)
- Default installation path
    - Installation path different from default? (Y/N)
    - If yes, explain
- Software version
- Maintenance contract information
- Software license
- Hosting server

Table D.8   Example of an Architecture Inventory

PURPOSE	DOCUMENT NAME (P)APER/ (E)LECTRONIC	LOCATION(S)	LAST UPDATED	OWNER
Network for building 500	P–Network Map 500	P–Off-site Vendor	04-30-02	O. L. Mysu
	E–NetMap_500.doc	E–Server/Path/ Document		
Finance application server	P–Finance Server	P–Corporate Library	01-08-02	C. S. Psyrvivour
	E–FINSERV.doc	E–Server/Path/ Document		

Call Tree

Call trees, or contact lists, an example of which is illustrated in Table D.9, must be kept up-to-date and should be included in every DR plan. Some decide to put this at the beginning of their DR plans, while others create lists for each member to carry on their person. This call tree will be used by anyone who is facing a potential disaster as defined previously in this document. Primary contacts from your emergency on-call, assessment, and recovery teams should be included in this list.

High-Profile Users

These are users of critical systems and should be notified in the event that their particular area has been affected. They will be instrumental in keeping the user population informed of the progress your DR team is making. Table D.10 shows a sample call tree for these high-profile users.

Table D.9 Example of a Call Tree

CONTACT	ADDRESS	PHONE #/	CELL PHONE/ PAGER NUMBER	HOME PHONE #/ ALT. PHONE #	TEAM

Table D.10 Example of a Call Tree for High-Profile Users

CONTACT	ADDRESS	PHONE #/	CELL PHONE/ PAGER NUMBER	HOME PHONE #/ ALT. PHONE #	APPLICATION

Local Authorities

It may seem far-fetched to include a call tree for local authorities, but you never know until you are faced with a disaster. Having these numbers at your fingertips will once again give you the ability to make proactive decisions and not reactive ones. Table D.11 shows an example of a call tree for local authorities. You may want to include local and state police, hospitals and emergency rooms, even Federal Emergency Management Agency (FEMA) numbers.

Contractor Contacts

Key lists of contractors or consultants who may have first-hand knowledge of the environment, applications, or other critical information necessary to the success of the recovery should be included in this plan. Again, the inclusion may be as simple as the example shown in Table D.12.

Table D.11   Example of a Call Tree for Local Authorities

CONTACT	ADDRESS	PHONE #/	CELL PHONE/ PAGER NUMBER	HOME PHONE #/ ALT. PHONE #	TEAM
Hospitals/ emergency rooms					
Poison control centers					
City police					
County/ state police					

Table D.12   Example of a List of Contractors

CONTACT/ COMPANY	ADDRESS	PHONE #/	CELL PHONE/ PAGER NUMBER	HOME PHONE #/ ALT. PHONE #	AREA OF EXPERTISE

Vendor Contacts

Any vendor that you may deem important during a disaster should be listed here. This could include hotels, office supply stores, airlines, and local carryout restaurants. This may require a bit of thinking outside the box, because you need to take into consideration that your response teams may be "living" at the recovery site until the disaster has been rectified. If you use one of the recovery services, they may have a list of this information depending the location of their recovery facilities. Talk with your recovery vendor and get that list to be included in your DR plan for each potential city that you would find yourself in performing your recovery. Table D.13 shows an example that you can use for your list of vendor contacts.

Table D.13   Example of a List of Vendor Contacts

CONTACT	ADDRESS	PHONE #/	CELL PHONE/ PAGER NUMBER	HOME PHONE #/ ALT. PHONE #	TEAM
Hardware/ software					
Auto/ truck rental					
Catering services					
Charter air services					
Courier services					
Delivery services					
Electrical contractors					
Forms suppliers					
Hotel/motel accom- modations					
Office equipment/ furniture and supply					

Table D.13   *(continued)*

CONTACT	ADDRESS	PHONE #/	CELL PHONE/ PAGER NUMBER	HOME PHONE #/ ALT. PHONE #	TEAM
Plumbing contractors					
Security guard services					
Temporary office services					
Trans- portation: Airlines- trains–buses					
Travel agencies					
Utilities: Electric- gas–water					

Team Meetings

Where would this plan be without team meetings to explore the status of the declaration? Plan an initial meeting to outline your particular plan of attack. Be thorough but concise, have prepared agendas, and include them in this plan. Remember, the primary reason for a DR plan is to limit the number of decisions that must be made during such an event. If you have included a sample agenda, or at least a boilerplate agenda, then you can begin your war-room meetings as soon as the teams are gathered. You should include predetermined time lines in the DR plan, as well as how often team meetings should be taking place. With each subsequent meeting, a progressive agenda should be included to aid in the flow of these meetings. To be as prepared for the meetings as possible, you should:

- Create boilerplate agendas to streamline the meetings during a disaster.

- Have predetermined time lines for status reports.

- Include as much information in this plan as possible.

Update Procedures

To maintain a consistent view of this plan, you should list the responsible plan's authors and editors, along with the location of each plan per author/editor, as shown in Table D.14.

The location of the electronic components of a DR plan should also be recorded, as shown in Table D.15.

Table D.14   Example of a List of Plan Authors and Editors

PLAN AUTHOR/ EDITOR/DATE LAST EDITED	DOCUMENT NAME/ PURPOSE	LOCATION: (P)APER/ (E)LECTRONIC
D.C. / D.L./12-09-02	DR Plan	P-Off-site E-SERV/PATH/DOCNAME
D.C./K.W./01-01-03	Backup Plan/Backup and Recovery Strategies	P-On-site/Off-site E-SERV/PATH/DOCNAME

Table D.15   Example of a Location List for Electronic Components of a DR Plan

PURPOSE	DOCUMENT NAME (P)APER/ (E)LECTRONIC	LOCATION(S)	LAST UPDATED	OWNER
Disaster Recovery	P-DR Plan E-DR_120502.doc	P-Room 1202 E-Server/Path/ Document	08-19-02	J. Dekrator
Oracle Recovery	P-Oracle Recovery Guide E-ORA_RG.doc	P-DBA Filing Cabinet and Off-site Vendor E-Server/Path/ Document	08-30-02	D. Alvish
Ops Guide	P-NBU Operations E-NBUOPS.doc	P-NONE E-Server/Path/ Document	11-20-02	T. Traansman
BIA for Sales	P-BIA Assessment for Sales Division E-BIA_SALES.doc	P-USA Bank Safe Deposit Box E-Server/ Path/Document	3-19-02	A. Prenzes

Determine your company's policy for updates and list them here. Perhaps your company will choose to update every six months or annually at the very minimum. The wording need not be exhaustive; be simple and concise to reduce complexity. The following is an example of a brief statement you might include in your company's DR testing policy plan:

The DR plan must be reviewed and updated annually at the very minimum. All members of the DR team should participate in the review and update of the plan. The next planned meeting is December 14, 2003. The Management Team will be responsible for sending out a reminder email as the date approaches.

Note that the paragraph indicates the next scheduled meeting. This is very important to maintain a consistency in your testing, review, and maintenance of your DR plan.

Developing a Test Plan

What good is a DR plan if it is not tested? Not very good—especially since the whole purpose for putting together a DR plan is to be prepared in the event you suffer any measured loss of data, equipment or services. This plan is supposed to give us an edge on such events, but if we do not test it, our planned outcome may be entirely different. Therefore, take this very simple methodology to heart as you begin this process: Plan your test, then test your plan. This very simple statement means that you must define a scope for your test because it is within this scope that you will find success or failure of your DR plan. If you fail to do this, you lose consistency and repeatability of your DR plan. Remember, we are testing the DR plan so we are prepared; failure during a test that is documented and addressed is actually a success. However, failures that are ignored remain failures.

Planning the Test

When you begin the process of planning your test, start at the result and work backward, much like we described at the beginning of this appendix. If you can define your results as goals, you should be able to build the steps necessary to achieve each goal. For example, the end result of your DR plan is that you would have your Online Reservations System (ORS) up and available within 14 hours. To accomplish that in the face of a declared disaster, you need to take the following steps:

1. Disaster is declared: Assumption—Facility inaccessible. To successfully test, you must make assumptions in order to test each level of the response teams. Other examples are as follows:

   a. System failure

   b. Application corruption

   c. Advancing weather conditions

2. Contact response teams, including

   a. Management team lead

   b. Emergency on-call team lead

   c. Assessment team lead

   d. Recovery team lead

3. Hot-site facility must be notified if this is required.

4. Off-site vendor must be notified and most recent tapes need to be delivered to hot-site facility.

5. Install/configure backup server.

6. Recover backup server's database.

7. ORS recovery machine is installed/configured with an OS and backup client software.

8. Import/inventory off-site tapes.

9. Begin recovery of data.

In this example, each step may have substantially more detail that can be expanded upon, but it gives you a good idea of where you need to go with planning your test. Again, the more detailed your test plan, the greater the probability is that you will find success during its execution. Do not let verbosity be the guiding light for whether or not a test plan is adequate; begin where you are with what you have and use the results of the tests, including both failures and successes, to build a stronger, more resilient plan. You may want to test only certain components of your disaster recovery plan, such as the restore component. In that case, make your test plan modular; in other words, create it in such a way that you can pull out certain components without compromising consistency. We strongly recommend that you perform these tests on your off-site media at least every six months— preferably quarterly, if you are allowed. Just remember to stay within the scope of your test plan as you are executing the test plan, so you can see the holes. Do not stop, rather, continue until you can go no further. Then document everything so you can plan your test better the next time.

Summary

When you have completed your DR plan, test, test, test. This should be done as often as your company requires it, but at a minimum, it should be done annually. Some companies perform these tests every six months; some test components of the plan more often. Keep in mind that this is not a static document. Your data storage continues to grow and new challenges present themselves in managing this growth. This growth will have an impact on your DR plan; therefore, the plan needs to be dynamic and should be reviewed and updated regularly. Be as thorough as you possibly can. As mentioned in the beginning of this appendix, this is not an exhaustive planning kit. Rather, it is a beginning. Take as much into consideration as you possibly can, talk with as many people as possible, and get your legal counsel involved to help create this plan. Then continue to work the plan consistently. Hopefully, you will never have to use it, but if you do, it will be nice to know that the teams all know and understand their roles and will be able to carry out their tasks with some level of confidence because of the extensive testing you have regularly performed.

One of the items we have not covered in this appendix is your backup operations guide. You must ensure this process is documented with the same discipline as your DR plan, and you must make sure it is updated regularly. If you do not have an operations guide, I have developed one specifically for NetBackup that you may obtain by contacting DataStaff, Inc. (www.datastaff.com).

Business Impact Analysis Planning Kit: The Storm Before the Calm

The storm before the calm? It makes sense when you think about it. When you start addressing the business at a business level, you may stir up a few things. For example, a client retains their data "forever" off-site. Why, you ask? Very good question. First, it is a legal powder keg: Should anyone file suit, they would be able to subpoena all of those records. Second, it costs a lot of money for those tape cartridges. The answer I received was innocent enough: We don't know how to categorize our data properly and differentiate its importance. The more I probed, the more uncomfortable things became at the business level, because we uncovered an area that the business really needed to address but had been left undone for many years.

This planning kit provides the initial information necessary to create a compelling business impact analysis (BIA) that will help you identify the critical components of your environment and the cost associated with their unavailability. We hope using this planning kit helps you achieve a sense of calm knowing that you will be well prepared in the event your company experiences a disaster.

An Introduction to BIA

We touched on BIAs in Appendix D. In this appendix, we go into greater detail. Let's begin with defining exactly what a business impact analysis is. As mentioned in the previous appendix, a BIA is an evaluation of your company's strengths and weaknesses with respect to its ability to recover from a severe business interruption to a complete disaster. While the BIA can stand on its own, it should also be included as a component of the DR plan. Here's what you should look at as you conduct this type of analysis:

- Intellectual property, critical hardware, software, and any custom applications
- Your time to recovery, based on the amount of money your company will stand to lose, plus the level of importance for this particular application, server, or service
- The conditions your data should be in at the very least in order to recover successfully, including how old the data is

When planning for DR, you should take into consideration the entire process of determining, implementing, and documenting everything that must be done in order to return some critical component of your business to its normal working order following a disaster. There is a common methodology used by a number of clients for DR planning that involves seven steps. If you have the DR planning kit, you will be familiar with these steps, listed here:

1. Perform BIA.
2. Perform risk assessment.
3. Determine recovery strategies.
4. Update/develop backup plan and operations guide.
5. Update/develop a recovery plan.
6. Test.
7. Update and maintain the DR plan.

We will be concerned with only Step 1 in this planning kit. The use of BIAs in a DR plan will help address the needs of the business and the business units with respect to data protection and availability by providing a means to define the importance of each component of the business unit and how each will have an impact should it become unavailable for a period of time. What you should find as a result of conducting BIAs is that you now have the basis for all the other steps in your DR planning process.

As you begin the process of interviewing the business unit managers, data owners, and administrators, you will begin to identify certain areas and associated costs that may not line up with the financial expectations for this business unit's recovery. Therefore, a second interview with the business unit managers would be required to resolve or reprioritize their goals so that they fall in line with the financial picture. However, you may find that recovering this business unit's applications would require more money than otherwise financially allocated. Based on which direction this goes, it may in fact force changes to be made to the backup plan, DR plan, or even the budgets.

The BIA is a methodology that helps to identify the impact of losing access to a particular system or application to your organization. The BIA process is primarily an information-gathering process. In the end you will take away several key components for each of the business units you have worked with, some of which we have listed here:

1. The criticality a particular system or application has to the organization

2. How quickly it must be recovered in order to minimize the company's risk of exposure

3. How current the data must be at the time of recovery

This information is essential to your DR and backup plans, as it describes the business requirements for backup and recovery.

In the past, most organizations viewed the IT staff as the bits-and-bytes types who didn't interface well with others. That is starting to change, and performing things like a DR plan and a BIA help a great deal in our marketing effort and in fostering relationships with the various business areas. The business unit managers will be attracted to the relationship by the information you provide to them, such as the impact to the business a disaster could bring to this particular unit.

The information that is collected during the interview process will be the basis for the analysis, which in turn will be used within the DR plan. We have included sample lists and forms to use during your interview process. You may choose to use these or create your own. Whatever you decide, we strongly recommend that you use something and maintain a level of consistency throughout your analysis.

Scope

The scope of your BIA is really quite logical, but it does take time to consider all areas. To facilitate your analysis, we have included a phased approach that you may want to consider taking during this process while you build the information portfolio for the particular application/service you have selected.

- *Phase I*—Identify which server, system, service, or application you want to analyze.

- *Phase II*—Find out which data owners, application administrators, system administrators, database administrators (DBAs), and business unit managers you would like to interview. *Hint:* During the interview process, ask the interviewees whom else you should be speaking to regarding this particular system.

- *Phase III*—Meet with these individuals or groups to start building your information portfolio on this business unit.

- *Phase IV*—Generate a report from the information portfolio.

Phase I

What is it that you will be analyzing? Remember that as you begin this process, it will begin to waterfall into other BIAs. Here is what we mean:

- Identify the name of the system or service.

- Start a new information portfolio for this service, application, or system.

- Identify the components required for this service, application, or system to be recovered. This includes hardware and software components as well.

Start where you are familiar and move on from there. For example, you know that accounts receivable (AR) is fairly important; begin analyzing that and soon you may find that there is a much larger package that contains AR you should be analyzing.

Since this has been written for the purposes of analyzing IT functions, you may want to create a form that is fairly generic as it pertains to systems, services, or applications. You will bring into your organization a much higher level of consistency, which is key when it comes to delegating the task of conducting BIAs to other team members.

Phase II

Now that you have the name of the system or service that you want to analyze, you should have enough information to begin building your contact list for interviews. When you choose whom to talk to, start at the highest level and work your way down. This accomplishes two things:

1. If you get the audience with the first person you talk to, you know you are getting someone who will understand the impact to the business.

2. If this person asks you to speak with someone who reports to him or her, you know that you will get his or her full cooperation having been told by a superior to work with you.

We have found that some people do not like talking about the likelihood of a disaster and subsequent impact to their business units, mainly because a process such as this exposes more than just the systems; it may also expose policies and procedures that need to be changed within the business unit. Unfortunately, those of us who conduct BIAs are often viewed in the same light as an auditor. Yet although the process may be painful, the end result makes for a much stronger company and organization.

Moving on, continue to build your information portfolio and schedule your appointments Here are some points you may want to follow during this process:

- Identify the parties with an interest in the components you have identified in Phase I.

- Make sure you have listed the data owners, application administrators, system administrators, DBAs, and so on.

- Make contacts and set up interview appointments.

Play detective—assume nothing and ask everything. Let the interviewees give you the information and avoid the tendency to "help" with the answers. It is even a good idea if you have a junior staff member or the IT staff administrator assist in the interview process so as not to taint the answers with your own. You will then get a better image of what the business unit perspective is.

Some of the areas to cover in this interview process are as follows:

- What are the areas of impact to the business should this system or service become unavailable? Remember, different levels of individuals will have different perspectives on the impact, so interview as many people as possible.

- What other business units rely on this component of the organization?

- Is this a revenue-generating application or activity?

- What financial impact would it have if it were down?

- What, if any, service level agreements (SLAs) are in place with either internal or external customers?

- What monetary impact does that SLA have with either internal or external customers?

- If you are a publicly held company, how much exposure could you stand before you begin to lose shareholder confidence? How would a loss affect your reputation on Wall Street?

Phase III

Now that you have a list of people to talk to, kindly ask them to allocate 60 to 90 minutes of their time in the next couple of weeks in order to complete this analysis. Always work with an agenda, especially if you are at the upper management level. Their time is limited, and without an agenda prepared at least 48 hours prior to the interview, you may find yourself having to reschedule and thus lose some level of credibility. Remember, this is as much a marketing campaign for the IT team as it is an investigation of the particular systems or services that need to be protected. Be sure to send out reminder emails. You should send at least three:

- One after you first schedule the appointment

- Another when you send the agenda, at least 48 hours prior to the meeting

- A third 24 hours before the meeting

It won't seem like you are badgering them, and it will be enough to get your point across. You are saying that this is important, you are taking it seriously, and you intend on running this analysis with as much professionalism as possible.

That was scheduling 101, so now let's jump into the interview process itself. The agenda you sent out should list the scope of this meeting. In other words, you should have done enough investigative work at this point to be able to outline to the interviewees just what it is you are trying to accomplish and with what system or service. It's also important for them to know that this is a business-critical function and in order for the company to become aware of the impact of a loss, this meeting must take place.

With each subsequent meeting with an individual or group of individuals, be sure to use separate interview forms that will be placed in your information portfolio. Document everything, and if possible, ask the person(s) for permission to record the conversation in order to be as thorough as possible during this analysis. The information out of these meetings is very important; it will dictate the direction for the DR plan as it pertains to this particular business unit's system or service. At this point in the interview process, you do not want to dispute with the managers, saying such things as "Oh that would cost too much money to recover it in that way!" Show some restraint and just write down or record their responses to your questions. It's okay to let them know that the shorter the recovery time, the higher the cost associated with it. However, your analysis will have a far greater impact on the managers after you have summarized your report and presented them with the costs of recovery based on their level of expectation than if you try to convince them during the interview. Also try to remember that you invited them to this meeting, so you should listen to what they have to say about their business needs. If you sound as though you are cutting them off at every step, they will be less apt to want to help you during your interview time. Your ability to recover their system is going to be solely based on what they tell you during this meeting. Remember, it's all about IT marketing.

Following are some items to keep in perspective when talking about recovery:

- Legal requirements, such as in an SLA, if any.

- Corporate image. If you are a leader in data widgets and lose a critical data center that tracks the production of your data widgets, what kind of consumer confidence will that build or destroy? What about Wall Street if you are a publicly traded company?

- How much money will you be losing if you can't access this system?

You can create your own forms or use the templates we have here, but basically you should identify the costs associated with a particular system or service unavailability. As you do this, remember to factor in the other components that are dependent on this system as well. You will have to work with your finance team or an outside risk assessment team to come up with some average figures for your industry to qualify how heavy the financial impact would be on your organization. Many of the industry research firms will have this type of information, so if your company subscribes to their service, perhaps you should query their database of information to add into your BIA forms. Suffice it to say that the levels of severity will be driven by the financial impact to be felt. It may be a good idea to frame it in such as way that the financial impacts are in ranges of your selection from 1 to 10 and to associate each level with a recovery window, with 10 having the most financial impact and probably requiring the shortest time of recovery. You will have to determine what these ranges are for your organization.

Phase IV

This is where the real work starts. You need to begin summarizing the information gathered from all of the interviews you conducted. Make sure you include in this report any red flags you have noted, along with risks, business impact, length of time this service or system could be down—including the amount of money lost per day, per hour, or per minute depending on the type of service it is—and the recovery steps. The recovery steps are based on assumptions you have made in the scope of your DR plan; so if you haven't planned to recover from a complete facility loss, do not attempt to build the recovery steps to do so here. Having said that, what you can do is create a list of what is required in order to recover this system, including the following:

- Hardware.
- Software, including OS, applications, and so on.
- Data, include how current the data must be.
- Recovery time, which is dictated by the business unit manager. This is not something we contradict during the initial meeting. At most companies, if the business unit managers believe the recovery of their service must happen in a particular time frame, the cost of building the resiliency they require would come out of their budgets. If that's not the case at your company, we recommend that you still hold back until you deliver your report. We still think that it has a much bigger impact.
- An impact report, listing the financial impact, consumer confidence impact, and so on. This report is at the heart of the BIA and is of critical importance to the business unit and upper management.

Email Examples

Here we have included some email examples you can use as is or modify to make this process a little easier. Figure E.1 briefly outlines what we plan to accomplish and requests the presence of this individual at the discovery meeting.

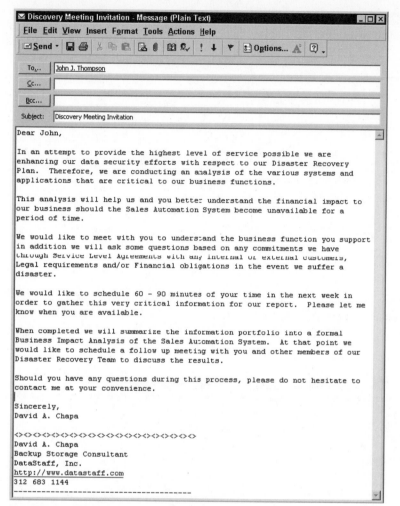

Figure E.1 Discovery meeting invitation.

Figure E.2 shows an example of an email that should be sent out within 24 hours of receiving a confirmation from the interviewee that he or she will be attending the meeting.

Figure E.3 is the agenda email that should be sent at least 48 hours prior to the actual meeting.

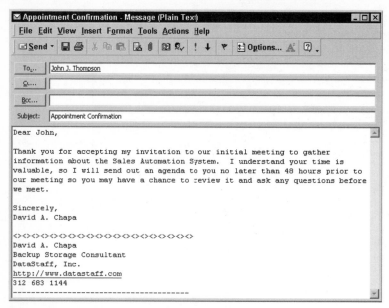

Figure E.2 Appointment confirmation email.

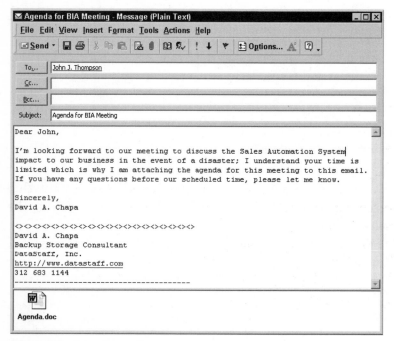

Figure E.3 Agenda email.

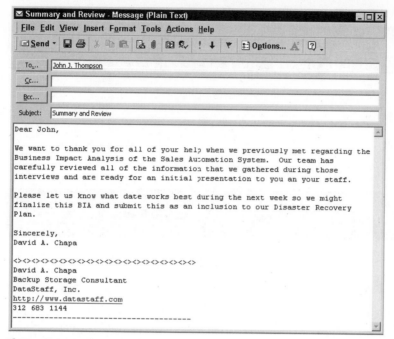

Figure E.4 Review email.

Figure E.4 shows the email that should be sent out after the meeting. In it, you should summarize the discussion and review any remaining issues that will need to be followed up on.

Forms and Resources

Building your information portfolio begins with a formal process. Therefore, it is important to have some level of consistency when you begin. We have included some sample forms and reports that you might find useful in your organization. If you choose not to use these forms, at least use something that can be reused by other members of your team. Inconsistent information portfolios are basically worthless when you are trying to coordinate disaster recovery plans. To begin the information portfolio, use this first worksheet shown in Table E.1, Preliminary List, as a brainstorming tool to identify as many systems or applications you are aware of. Once you decide what application or service you want to assess, you should next use the BIA Assessment Sheet to begin your investigative work and gather the other information listed.

Table E.1 Preliminary List

DATE:				
APP/SERVER/ SERVICE	**SYS. ADMIN/ DATA OWNER**	**BUSINESS UNIT**	**PHONE #**	**BIA (Y/N)**
Dependencies, additional contacts, misc. information:				

DATE:				
APP/SERVER/ SERVICE	**SYS. ADMIN/ DATA OWNER**	**BUSINESS UNIT**	**PHONE #**	**BIA (Y/N)**
Dependencies, additional contacts, misc. information:				

DATE:				
APP/SERVER/ SERVICE	**SYS. ADMIN/ DATA OWNER**	**BUSINESS UNIT**	**PHONE #**	**BIA (Y/N)**
Dependencies, additional contacts, misc. information:				

BIA Assessment Sheet

The BIA Assessment Sheet is the beginning of the information portfolio. This will only be as complete as you are thorough; therefore, never think it unprofessional to ask additional questions and for additional information. Remind the individuals that you are gathering this information only to ensure that this report is sufficiently complete to make a recovery as smooth as possible.

Your assessment sheet should include the following:

- Date the report is created
- Application/system being used
- System administration support person's name and phone number
- Business unit manager's name and phone number

Be as thorough as you can in your report, but remember that some of this information will come out in the interviews you conduct. For the application/system, list all other applications or services it depends on. If this is a server, then list all of the applications that it supports and that must be recovered in the event of a disaster. Also make note of what areas of the company would be affected if any of those applications or servers listed were lost.

Start building your interview list. Remember to start at the top and work your way down. For example, start with a vice president of the business unit and explain the situation to him or her, then continue from there. You should definitely interview the system administrator for the server that is being assessed.

Lastly, always leave yourself some room for issues that arise either during the initial conversations regarding the meetings or just when you have an idea. This will eliminate many loose pieces of paper and the potential for loss or misplacement of them.

Overall Impact Assessment Sheet

The overall impact assessment sheet will help you define during your meetings the financial impact a failure would have on the particular business area you are assessing, corporate image, customer confidence, and any legal ramifications to be concerned with as a result of losing this particular business area's functions for a period of time. The following information should be included in your report:

- Date report is created
- Business area/unit being assessed
- System administration support person's name and phone number
- Business unit manager's name and phone number

Also note what financial loss the company would expect to see should this particular business area experience a disaster, based on the level of importance it holds for the overall business. Table E.2 shows a sample form where you can record this information.

Table E.2 Financial Loss per Outage Duration

OUTAGE DURATION	< 1 HOUR	1 – 12 HOURS	1 DAY	1 WEEK
\<Business Component\>	Enter $$ Amount	Enter $$ Amount	Enter $$ Amount	Enter $$ Amount
\<Business Component\>	Enter $$ Amount	Enter $$ Amount	Enter $$ Amount	Enter $$ Amount
\<Business Component\>	Enter $$ Amount	Enter $$ Amount	Enter $$ Amount	Enter $$ Amount
\<Business Component\>	Enter $$ Amount	Enter $$ Amount	Enter $$ Amount	Enter $$ Amount

NOTE Before completing this form, you should first determine the loss ranges per outage duration.

You will also need to note the following in your report:

- Could this loss have impact on the corporate image?
  - At what point would it impact image negatively?
- What would be the impact to the customers?
  - At what point would it impact the customers negatively?
- Are there any legal ramifications to be concerned with as a result of this loss?
  - At what point would it impact the company legally?

Internet Resources

So many resources are available that we decided to list only a few in Table E.3 to help you with your research. Since the BIAs can be used for all levels of your business, you will find a broad sampling of resources and links that you can visit.

Table E.3   Internet Resources

RESOURCES AND LINKS	URL
Disaster Recovery Journal	www.drj.com
Contingency Planning and Management Magazine	www.contingencyplanning.com
Disaster Recovery Institute International	www.dr.org
FEMA	www.fema.gov
Disaster Links	www.Disasterlinks.com
Disaster Prevention and Recovery Guide	www.system.missouri.edu/records/disaster.html
X-Force Threat Analysis Service	http://xforce.iss.net
The Business Continuity Institute	www.thebci.org
Disaster Recovery Information Exchange	www.drie.org
State of Kansas Business Contingency Planning	http://da.state.ks.us/disc/dr/
SOME VENDORS TO KNOW ABOUT	**URL**
On-Track Data Recovery	www.ontrack.com
Media Recovery	www.mediarecovery.com
ServiceMaster Recovery Management	www.servicemasterrecovery.com/

Summary

This appendix should give you a jump-start on creating business impact analyses for your company or organization. Remember to use an agenda when you conduct an interview and keep it on a professional level at all times. This is a very critical business function you are attempting to document and thus requires focus. Stay with the agenda, keep focused, and if you have a difficult time with the interviews or are not comfortable with interviewing, then we suggest you role-play with other members of your IT staff. Write down notes for yourself if you find that you drift during the role-playing, and create scenarios to help the individuals you are inter-viewing properly appreciate the level of severity you are attempting to plan for. This is a dynamic process, so as the interview takes place, you may have other questions that come up. Write them down on your agenda, and make sure to ask them during the meeting, keeping in mind that the question should be within the context of the agenda you have set forth. Also, ask if you can record the meeting for the purposes of increasing the quality of your analysis.

Performance Test Tech Note

Introduction

This document has been compiled from notes that have been made over the past several years working with NetBackup. Some of the information is original and some has come from other NetBackup Professional Consultants. This was created to assist in the troubleshooting of network performance issue as it relates to NetBackup. Some of the following are undocumented and "unsupported" by Veritas Software, and are provided merely for testing purposes only.

Testing Performance with NetBackup

There are a variety of tests one can perform to identify where the "problems" exist within ones backup environment. This document only covers a few that I have found to be most useful in my capacity as a Consultant working with NetBackup. This document will briefly expose you to some of these ideas and concepts.

Where to Begin

So you have identified that there is some performance problem with some of your backup clients. Perhaps you have noticed it because of some errors you have been receiving or you have been using my clnt_thruput.sh script and started to see a decline in performance for a particular client. Whatever the case may be, you are now here looking at ways to troubleshoot this issue. We have many connection points that could be potential bottlenecks for our backup client. From the client we have CPU, MEMORY, DISK, NIC, just to name a few with a NETWORK in between the client and the server. We could be seeing similar issues with the server as well. So simply saying that we have performance problems is a very broad statement and requires us to "drill down" and narrow that statement a bit. The way we do this is to attempt to divide these areas up as much as possible in order to troubleshoot with as high a level of consistency as possible. Network performance is probably blamed for 90% of the backup performance problems. Why? Because network is the easiest target, well here's to the defense of the network groups out there, it may be your backup server, or the client's disk. It may also be the network, but this document will help us better discern where the problem lies.

Dumping to the "Bit-Bucket"

Now there are a couple of thing that can be done to eliminate the many variables that exist between the client and the server. For our first example, we make an assumption that the client and server are two different machines and therefore will take the network and the server out of the equation and focus solely on the client. What we want to do is test how fast the client can "read" data off of the disk. We do this by having it sent to an infinitely fast device, the bit-bucket or NUL.

From the Client

To see if the client is the bottleneck in the network performance, perform the following using bpbkar, which is in the bin directory where your Net-Backup software is installed. For information's sake, bpbkar is the backup/archive process or daemon that is responsible for file collection and creating the image that will eventually be put on the tape or disk being used for backup. In our example however, we will not be sending data across the network, but redirect STDOUT to NUL and STDERR to a file to be reviewed later. This file will give you the number of files that it processed and the size of the "backup image" that was created, but ultimately sent to

NUL. When you begin this process, you want to select a sizeable amount of data in order to get a fairly accurate representation and you want to simply track the amount of time it takes to process this command. Do not write to the same device you are reading from, this will skew your results.

NT/2000:

This test will use just bpbkar writing to /dev/null (the bit bucket), which eliminates the network portion of the equation.

```
c:\Veritas\Netbackup\bin\bpbkar32.exe -nocont  > NUL 2>   (for NT)
```

```
i.e. c:\Veritas\Netbackup\bin\bpbkar32.exe -nocont c:\ > NUL 2> temp.f
```

temp.f will contain all of the files that bpbkar has collected. This will grow considerably if there is a large file system or directory structure you are testing with. BE WARNED.

From Unix:

```
/usr/openv/netbackup/bin/bpbkar -nocont / > /dev/null 2>
/tmp/files.out
```

Same idea.

From the Server

So now we have taken the testing from the client to the server. Both of these tests will have left the network completely out of the respective equations. If your testing of the client has left you with reasonable results, then it is time to test the server. This may be moot especially if your overall backup performance is good with the exception of a few clients. But as good-natured System Administrators we want to make sure that we have adequate test documentation before we address our network group. Besides it's always good to perform these self-assessments every now and then.

There is an undocumented feature with NetBackup that allows you to eliminate the tape subsystems, disk and drive controllers from the equation and simply write your backups to, yes, the bit-bucket. As I mentioned before this is an infinitely fast device, if we could only write to NUL for all of our backups, our performance issues would go away, but alas we would have no data to show for it, *so we can't*. If you would like to do this, you must understand that there are several CAVEATS and WARNINGS that if you do not heed will have negative effects on your environment. Particularly with this one, will be your inability to restore any data from disk storage units, because the data will just simply not be there.

So here's the reason we want to run this type of test. First of all it will let us know how NetBackup is processing the data. Could there be anything inherently wrong with our NetBackup configuration? Hopefully part one of this test will help us to see that a bit clearer. The second reason we want to run this test, is after we validate our NetBackup Server configuration has been ruled out as the culprit, our client is performing well with its local test, we can test the backup from the client to the server across the network.

Here's how we begin:

1. Create a disk storage unit; even if you already have some created I recommend that you create a new one and call it DISK_STU_TEST or something similar.

2. Now touch /usr/openv/netbackup/bpdm_dev_null or for the WINTEL systems, create an empty file call bpdm_dev_null in the NetBackup directory.

3. Run your test backup.

I usually create a backup policy called special that I use for adhoc backups or testing. You may want to do something similar to avoid any modifications of your production backup policies. Whatever you decide to do, make sure you select the DISK_STU_TEST storage unit to be used by the test backup policy. When this backup job runs, the fragments will be created but the file length will remain 0 and bpdm will write the image to the bit-bucket (i.e. /dev/null).

NOTE When you back up to a disk storage unit, bptm (backup tape manager) daemon or process will not be invoked, rather bpdm (backup disk manager) will be. Therefore if the test proves to be successful, then we may be looking at a tuning issue with regard to shared memory and/or tape buffers.

Since we are sending all of the image data to NUL, we will not be able to restore any of this data that we backed up during our test. This is true for ALL disk storage units created on this particular media server. You must remember to DELETE bpdm_dev_null after your testing is complete.

If you touch the file, you should see the following in bpdm debug log for backups:

```
> really writing to /dev/null
```

This tells us that we have created the storage unit correctly for this test and that any other subsequent backups to a disk storage unit on this media server will really write to /dev/null.

Caveats:

- Don't try restores.

- Doing this affects ALL disk-based backups on the server (all go to null).

- I have been told that while it has yet to be proven, it may cause problems with tape based backups as well. I personally haven't had this experience.

- Doing this leaves extra information lying around in NB databases.

- Expire any images that you create with this test after the test is over using the bpexpdate command.

- When you are done remove the /usr/openv/netbackup/ bpdm_dev_null file.

Using FTP

The final test is simply using FTP. We have now tested and timed the backup at the client to the bit bucket, client to the server to the bit bucket and now we want to try the network, from the client to the server. This will tell us if we are looking at a client issue, server issue or network issue. If anything it will give us good information as to how to proceed resolving our performance problem.

Run this test from the client, then from the server and evaluate both findings to determine the next step.

1. FTP from the client to the server, then server to client.

2. FTP something large enough to measure (1 GB preferably).

While this may not seem like a real test, it does accomplish something for us. We are able to transfer data OUTSIDE of the backup application, allowing us to compare the times with FTP and the times with backup. With all of this information and testing complete, the profile of the client backup should be relatively clear and we should be able to at least determine where the root cause of the problem exists. If this is not the case, open a support call with VERITAS. Be prepared to submit all of your documentation to them, so you can avoid any lost time resolving your issue.

Summary

These tests should prove quite helpful to you. I'm sure there are a dozen more that I haven't even thought of, but these have always worked well for me. If there is a final word I can leave with you it would be to document, document, document. As much as we all loathe the thought, it is central to everything we do. Our environments would be completely unmanageable without it. Every ounce of documentation gives you and your staff the confidence to administer, maintain and troubleshoot your NetBackup environment.

NetBackup Performance Tuning on Windows

Document Description

This document contains information on ways to optimize NetBackup on Windows systems. It is relevant for NetBackup 4.5 and for earlier releases. This document is intended, primarily for system administrators, to provide a guide for NetBackup performance evaluation. It is not intended to provide tuning advice for particular systems. If you would like help fine-tuning your system, please contact the VERITAS consulting service.

Introduction to NetBackup Performance

Before we examine the factors that affect backup performance, please note that an important first step is to ensure that your system meets Net-Backup's recommended minimum requirements. Refer to your *NetBackup Installation Guide* and *Release Notes* for information about these requirements. Additionally, we recommend that you have the most recent Net-Backup software patch installed. For example, if you are testing with NetBackup 3.4x, patch 341_2 includes significant restore performance enhancement to tar32.exe.

The final measure of performance is the length of time required for backup operations to complete (usually known as the *backup window*), or the length of time required for a critical restore operation to complete. However, in order to measure performance and then use those measurements to implement changes to improve performance, a performance metric more reliable and reproducible than simple wall clock time should be used. We will discuss these types of metrics in this document.

Many performance issues can be traced to hardware or other environmental issues. A basic understanding of the *entire data transfer path* is essential in determining the maximum obtainable performance in your environment. Poor performance is often the result of poor planning, which can be based on unrealistic expectations of any particular component of the data transfer path.

The slowest component in the data transfer path (for a backup, the path usually starts at the data on the disk and ends with a backup copy on tape) will be the bottleneck that will limit the overall performance of NetBackup. For example, a fast tape drive combined with an overloaded server will yield poor performance. Similarly, a slow network combined with a fast tape drive will also yield poor performance.

This document subdivides the standard NetBackup data transfer path into four basic components: the NetBackup client, the network, the NetBackup server, and the storage device. While it may be useful to subdivide the data transfer path even further in some installations, to identify and ease specific bottlenecks, these four components offer a good general approach to illustrate the 'divide and conquer' approach to improving overall NetBackup performance.

This document discusses NetBackup performance evaluation and improvement from a testing perspective. It describes ways to isolate performance variables in order to get a sense of the effect each variable has on overall system performance, and to optimize NetBackup performance with regTard to that variable. It may not be possible to optimize every variable on your production system.

This document was written with file system backups in mind. Database backups may have different requirements.

Measuring NetBackup Performance

Once you have established an accurate metric as described here, you can measure the current performance of NetBackup and your system components to compile a baseline performance benchmark. Once you have a baseline, you can apply changes in a controlled way. By measuring performance after each change, you can accurately measure the effect of each change on NetBackup's performance.

The following topics are covered in this section:

- Controlling system variables for consistent testing conditions
- Evaluating performance through the Activity Monitor and the All Log Entries report
- Evaluating system components, such as your CPU and memory

Controlling System Variables for Consistent Testing Conditions

For reliable performance evaluation, eliminate as many unpredictable variables as possible in order to create a consistent backup environment. Only a consistent environment will produce reliable and reproducible performance measurements. Some of the variables to consider are described below as they relate to the NetBackup server, the network, the NetBackup client, or the data itself.

Server Variables

Of course, it is important to eliminate all other NetBackup activity from your environment when you are measuring the performance of a particular NetBackup operation. One area which you must consider during this process is the automatic scheduling of backup jobs by the NetBackup scheduler.

When policies are created, they are usually set up to allow the Net-Backup scheduler to initiate the backups. The NetBackup scheduler will initiate backups based on the traditional NetBackup frequency-based scheduling or on certain days of the week, month, or other time interval. This process is called calendar-based scheduling and is new in NetBackup 4.5. As part of the backup policy definition, the **Start Window** is used to indicate when the NetBackup scheduler can start backups using either frequency-based or calendar-based scheduling. When you perform backups for the purpose of performance testing, this setup might interfere since the NetBackup scheduler may initiate backups unexpectedly; especially if the operations you intend to measure run for an extended period of time.

The simplest way to prevent the NetBackup scheduler from running backup jobs during your performance testing (assuming you are testing the performance of a backup job), is to create a new policy specifically for use in performance testing and to leave the **Start Window** field blank in the schedule definition for that policy. This prevents the NetBackup scheduler from initiating any backups automatically for that policy. After creating the policy, you can run the backup on demand by using the `Manual Backup` command from the NetBackup Administration Console.

To prevent the NetBackup scheduler from running backup jobs unrelated to the performance test, you may want to set all other backup policies to inactive by using the `Deactivate` command from the NetBackup Administration Console. Of course, you must reactivate the policies to start running backups again.

You can use a user-directed backup to run the performance test as well. However, we suggest using the manual backup option for a policy, (or immediate backup, as it is sometimes called) instead of a user-directed backup to more closely simulate initiation of a backup job by the NetBackup Scheduler. Additionally, if you use a manual backup, the backup policy will contain the entire definition of the backup job, including the clients and files that are part of the performance test. Confining the definition of the backup job to a single location makes it easier to manage changes to the definition, which in turn makes reliable performance test results more likely.

You may want to consider changing the wakeup interval for the NetBackup Scheduler to a larger value for the duration of performance testing. Use the Global NetBackup Attributes tab of the Master Server Properties dialog to modify the wakeup interval. Access the Master Server Properties dialog through the Host Properties node of the NetBackup Administration Console in release 4.5, or the Configure NetBackup GUI in earlier releases. The wakeup interval controls how often the NetBackup Scheduler examines the policy definitions on the master server to determine if there are any new backup jobs to start. If there are a large number of NetBackup policies defined for the master server, this action by the Scheduler may affect the performance test. Setting the wakeup interval to a large value, such as 1440 (24 hours) will avoid any impact of this processing on the performance test.

Be aware that changing the wakeup interval will not reflect performance in your actual production environment. For more realistic results, use the wakeup interval specified in your production environment.

Before you start the performance test, check the Activity Monitor to make sure there is no NetBackup processing currently in progress. Similarly, check the Activity Monitor after the performance test for unexpected activity (such as an unanticipated restore job) that may have occurred during the test.

Additionally, check for non-NetBackup activity on the server during the performance test and try to reduce or eliminate it.

Network Variables

Network performance is key to achieving optimum performance with NetBackup. Ideally, you would use a completely separate network for performance testing to avoid the possibility of skewing the results by encountering unrelated network activity during the course of the test.

In many cases, a separate network is not available. Ensure that non-NetBackup activity is kept to an absolute minimum during the time you are evaluating performance. If possible, schedule testing for times when backups are not active. Even occasional short bursts of network activity may be enough to skew the results during portions of the performance test. If you are sharing the same network as any production backups occurring for other systems, you must account for this activity during the performance test.

Another network variable you must consider is host name resolution. NetBackup depends heavily upon a timely resolution of host names to operate correctly. If you have any delays in host name resolution, including reverse name lookup to identify a server name from an incoming connection from a certain IP address, you may want to eliminate that delay by using the HOSTS file for host name resolution on systems involved in your performance test environment.

Client Variables

Make sure the client system is in a relatively quiescent state during performance testing. A lot of activity, especially disk-intensive activity such as virus scanning, will limit the data transfer rate and skew the results of your tests.

One possible mistake is to allow another NetBackup server, such as a production backup server, to have access to the client during the course of the test. This may result in NetBackup attempting to backup the same client to two different servers at the same time, which would severely impact the results of a performance test in progress at that time.

Different file systems have different performance characteristics. For example, comparing data throughput results from operations on a FAT file system to those from operations on an NTFS system may not be valid, even if the systems are otherwise identical. If you do need to make such a comparison, factor the difference between the file systems into your performance evaluation testing, and into any conclusions you may draw from that testing.

Take care when OTM (Open Transaction Manager) is enabled to back up open files on the client during performance testing. OTM will delay for a certain amount of time waiting for the disk drive to quiesce. This delay can vary from one performance test run to the next, causing unreliable results. You may want to disable OTM on the client during performance testing if it is not needed to back up open files and avoid this unpredictable delay.

Data Variables

Monitoring the data you are backing up improves the repeatability of performance testing. If possible, move the data you will use for testing backups to its own drive or logical partition (not a mirrored drive), and defragment the drive before you begin performance testing. For testing restores, start with an empty disk drive or a recently defragmented disk drive with ample empty space. This will help reduce the impact of disk fragmentation, etc., on the NetBackup performance test run and yield more consistent results between test runs.

Similarly, for testing backups to tape, always start each test run with an empty piece of media. You can do this by expiring existing images for that piece of media through the Catalog node of the NetBackup Administration Console (new in release 4.5), or by running the bpexpdate command. Another approach is to use the bpmedia command to freeze any media containing existing backup images so that NetBackup selects a new piece of media for the backup operation. This step will help reduce the impact of tape positioning, etc., on the NetBackup performance test run and will yield more consistent results between test runs. When you test restores from tape, always restore from the same backup image on the tape to achieve consistent results between test runs.

In general, using a large data set will generate a more reliable and reproducible performance test than a small data set. A performance test using a small data set would probably be skewed by startup and shutdown overhead within the NetBackup operation. These variables are difficult to keep consistent between test runs and are therefore likely to produce inconsistent test results. Using a large data set will minimize the effect of start up and shutdown times.

Design the makeup of the dataset to represent the makeup of the data in the intended production environment. For example, if the data set in the production environment contains many small files on file servers, then the data set for the performance testing should also contain many small files.

A representative test data set will more accurately predict the NetBackup performance that you can reasonably expect in a production environment.

The type of data can help reveal bottlenecks in the system. Files consisting of non-compressible (random) data cause the tape drive to run at its lower rated speed. As long as the other components of the data transfer path are keeping up, you may identify the tape drive as the bottleneck. On the other hand, files consisting of highly-compressible data can be processed at higher rates by the tape drive when hardware compression is enabled. This scenario may result in a higher overall throughput and possibly expose the network as the bottleneck.

Many values in NetBackup provide data amounts in KB and rates in KB/Sec. For greater accuracy, divide by 1024 rather than rounding off to 1000 when you convert from KB to MB or from KB/Sec. to MB/Sec.

Evaluating Performance

There are two primary locations from which NetBackup data throughput performance statistics can be obtained for a NetBackup operation: the NetBackup Activity Monitor and the NetBackup All Log Entries report. The choice of which location to use is determined by the type of NetBackup operation you are measuring: non-multiplexed backup, restore, or multiplexed backup.

You can obtain statistics for all three types of operations from the NetBackup All Log Entries report. You can obtain statistics for non-multiplexed backup or restore operations from the NetBackup Activity Monitor (statistics for restore operations are newly available in the Activity Monitor with the 4.5 release). For multiplexed backup operations, you can obtain the overall statistics from the All Log Entries report after all the individual backup operations which are part of the multiplexed backup are complete. In this case, the statistics available in the Activity Monitors for each of the individual backup operations are relative only to that operation, and do not reflect the actual total data throughput to the tape drive.

There may be small differences between the statistics available from these two locations due to slight differences in rounding techniques between the entries in the Activity Monitor and the entries in the All Logs report. Therefore, we suggest you pick one location from which to obtain statistics and consistently use it to compare performance between test runs.

Evaluating Performance Through the NetBackup Activity Monitor

1. Run the backup or restore job (restore job statistics available only in the 4.5 release).

2. Open the NetBackup Activity Monitor.

3. Verify the backup or restore job completed successfully.

   A **0** should appear in the status column.

4. View the details for the job by selecting the **Details** menu option, or by double-clicking on the entry for the job.

5. Select the **Detailed Status** tab.

6. Obtain the NetBackup performance statistics from the following fields:

   - **Started/Ended:** These fields show the time window during which the backup or restore job took place.

   - **Elapsed:** This field shows the total elapsed time from when the job was initiated to job completion and can be used as an indication of total wall clock time for the operation.

   - **KB/sec:** This is the data throughput rate.

   - **Current Kilobytes Written:** Compare this value to the amount of data. Although it should be comparable, the NetBackup data amount will be slightly higher because of administrative information, known as metadata, saved for the backed up data.

   For example, if you display properties for a directory containing 500 files, each 1 MB in size, the directory shows a size of 500 MB, or 524,288,000 bytes, which is equal to 512,000 KB. The NetBackup report may show 513,255 KB written, reporting an extra 1,255 KB than provided through viewing the directory's properties. This is true for a flat directory. Subdirectory structures may diverge due to the way the operating system tracks used and available space on the disk. Also, be aware that the operating system may be reporting how much space was allocated for the files in question, not just how much data is actually there. For example, if the allocation block size is 1 KB, 1000 1 byte files will report a total size of 1 MB, even though 1 KB of data is all that exists. The greater the number of files, the larger this discrepancy may become.

Evaluating Performance Using the All Log Entries Report

1. Run the backup or restore job.

2. Run the All Log Entries report from the NetBackup reports node in the NetBackup Administrative Console in release 4.5, or the Net-Backup Reports GUI in earlier releases. Be sure that the Date/Time Range that you select covers the time period during which the job was run.

3. Verify that the job completed successfully by searching for an entry such as "the requested operation was successfully completed" for a backup, or "successfully read (restore) backup id . . . " for a restore.

4. Obtain the NetBackup performance statistics from the following entries in the report. (Note that the entries shown here are based on release 4.5. The entries for earlier releases will be the same or similar.)

ENTRY	STATISTIC
`started backup job for client <`*name*`>, policy <`*name*`>, schedule <`*name*`> on storage unit <`*name*`>`	The **Date** and **Time** fields for this entry show the time at which the backup job started.
`successfully wrote backup id <`*name*`>, copy <`*number*`>, <`*number*`> Kbytes`	For a multiplexed backup, this entry shows the size of the individual backup job and the **Date** and **Time** fields show the time at which the job finished writing to the storage device. The overall statistics for the multiplexed backup group, including the data throughput rate to the storage device, are found in a subsequent entry below.
`successfully wrote <`*number*`> of <`*number*`> multiplexed backups, total Kbytes <`*number*`> at Kbytes/sec`	For multiplexed backups, this entry shows the overall statistics for the multiplexed backup group including the data throughput rate.
`successfully wrote backup id <`*name*`>, copy <`*number*`>, fragment <`*number*`>, <`*number*`> Kbytes at <`*number*`> Kbytes/sec`	For non-multiplexed backups, this entry essentially combines the information in the previous two entries for multiplexed backups into one entry showing the size of the backup job, the data throughput rate, and the time, in the **Date** and **Time** fields, at which the job finished writing to the storage device.

(continued)

ENTRY	STATISTIC
`the requested operation was successfully completed`	The **Date** and **Time** fields for this entry show the time at which the backup job completed. This value is later than the "successfully wrote" entry above because it includes extra processing time at the end of the job for tasks such as NetBackup image validation.
`begin reading backup id <`*name*`>, (restore), copy <`*number*`>, fragment <`*number*`> from media id <`*name*`> on drive index <`*number*`>`	The **Date** and **Time** fields for this entry show the time at which the restore job started reading from the storage device. (Note that the latter part of the entry is not shown for restores from disk, as it does not apply.)
`successfully restored from backup id <`*name*`>, copy <`*number*`>, <`*number*`> Kbytes`	For a multiplexed restore (generally speaking, all restores from tape are multiplexed restores as non-multiplexed restores require additional action from the user), this entry shows the size of the individual restore job and the **Date** and **Time** fields show the time at which the job finished reading from the storage device. The overall statistics for the multiplexed restore group, including the data throughput rate, are found in a subsequent entry below.
`successfully restored <`*number*`> of <`*number*`> requests <`*name*`>, read total of <`*number*`> Kbytes at <`*number*`> Kbytes/sec`	For multiplexed restores, this entry shows the overall statistics for the multiplexed restore group, including the data throughput rate.
`successfully read (restore) backup id media <`*number*`>, copy <`*number*`>, fragment <`*number*`>, <`*number*`> Kbytes at <`*number*`> Kbytes/sec`	For non-multiplexed restores (generally speaking, only restores from disk are treated as non-multiplexed restores), this entry essentially combines the information from the previous two entries for multiplexed restores into one entry showing the size of the restore job, the data throughput rate, and the time, in the **Date** and **Time** fields, at which the job finished reading from the storage device.

Additional Information

The NetBackup All Log Entries report will also have entries similar to those described above for other NetBackup operations such as image duplication operations used to create additional copies of a backup image. Those entries have a very similar format and may be useful for analyzing the performance of NetBackup for those operations.

The `bptm` debug log file will contain the entries that are in the All Log Entries report, as well as additional detail about the operation that may be useful for performance analysis. One example of this additional detail is the intermediate data throughput rate message for multiplexed backups, as shown below:

```
... intermediate after <number> successful, <number> Kbytes at <number>
Kbytes/sec
```

This message is generated whenever an individual backup job completes that is part of a multiplexed backup group. In the debug log file for a multiplexed backup group consisting of three individual backup jobs, for example, there could be two intermediate status lines, then the final (overall) throughput rate.

For a backup operation, the `bpbkar` debug log file will also contain additional detail about the operation that may be useful for performance analysis. One such example would be data regarding the delay involved in initializing OTM to back up open files on the NetBackup client.

Keep in mind, however, that writing the debug log files during the NetBackup operation introduces some overhead that would not normally be present in a production environment. Factor that additional overhead into any calculations done on data captures while debug log files are in use.

See the *NetBackup Troubleshooting Guide* to learn how to set up NetBackup to write these debug log files during the NetBackup operation.

Evaluating System Components

In addition to evaluating NetBackup's performance, you should also verify that common system resources are in adequate supply. You may want to use the Windows Performance Monitor utility included with Windows NT or Windows 2000. For information about using the Performance Monitor, refer to your Microsoft documentation.

The Performance Monitor organizes information by *object*, *counter*, and *instance*.

An *object* is a system resource category, such as a processor or physical disk. Properties of an object are *counters*. Counters for the **Processor** object include **%Processor Time**, which is the default counter, and **Interrupts/sec**. Duplicate counters are handled via *instances*. For example, to monitor the **%Processor Time** of a specific CPU on a multiple CPU system, the **Processor** object is selected, then the **%Processor Time** counter for that object is selected, followed by the specific CPU instance for the counter.

When you use the Performance Monitor, you can view data in real time format or collect the data in a log for future analysis. Specific components to evaluate include CPU load, memory use, and disk load.

Monitoring CPU Load

To determine if the system has enough power to accomplish the requested tasks, monitor the **% Processor Time** counter for the **Processor** object to determine how hard the CPU is working, and monitor the **Process Queue Length** counter for the **System** object to determine how many processes are actively waiting for the processor.

For **% Processor Time**, values of 0 to 80 percent are generally considered safe. Values from 80 percent to 90 percent indicate that the system is being pushed hard, while consistent values above 90 percent indicate that the CPU is a bottleneck.

Spikes approaching 100 percent are normal and do not necessarily indicate a bottleneck. However, if sustained loads approaching 100 percent are observed, efforts to tune the system to decrease process load or an upgrade to a faster processor should be considered.

Sustained **Processor Queue Lengths** greater than two indicate too many threads are waiting to be executed. To correctly monitor the **Processor Queue Length** counter, the Performance Monitor must be tracking a thread-related counter. If you consistently see a queue length of 0, verify that a non-zero value can be displayed.

The default scale for the **Processor Queue Length** may not be equal to 1. Be sure to read the data correctly. For example, if the default scale is 10x, then a reading of 40 actually means that only 4 processes are waiting.

Monitoring Memory Use

Memory is a critical resource for increasing the performance of backup operations. When you examine memory usage, view information on:

Committed Bytes.   Committed Bytes displays the size of virtual memory that has been committed, as opposed to reserved. Committed memory must have disk storage available or must not require the disk storage because the main memory is large enough. If the number of Committed Bytes approaches or exceeds the amount of physical memory, you may encounter problems with page swapping.

Page Faults/sec.   Page Faults/sec is a count of the page faults in the processor. A page fault occurs when a process refers to a virtual memory page that is not in its Working Set in main memory. A high Page Fault rate may indicate insufficient memory.

Monitoring Disk Load

To use disk performance counters to monitor the disk performance in Performance Monitor, you may need to enable those counters. Windows may not have enabled the disk performance counters by default for your system.

For more information about disk performance counters, from a command prompt, type:

```
diskperf -help
```

To enable these counters and allow disk monitoring:

1. From a command prompt, type:

    ```
    diskperf -y
    ```

2. Reboot the system.

To disable these counters and cancel disk monitoring:

1. From a command prompt, type:

    ```
    diskperf -n
    ```

2. Reboot the system.

When you monitor disk performance, use the **%Disk Time** counter for the **PhysicalDisk** object to track the percentage of elapsed time that the selected disk drive is busy servicing read or write requests.

Also monitor the **Avg. Disk Queue Length** counter and watch for values greater than 1 that last for more than one second. Values greater than 1 for more than a second indicate that multiple processes are waiting for the disk to service their requests.

Several techniques may be used to increase disk performance, including:

Check the fragmentation level of the data.   A highly fragmented disk limits throughput levels. Use a disk maintenance utility to defragment the disk.

Consider adding additional disks to the system to increase performance.   If multiple processes are attempting to log data simultaneously, dividing the data among multiple physical disks may help.

Determine if the data transfer involves a compressed disk.   The use of Windows NT compression to automatically compress the data on the drive adds additional overhead to disk read or write operations, adversely affecting the performance of NetBackup. Only use Windows NT compression if it is needed to avoid a disk full condition.

Consider converting to a system based on a Redundant Array of Inexpensive Disks (RAID).   Though more expensive, RAID devices generally offer greater throughput, and, (depending on the RAID level employed), improved reliability.

Determine what type of controller technology is being used to drive the disk.   Consider if a different system would yield better results. The following table shows some typical throughput rates for common controllers:

CONTROLLER TECHNOLOGY	MAX TRANSFER RATE	# DEVICES
BIOS Hard disk (MFM, RLL, ESDI)	8MB/s	2
IDE	5MB/s	2
SCSI	5MB/s	7
SCSI-2 Fast	10MB/s	7
SCSI-2 Wide	20MB/s	7
SCSI-2 F/W	40MB/s	7
Ultra SCSI	80MB/s	15

NetBackup Client Performance

This section lists some factors to consider when you evaluate the NetBackup client component of the NetBackup data transfer path. Examine these conditions to identify possible changes that may improve the overall performance of NetBackup.

Disk Fragmentation.   Fragmentation is a condition where data is scattered around the disk in non-contiguous blocks. This condition severely impacts the data transfer rate from the disk. Fragmentation can be repaired using hard disk management utility software offered by a variety of vendors.

Virus Scanning.   If virus scanning is turned on for the system, it may severely impact the performance of the NetBackup client during a backup or restore operation. This may be especially true for systems such as large NT file servers. You may wish to disable virus scanning during backup or restore operations to avoid the impact on performance.

NetBackup Notify Scripts.   The `bpstart_notify.bat` and `bpend_notify.bat` scripts are very useful in certain situations, such as shutting down a running application to back up its data. However, these scripts must be written with care to avoid any unnecessary lengthy delays at the start or end of the backup job. If the scripts are not performing tasks essential to the backup operation, you may want to remove them.

NetBackup Software Location.   If the data being backed up is located on the same physical disk drive as the NetBackup installation, performance may be adversely affected, especially if NetBackup debug log files are being used. If they are being used, the extent of the degradation will be greatly influenced by the NetBackup verbose setting for the debug logs. If possible, install NetBackup on a separate physical disk drive to avoid this disk drive contention.

Open Transaction Manager (OTM).   When OTM is enabled, there is a delay at the start of the backup while information is gathered about the volumes being snapped and while the OTM driver is waiting for the disk activity to quiesce. In some cases, there will be an additional delay while OTM creates the snapshot cache file. NetBackup transfer rates are affected by this delay because NetBackup treats the start of the data transfer as the time that the backup process is started on the client. You may wish to disable OTM to eliminate this delay unless it is needed to back up open files.

Job Tracker.   If the NetBackup Client Job Tracker is running on the client, then NetBackup will gather an estimate of the data to be backed up prior to the start of a backup job. Gathering this estimate will affect the startup time, and therefore the data throughput rate, because no data is being written to the NetBackup server during this estimation phase. You may wish to avoid running the NetBackup Client Job Tracker to avoid this delay.

Client Location.   You may wish to consider adding a locally attached tape device to the client and changing the client to a NetBackup media server if you have a substantial amount of data on the client. For example, backing up 100 GBs of data to a locally attached tape drive will generally be more efficient than backing up the same amount of data across a network connection to a NetBackup server. Of course, there are many variables to consider, such as the bandwidth available on the network, that will affect the decision to back up the data to a locally attached tape drive as opposed to moving the data across the network.

Determining the Theoretical Performance of the NetBackup Client Software. There is a useful feature in the NetBackup client software utility `bpbkar32` that may be used to determine the speed at which the NetBackup client can read the data to be backed up from the disk drive. This feature can be used to eliminate as a possible performance bottleneck the speed at which the data can be read when you are attempting to improve a poorly performing NetBackup installation. Use the following syntax for this utility:

```
bpbkar32 -nocont <filepath> > NUL 2 > NUL
```

In the above syntax, *<filepath>* would be replaced with the path to the data to be read from the disk, C:\ for example. Using this syntax simulates an infinitely fast speed for the other components of the NetBackup data transfer path, such as the network.

You can view the performance statistics of the operation in the `bpbkar` debug log file, or use a stopwatch to time the operation and then manually calculate the performance statistics.

NetBackup Network Performance

This section lists some factors to consider when you evaluate the network component of the NetBackup data transfer path to identify possible changes that may improve the overall performance of NetBackup.

Network Load.   There are two key considerations to monitor when you evaluate remote backup performance:

- The amount of network traffic
- The amount of time that network traffic is high

Small bursts of high network traffic for short durations will have some negative impact on the data throughput rate. However, if the network traffic remains consistently high for a significant amount of time during the operation, the network component of the NetBackup data transfer path will very likely be the bottleneck. Always try to schedule backups during times when network traffic is low. If your network is heavily loaded, you may wish to implement a secondary network which can be dedicated to backup and restore traffic.

NetBackup Media Server Network Buffer Size.   The NetBackup media server has a tunable parameter that you can use to adjust the size of the Winsock2 network communications buffer used to receive data from the network (a backup) or write data to the network (a restore). This parameter specifies the value that is used to call the setsockopt() Winsock2 API to set the network buffer size for backups (SO_RCVBUF) and restores (SO_SNDBUF).

The default value for this parameter in release 3.4.1 and earlier is 32032 bytes. In release 4.5, the default value for this parameter is derived from the NetBackup data buffer size (see below for more information about the data buffer size) using the following formula:

For backup jobs: (*<data_buffer_size>* * 4) + 1024

For restore jobs: (*<data_buffer_size>* * 2) + 1024

Because the default value for the NetBackup data buffer size is 65536 bytes, this formula results in a default value of 263168 bytes for backups and 132096 bytes for restores.

To set this parameter, create the following files:

> *<install_path>*\NetBackup\NET_BUFFER_SZ
>
> *<install_path>*\NetBackup\NET_BUFFER_SZ_REST
>
> (new in 4.5, not used in earlier releases)

These files contain a single integer specifying the network buffer size in bytes. For example, to use a network buffer size of 64 KB, the file would contain 65536. If the files contain the integer 0 (zero), the setsockopt() Winsock2 API call will be skipped and the system default value for the network buffer size will be used.

If the NET_BUFFER_SZ file exists, its contents will be used to specify the network buffer size for both backup and restores.

If the NET_BUFFER_SZ_REST file exists (only in 4.5), its contents will be used to specify the network buffer size for restores.

If both files exist, the NET_BUFFER_SZ file will be used to specify the network buffer size for backups, and the NET_BUFFER_SZ_REST file will be used to specify the network buffer size for restores.

Because local backup or restore jobs on the media server do not send data over the network, this parameter has no effect on those operations. It is used only by the NetBackup media server processes which read from or write to the network, specifically, the bptm or bpdm processes. It is not used by any other NetBackup for Windows processes on a master server, media server, or client.

This parameter is the counterpart on the media server to the Communications Buffer Size parameter on the client, which is described below. The network buffer sizes are not required to be the same on all of your NetBackup systems for NetBackup to function properly, however, setting the Network Buffer Size parameter on the media server and the Communications Buffer Size parameter on the client (see below) to the same value has achieved the best performance in some NetBackup installations.

Similarly, the network buffer size does not have a direct relationship with the NetBackup data buffer size (see below). They are separately tunable parameters. However, as you can see by the default value for network buffer size in release 4.5, setting the network buffer to a substantially larger value than the data buffer has achieved the best performance in many NetBackup installations.

Tuning this parameter along with the Communications Buffer Size parameter on the client has resulted in significant improvements in the throughput of the network component of the NetBackup data transfer path in some NetBackup installations.

NetBackup Client Communications Buffer Size. The NetBackup client has a tunable parameter that you can use to adjust the size of the Winsock2 network communications buffer used to write data to the network for backups. This parameter specifies the value that is used to call the setsockopt() Winsock2 API to set the network buffer size for backups (SO_SNDBUF).

This parameter is the counterpart on the client to the Network Buffer Size parameter on the media server, described above. As mentioned, the network buffer sizes are not required to be the same on all of your NetBackup systems for NetBackup to function properly. However, setting the Network Buffer Size parameter on the media server (see above) and the Communications Buffer Size parameter on the client to the same value achieves the best performance in some NetBackup installations.

To set the Communications Buffer Size parameter:

1. From **Host Properties** in the NetBackup Administration Console in release 4.5, or from the Configure NetBackup GUI in earlier releases, open the **Client Properties** dialog for the client on which the parameter is to be changed.

2. From the Windows Client tab, set the Communications buffer size: field.

This parameter is specified in number of kilobytes. The default value is 32. An extra kilobyte is added internally for backup operations (SO_SNDBUF). Therefore, the default network buffer size for backups is 33792 bytes. In some NetBackup installations, this default value is too small. Increasing the value to 128 improves performance in these installations.

Another way to set this parameter is to configure the Buffer_Size parameter in the registry.

Locate the following key under HKEY_LOCAL_MACHINE

```
Software/VERITAS/NetBackup/CurrentVersion/Config
```

Add or modify the Buffer_Size value, which is a REG_DWORD value. Set it to 0x20.

Because local backup jobs on the media server do not send data over the network, this parameter has no effect on these local operations. This parameter is used by only the NetBackup client processes which write to the network, specifically, the bpbkar32 process. It is not used by any other NetBackup for Windows processes on a master server, media server, or client.

NetBackup Server Performance

This section lists some factors to consider when you evaluate the NetBackup server component of the NetBackup data transfer path to identify possible changes that may improve the overall performance of NetBackup.

Number and Size of Shared Data Buffers. By default, NetBackup uses eight shared data buffers for a multiplexed backup, 16 shared data buffers for a non-multiplexed backup, 12 shared data buffers for a multiplexed restore, and 16 shared data buffers for a non-multiplexed restore.

To change these settings, create the following file(s):

```
<install_path>\NetBackup\db\config\NUMBER_DATA_BUFFERS
<install_path>\NetBackup\db\config\NUMBER_DATA_BUFFERS_RESTORE
```

These files contain a single integer specifying the number of shared data buffers NetBackup will use.

If the NUMBER_DATA_BUFFERS file exists, its contents will be used to determine the number of shared data buffers to be used for multiplexed and non-multiplexed backups.

If the NUMBER_DATA_BUFFERS_RESTORE file exists, its contents will be used to determine the number of shared data buffers to be used for multiplexed restores.

By default, NetBackup uses 64 KB (65536 bytes) as the size of each shared data buffer. A single tape I/O operation is performed for each shared data buffer. Therefore, this size must not exceed the maximum block size for the tape device or operating system. For Windows systems, the maximum block size is generally 64 KB, although in some cases customers are using a larger value successfully.

For this reason, the terms 'tape block size' and 'shared data buffer size' are synonymous in this context.

The NetBackup media server will query the tape device for its maximum block size, and cause the backup operation to fail if the shared data buffer size exceeds the value that is returned.

NOTE Some tape devices may not reliably return this information. Therefore, it is critical to perform both backup and restore testing if the shared data buffer size value is changed. If all NetBackup media servers are not running in the same operating system environment, it is critical to test restores on each of the NetBackup media servers that may be involved in a restore operation. For example, if a UNIX NetBackup media server is used to write a backup to tape with a shared data buffer (block size) of 256 KB, then it is possible that a Windows NetBackup media server will not be able to read that tape. In general, we strongly recommend you test restore as well as backup operations.

To change the size of the shared data buffers, create the following file:

```
<install_path>\NetBackup\db\config\SIZE_DATA_BUFFERS
```

This file contains a single integer specifying the size of each shared data buffer in bytes. For example, to use a shared data buffer size of 32 KB, the file would contain the integer 32768.

Note that the size of the shared data buffers used for a restore operation is determined by the size of the shared data buffers in use at the time the backup was written. This file is not used by restores.

In general, the number and size of the shared data buffers can be used to calculate the amount of shared memory required by NetBackup using this formula:

*(number_data_buffers * size_data_buffers) * number_tape_drives * max_multiplexing_setting*

For example, assume that the number of shared data buffers is 16, the size of the shared data buffers is 64 KB, there are two tape drives, and the maximum multiplexing setting is four. Following the formula above, the amount of shared memory required by NetBackup is:

```
(65536 * 16) * 2 * 4 = 8 MB
```

See below for information about how to determine if you should change these settings.

Parent/Child Delay Values.   Although rarely changed, it is possible to modify the parent and child delay values for a process.

To change these values, create the following files:

```
<install_path>\NetBackup\db\config\PARENT_DELAY
<install_path>\NetBackup\db\config\CHILD_DELAY
```

These files contain a single integer specifying the value in milliseconds to be used for the delay corresponding to the name of the file. For example, to use a parent delay of 50 milliseconds, the PARENT_DELAY file would contain the integer 50.

See below for more information about how to determine if you should change these values.

The following section refers to the bptm process on the media server during back up and restore operations from a tape storage device. If you are backing up to or restoring from a disk storage device, substitute bpdm for bptm throughout the section. For example, to activate debug logging for a disk storage device, the following directory must be created:

```
<install_path>\NetBackup\logs\bpdm
```

Using NetBackup Wait and Delay Counters

During a backup or restore operation the NetBackup media server uses a set of shared data buffers to isolate the process of communicating with the tape from the process of interacting with the disk or network. Through the use of *Wait* and *Delay counters*, you can determine which process on the NetBackup media server, the data producer or the data consumer, has to wait more often.

Achieving a good balance between the data producer and the data consumer processes on the NetBackup media server is an important factor in achieving optimal performance from the NetBackup server component of the NetBackup data transfer path.

Understanding the Two-Part Communication Process

The two-part communication process differs depending on whether the operation is a backup or restore and whether the operation involves a local client or a remote client.

Local Clients

When the NetBackup media server and the NetBackup client are part of the same system, the NetBackup client is referred to as a local client.

Backup of Local Client.   For a local client, the bpbkar32 process reads data from the disk during a backup and places it in the shared buffers. The bptm process reads the data from the shared buffer and writes it to tape.

Restore of Local Client.   During a restore of a local client, the bptm process reads data from the tape and places it in the shared buffers. The *tar32* process reads the data from the shared buffers and writes it to disk.

Remote Clients

When the NetBackup media server and the NetBackup client are part of two different systems, the NetBackup client is referred to as a remote client.

Backup of Remote Client.   The bpbkar32 process on the remote client reads data from the disk and writes it to the network. Then a child bptm process on the media server receives data from the network and places it in the shared buffers. The parent bptm process on the media server reads the data from the shared buffers and writes it to tape.

Restore of Remote Client. During the restore of the remote client, the parent bptm process reads data from the tape and places it into the shared buffers. The child bptm process reads the data from the shared buffers and writes it to the network. The tar32 process on the remote client receives the data from the network and writes it to disk.

Roles of Processes during Backup and Restore Operations

When a process attempts to use a shared data buffer, it first verifies that the next buffer in order is in a correct state. A data producer needs an empty buffer, while a data consumer needs a full buffer. The following chart provides a mapping of processes and their roles during backup and restore operations:

OPERATION	DATA PRODUCER	DATA CONSUMER
Local Backup	bpbkar32	bptm
Remote Backup	bptm (child)	bptm (parent)
Local Restore	bptm	tar32
Remote Restore	bptm (parent)	bptm (child)

If a full buffer is needed by the data consumer but is not available, the data consumer increments the Wait and Delay counters to indicate that it had to wait for a full buffer. After a delay, the data consumer will check again for a full buffer. If a full buffer is still not available, the data consumer increments the Delay counter to indicate that it had to delay again while waiting for a full buffer. The data consumer will repeat the delay and full buffer check steps until a full buffer is available.

This sequence is summarized in the following algorithm:

```
while (Buffer_Is_Not_Full) {
        ++Wait_Counter;
  while (Buffer_Is_Not_Full) {
    ++Delay_Counter;
    delay (DELAY_DURATION);
     }
 }
```

If an empty buffer is needed by the data producer but is not available, the data producer increments the Wait and Delay counter to indicate that it had to wait for an empty buffer. After a delay, the data producer will check again for an empty buffer. If an empty buffer is still not available, the data producer increments the Delay counter to indicate that it had to delay again while waiting for an empty buffer. The data producer will relate the delay and empty buffer check steps until an empty buffer is available.

The algorithm for a data producer has a similar structure:

```
while (Buffer_Is_Not_Empty) {
   ++Wait_Counter;
   while (Buffer_Is_Not_Empty) {
     ++Delay_Counter;
delay (DELAY_DURATION);
     }
   }
```

Analysis of the *Wait* and *Delay* counter values indicates which process, producer or consumer, has had to wait most often and for how long.

There are four basic *Wait and Delay Counter* relationships:

Data Producer >> Data Consumer. The data producer has substantially larger Wait and Delay counter values than the data consumer.

The data consumer is unable to receive data fast enough to keep the data producer busy. Investigate means to improve the performance of the data consumer. For a back up operation, check if the data buffer size is appropriate for the tape drive being used (see below).

If data consumer still has a substantially large value in this case, try increasing the number of shared data buffers to improve performance (see below).

Data Producer = Data Consumer. The data producer and the data consumer have very similar Wait and Delay counter values, but those values are relatively large.

This may indicate that the data producer and data consumer are regularly attempting to use the same shared data buffer. Try increasing the number of shared data buffers to improve performance (see below).

Data Producer = Data Consumer. The data producer and the data consumer have very similar Wait and Delay counter values, but those values are relatively small.

This indicates that there is a good balance between the data producer and data consumer, which should yield good performance from the NetBackup server component of the NetBackup data transfer path.

Data Producer << Data Consumer. The data producer has substantially smaller Wait and Delay counter values than the data consumer.

The data producer is unable to deliver data fast enough to keep the data consumer busy. Investigate means to improve the performance of the data producer. For a restore operations, check if the data buffer size (see below) is appropriate for the tape drive being used.

If the data producer still has a relatively large value in this case, try increasing the number of shared data buffers to improve performance (see below).

The points above describe the four basic relationships possible. Of primary concern is the relationship and the size of the values. Information on determining substantial versus trivial values appears on the following pages. The relationship of these values only provides a starting point in the analysis. Additional investigative work may be needed to positively identify the cause of a bottleneck within the NetBackup data transfer path.

Determining Wait and Delay Counter Values

Wait and Delay counter values can be found by creating and reading debug log files on the NetBackup media server.

NOTE Writing the debug log files introduces some additional overhead and will have a small impact on the overall performance of NetBackup. This impact will be more noticeable for a high verbose level setting. Normally, you should not need to run with debug logging enabled on a production system.

To determine Wait and Delay counter values for a local client backup:

1. Activate debug logging by creating these two directories on the media server:

    ```
    <install_path>\NetBackup\Logs\bpbkar
    <install_path>\NetBackup\Logs\bptm
    ```

2. Execute your backup.

3. Look at the log for the data producer (bpbkar32) process in:

    ```
    <install_path>\NetBackup\Logs\bpbkar
    ```

    The line you are looking for should be similar to the following, and will have a timestamp corresponding to the completion time of the backup:

    ```
    ... waited 224 times for empty buffer, delayed 254 times
    ```

    In this example the Wait counter value is 224 and the Delay counter value is 254.

4. Look at the log for the data consumer (bptm) process in:

    `<install_path>\NetBackup\Logs\bptm`

    The line you are looking for should be similar to the following, and will have a timestamp corresponding to the completion time of the backup:

    `... waited for full buffer 1 times, delayed 22 times`

    In this example, the Wait counter value is 1 and the Delay counter value is 22.

To determine Wait and Delay counter values for a remote client backup:

1. Activate debug logging by creating this directory on the media server

    `<install_path>\NetBackup\Logs\bptm`

2. Execute your backup.

3. Look at the log for the bptm process in:

    `<install_path>\NetBackup\Logs\bptm`

    Delays associated with the data producer (bptm child) process will appear as follows:

    `... waited for empty buffer 22 times, delayed 151 times, ...`

    In this example, the Wait counter value is 22 and the Delay counter value is 151.

    Delays associated with the data consumer (bptm parent) process will appear as:

    `... waited for full buffer 12 times, delayed 69 times`

    In this example the Wait counter value is 12, and the Delay counter value is 69.

To determine Wait and Delay counter values for a local client restore:

1. Activate logging by creating the following two directories on the NetBackup media server:

    `<install_path>\NetBackup\Logs\bptm`

    and

    `<install_path>\NetBackup\Logs\tar`

2. Execute your restore.

3. Look at the log for the data consumer (`tar32`) process in:

   `<install_path>\NetBackup\Logs\tar`

   The line you are looking for should be similar to the following, and will have a timestamp corresponding to the completion time of the restore:

   ```
   ... waited for full buffer 27 times, delayed 79 times
   ```

   In this example, the Wait counter value is 27, and the Delay counter value is 79.

4. Look at the log for the data producer (`bptm`) process in:

   `<install_path>\NetBackup\Logs\bptm`

   The line you are looking for should be similar to the following, and will have a timestamp corresponding to the completion time of the restore:

   ```
   ... waited for empty buffer 1 times, delayed 68 times
   ```

   In this example, the Wait counter value is 1 and the delay counter value is 68.

To determine Wait and Delay counter values for a remote client restore:

1. Activate debug logging by creating the following directory on the media server:

   `<install_path>\NetBackup\Logs\bptm`

2. Execute your restore.

3. Look at the log for bptm in:

   `<install_path>\NetBackup\Logs\bptm`

4. Delays associated with the data consumer (`bptm` child) process will appear as follows:

   ```
   ... waited for full buffer 36 times, delayed 139 times
   ```

   In this example, the Wait counter value is 36 and the Delay counter value is 139.

   Delays associated with the data producer (`bptm` parent) process will appear as follows:

   ```
   ... waited for emtpy buffer 95 times, delayed 513 times
   ```

In this example the Wait counter value is 95 and the Delay counter value is 513.

NOTE When you run multiple tests, you can rename the current log file. NetBackup will automatically create a new log file, which prevents you from erroneously reading the wrong set of values.

Deleting the debug log file will not stop NetBackup from generating the debug logs. You must delete the entire directory. For example, to stop `bptm` logging, you must delete the bptm subdirectory. NetBackup will automatically generate debug logs at the specified verbose setting whenever the directory is detected.

Using Wait and Delay Counter Values to Analyze Problems

You can use the `bptm` debug log file to verify that the following tunable parameters have successfully been set to the desired values. You can use these parameters and the Wait and Delay counter values to analyze problems. These additional values include:

Data buffer size.   The size of each shared data buffer can be found on a line similar to:

```
... io_init: using 65536 data buffer size
```

Number of data buffers.   The number of shared data buffers may be found on a line similar to:

```
... io_init: using 16 data buffers
```

Parent/child delay values.   The values in use for the duration of the parent and child delays can be found on a line similar to:

```
... io_init: child delay = 20, parent delay = 30 (milliseconds)
```

NetBackup Media Server Network Buffer Size.   The values in use for the Network Buffer Size parameter on the media server can be found on lines similar to these (may only be part of 4.5 debug log files):

The receive network buffer is used by the `bptm` child process to read from the network during a remote backup.

```
...setting receive network buffer to 263168 bytes
```

The send network buffer is used by the `bptm` child process to write to the network during a remote restore.

```
...setting send network buffer to 131072 bytes
```

See the section on NetBackup Network Performance for more information about the Network Buffer Size parameter on the media server.

Suppose you wanted to analyze a local backup in which there was a 30-minute data transfer duration baselined at 5 MB/sec with a total data transfer of 9,000 MB. Because a local backup is involved, if you refer to the table under "Roles of Processes during Backup and Restore Operations," you can determine that bpbkar32 is the data producer and bptm is the data consumer.

You would next want to determine the Wait and Delay values for bpbkar32 and bptm by following the procedures described in the section "Determining Wait and Delay Counter Values." For this example, suppose those values were:

PROCESS	WAIT	DELAY
bpbkar32	29364	58033
bptm	95	105

Using these values, you can determine that the bpbkar32 process is being forced to wait by a bptm process which cannot move data out of the shared buffer fast enough.

Next, you can determine time lost due to delays by multiplying the Delay counter value by the parent or child delay value, whichever applies.

In this example, the bpbkar32 process uses the child delay value, while the bptm process uses the parent delay value. (The defaults for these values are 20 for child delay and 30 for parent delay.) The values are specified in milliseconds. See "Parent/Child Delay Values" under the "NetBackup Server Performance" section for more information on how to modify these values.

Use the following equations to determine the amount of time lost due to these delays:

bpbkar32	= 58033 delays X 0.020 seconds
	= 1160 seconds
	= 19 minutes 20 seconds
bptm	= 105 X 0.030 seconds
	= 3 seconds

This is useful in determining that the delay duration for the bpbkar32 process is significant. If this delay were entirely removed, the resulting transfer time of 10:40 (total transfer time of 30 minutes minus delay of 19 minutes and 20 seconds) would indicate a throughput value of 14 Mb/sec, nearly a threefold increase. This type of performance increase would warrant expending effort to investigate how the tape drive performance can be improved.

The number of delays should be interpreted within the context of how much data was moved. As the amount of data moved increases, the significance threshold for counter values increases as well.

Again, using the example of a total of 9,000 MB of data being transferred, assume a 64 KB buffer size. You can determine the total number of buffers to be transferred using the following equation:

Number_Kbytes	= 9,000 X 1024
	= 9,216,000 KB
Number_Slots	= 9,216,000 / 64
	= 144,000

The Wait counter value can now be expressed as a percentage of the total divided by the number of buffers transferred:

bpbkar32	= 29364 / 144,000
	= 20.39%
bptm	= 95 / 144,000
	= 0.07%

In this example, in the 20 percent of cases where the bpbkar32 process needed an empty shared data buffer, that shared data buffer has not yet been emptied by the bptm process. A value this large indicates a serious problem, and additional investigation would be warranted to determine why the data consumer (bptm) is having problems keeping up.

In contrast, the delays experienced by bptm are insignificant for the amount of data transferred.

You can also view the Delay and Wait counters as a ratio:

bpbkar32	= 58033/29364
	= 1.98

In this example, on average the bpbkar32 process had to delay twice for each wait condition that was encountered. If this ratio is substantially large, you may wish to consider increasing the parent or child delay value, whichever one applies, to avoid the unnecessary overhead of checking for a shared data buffer in the correct state too often. Conversely, if this ratio is close to 1, you may wish to consider reducing the applicable delay value to check more often and see if that increases your data throughput performance.

Keep in mind that the parent and child delay values are rarely changed in most NetBackup installations.

The preceding information explains how to determine if the values for Wait and Delay counters are substantial enough for concern. The Wait and Delay counters are related to the size of data transfer. A value of 1,000 may be extreme when only 1 MB of data is being moved. The same value may indicate a well-tuned system when gigabytes of data are being moved. The final analysis must determine how these counters affect performance by considering such factors as how much time is being lost and what percentage of time a process is being forced to delay.

Common Restore Performance Issues

This section details performance problems often seen with restore actions.

Improper Multiplex Settings.   If multiplexing is too high, needless tape searching may occur. The ideal setting is the minimum needed to stream the drives.

NetBackup Catalog Performance.   The disk subsystem where the Net-Backup catalog resides has a large impact on the overall performance of NetBackup. To improve restore performance, configure this sub-system for fast reads.

Fragment Size.   The *fragment size* affects where tape markers are placed and how many tape markers are used. Fewer tape marks can slow recovers if a fast locate block is not available. SCSI fast locate block positioning can help. A typical fragment size setting is 2048 MB.

MPX_RESTORE_DELAY setting.   NetBackup can perform multiple restores at the same time from a single multiplexed tape. The default delay setting is 30 seconds. If multiple restore requests are submitted within the time window indicated by this delay setting, they will be considered as candidates to be run at the same time, if possible. This may be a useful parameter to change if multiple stripes from a large database backup are multiplexed together on the same tape.

NetBackup Storage Device Performance

This section lists some factors to consider when you evaluate the storage device component of the NetBackup data transfer path to identify possible changes that may improve the overall performance of NetBackup.

Tape drive wear and tear is much less, and efficiency is greater if *the data stream matches the tape drive capacity* and is sustained. Generally speaking, most tape drives have much slower throughput than most disk drives. We recommend using no more than two high performance tape drives per SCSI/FC connection. The SCSI/FC connection should be able to handle both drives at the maximum rated throughput.

These are some of the factors which affect tape drives:

Media Positioning.   When a backup or restore is performed, the storage device must position the tape so that the data is over the read/write head. Depending on the location of the data and the overall performance of the media device, this can take a significant amount of time. When you conduct performance analysis with media containing multiple images, it is important to account for the time lag that occurs before the data transfer starts.

Tape Streaming.   If a tape device is being used at its most efficient speed, it is said to be streaming the data onto the tape. Generally speaking, if a tape device is streaming, there will be little physical stopping and starting of the media. Instead the media will be constantly spinning within the tape drive. If the tape device is not being used at its most efficient speed, it may continually start and stop the media from spinning. This behavior is the opposite of tape streaming and usually results in a poor data throughput rate.

Data Compression.   Most tape devices support some form of data compression within the tape device itself. Highly compressible data will yield a higher data throughput rate than incompressible data if the tape device supports hardware data compression. This will be true even if the tape device is able to stream the data onto the tape for both the highly compressible data and the incompressible data.

Tape devices typically come with two performance values: Maximum Throughput Rate and Nominal Throughput Rate. The maximum throughput rate is based on how fast compressible data can be written to the tape drive when hardware compression is enabled. The nominal throughput rates applies to less than ideal conditions.

In general, if your hardware device supports compression, you may not want to use software compression such as that available in NetBackup. If you do so, in some cases the size of the data as stored on the media may actually increase because the data has gone through more than one compression algorithm. However, there may still be other valid reasons to use the software compression in NetBackup, such as reducing the amount of data that must be transmitted across the network for a remote client backup.

Index